Nights
in Tents

Nights in Tents

On the Front Lines of the Occupy Movement

LAURA LOVE

YUCCA

Yucca Publishing books may be purchased in bulk at special discounts for sales promotion, corporate gifts, fund-raising, or educational purposes. Special editions can also be created to specifications. For details, contact the Special Sales Department, Yucca Publishing, 307 West 36th Street, 11th Floor, New York, NY 10018 or yucca@skyhorsepublishing.com.

Yucca Publishing® is an imprint of Skyhorse Publishing, Inc.®, a Delaware corporation.

Visit our website at www.yuccapub.com.

10 9 8 7 6 5 4 3 2 1

Library of Congress Cataloging-in-Publication Data is available on file.

Jacket design by Laura Klynstra
Jacket photo: iStockphoto/urbancow

Print ISBN: 978-1-63158-106-9
Ebook ISBN: 978-1-63158-112-0

Printed in the United States of America

There's a time when the operation of the machine becomes so odious—makes you so sick at heart—that you can't take part. You can't even passively take part. And you've got to put your bodies upon the gears and upon the wheels, upon the levers, upon all the apparatus, and you've got to make it stop. And you've got to indicate to the people who run it, to the people who own it that unless you're free, the machine will be prevented from working at all.

—Mario Savio, December 2, 1964, University of California, Berkeley Free Speech Movement

Nights in Tents

Chapter 1

The Beginning Is Near

October 21–25, 2011

"**M**ic check," boomed a basso profundo call from filthy cupped hands encircling the craggy, unshaven face of a shirtless man, clad only in floral, loose fitting cotton pants held up by a single frayed drawstring.

"MIC CHECK," echoed the energetic throng of people surrounding the sweaty, hairy, impossibly thin caller.

"Okay, there's like . . ." resumed the caller, pausing after the word, "like."

"OKAY, THERE'S LIKE . . ." repeated the crowd.

"a shitload of awesome . . ."

"A SHITLOAD OF AWESOME . . ."

"vegan, non-GMO . . ."

"VEGAN, NON-GMO . . ."

"gluten-free . . ."

"GLUTEN-FREE . . ."

"organic food being served right now in the kitchen."

"ORGANIC FOOD BEING SERVED RIGHT NOW IN THE KITCHEN."

Several hands shot skyward, fingers fluttering, while earthy faces beamed and shone with delight. As a first-time visitor to Zuccotti Park, I had no idea what was going on, so I too raised my hands in the air and copied the motions of the hundreds of people surrounding me. I soon learned that this demonstration was known to members of the Occupy Movement as "twinkle fingers," which is similar to "jazz hands," but signifies general approval for what's being said by the main speaker. The call and response delivery of the message is what I now know to be the "human microphone," whereby a single person can deliver an entire speech without the aid of a PA system to a large group of people, simply by having those nearest the caller repeat short sections of the message in unison to the outlying listeners. The process serves to deliver the communiqué to those further away who cannot hear the original caller. It reminded me of the old *Saturday Night Live* skit where TV pitchman, Garrett Morris, cups his hands and re-screams his original commercial message for the benefit of the hearing impaired.

"So like—if you fuckers are hungry . . ."

"SO LIKE—IF YOU FUCKERS ARE HUNGRY . . ."

"you need to head on over there—pronto—and check that out."

"YOU NEED TO HEAD ON OVER THERE—PRONTO— AND CHECK THAT OUT."

The smell of burning white sage met my nose and mingled with body odor, incense, and marijuana smoke. I didn't find the aroma pleasant, although I appreciated the act of "smudging," an ancient Native American ritual I was vaguely familiar with, having seen it performed by alternative type friends of mine, to purge and purify an area of negativity, harmful spirits, and general bad vibes. I remembered back to the eighties when I bought my first house in Seattle. Friends came over to perform the ceremony as a housewarming gift, since the place wasn't in a great neighborhood and had most likely been a drug shooting gallery or murder scene before I scored it.

Many took the caller's advice and headed over to the growing line at the "kitchen"—a series of tables and canopies providing shelter for a makeshift structure of propane burners, steam tables, Tibetan prayer flags, industrial cookware, washable plates, flatware, and cloth napkins. The scene enthralled me. There was even a gray water reclamation system that looked similar to moonshine stills I'd seen in pictures taken by government "revenuers" during Prohibition, just before they dismantled the works and hauled the manufacturers off to the hoosegow.

In September of 2011, I began hearing about a rogue band of disaffected young people in New York City who had taken their disgust with corporate greed and Wall Street excesses to the streets and set up an encampment in a park not far from the iconic bronze bull statue. The group had been inspired by a call to arms from the lefty, anticonsumerist Canadian magazine, *Adbusters*, who had asked their readers if they were "ready for a Tahrir Moment," referring to the Arab Spring protests that had captivated the imaginations of simmering malcontents all over the world with their populist uprisings and sudden overthrow of long-standing tyrants and dictators. The publication outlined its bold dare by declaring that, "On September 17, we want to see twenty thousand people flood into lower Manhattan, set up tents, kitchens, peaceful barricades and occupy Wall Street for a few months." Cannily, the group that answered the call was able to take advantage of a loophole in the city's laws that permitted them to bed down on the edges of New York sidewalks without being jailed. The burgeoning commune quickly became an embarrassing eyesore to multibillionaire mayor, Michael Bloomberg, who was soon gnashing his teeth and racking his brains to figure out a low profile, nonincendiary method to rid himself of the rebellious, noisy, stinky hippie plague of locusts that had descended upon his city's crowning jewel—the fabled Financial District. As bothersome as the incessant drumming, singing, marching, smudging, and chanting had become, nothing bore greater responsibility for the mayor's ire than the fact that this insouciant band of semiferal, bottom-feeding, ragtag, pseudo-intellectuals had appointed themselves arbiters of the fantastic, uniquely American system that had been working just fine for him. Not only were they attacking the institution of Wall Street, they were specifically targeting the very businesses and practices that had made him rich and the Bloomberg name famous. In a revolting display of cheekiness, they had frosted their nondairy, gluten-free cake by giving the operation a catchy Mad Men worthy title, in the form of a Twitter hashtag, #OccupyWallStreet, and a memorable poster of a reedy ballerina, arms outstretched, leg extended on tiptoe, atop the symbolic bull itself. Christ, where's the respect? The OWS brand was taking off and growing exponentially. The fact that its activities were reaching and intriguing a shut-in like me, in my off-grid home on a remote mountain in North Central Washington State, was ample evidence that things were spinning out of control and the upstart movement was creating a life of its own.

I came to this place with the intention of seeing for myself a movement I'd been waiting for most of my adult life. Even though I'd glimpsed it from the lens of mainstream media cameras and talking heads, it consumed me. Luckily, my occupation as a touring folk singer had landed me within a stone's throw of the Wall Street phenomenon I'd become so enamored with and hopeful about of late. It was pure coincidence that my "day job" as a traveling entertainer took me to that place, at that time, just when I needed it most. All it had taken to get me there was a single phone call from a friend who happened to be a legendary folk goddess who needed a backup singer on her comeback tour, after a much-needed two years off—an eternity in musician time.

It was Saturday, October 21, 2011. Folk singer/cultural activist, Holly Near, and I had just finished performing a concert for 250 or so gray- and white-haired people, mostly women, in a theater in Albany, the capital city of New York State. I marveled at how old I'd somehow gotten, as evidenced by our largely mature audience. I couldn't believe how swiftly life had flown by, and how the twenty-somethings had suddenly become sixty-somethings in what seemed like the skip of a stone. Over the years my stage dancing had turned to stage sitting and these days I was getting applause for simply standing up and leaving the comfort of my padded chair every once in awhile. As I sat there singing, I could feel the comforting bulge of credit cards and ID in my back pocket, however, now nestled between my driver's license and Visa, was an AARP card, a recent addition to my wallet.

Since I first became aware of her in the 1990s, I have admired Holly and her soul-deep commitment to fighting social injustice, war, poverty, sexism, racism, and all the other "isms" that screw everything up in this world. I learned that she had gone on the much-publicized "Free the Army" tour with Jane Fonda and Donald Sutherland in 1971, which caused quite a stir and blew a lot of minds. The event, which Fonda described as "Political Vaudeville," took the antiwar trio to military towns along the West Coast, with the purpose of establishing meaningful dialog with soldiers who were soon to be sent off to Vietnam to fight and perhaps die in that conflict. They eventually wound up in Southeast Asia, performing for and talking directly to American troops in a show that was meant to be a sort of counterpoint to Bob Hope's USO tours. It seemed fitting that I would be there with Holly in Albany, New York, on the very night that residents planned to launch their own tent city, much like the one I knew Occupy Wall Street had erected at Zuccotti Park in New York City on September 17.

I had been closely following the Occupy movement on TV and the Internet and was titillated by its grassroots, guerrilla activism aspects, as well as the "get you some justice now" urgency of the Wall Street activists. I was instantly drawn to it like a tornado to a trailer park. Holly's show, which had a casual living room feel to it, had somehow morphed that evening into an impromptu pep rally for Occupy Albany. She sang her rousing anthems, and I sang my civil rights songs, "Eyes on the Prize," and "We Shall Not Be Moved." After the performance, we were asked by concertgoers to lead a group to a nearby park around the Capitol Building. I'd been champing at the bit to get my feet wet in a real live Occupy event and on this night, a rally, protest, and demonstration were planned, followed by tent setups. It was widely known that the mayor and governor intended to enforce the 11:00 p.m. curfew and prevent any camping after that time. All of us, including many senior women, walked the half mile or so into a scene of primal drumming, chanting, electronic signs streaming the cost of wars in Afghanistan and Iraq, high pitched ululating, Guy Fawkes masks, face paint, and tribal dancing. I guessed that maybe five hundred to seven hundred people were gathered there. Chants of, "We are the 99%," "Ain't no power like the power of the people, 'cause the power of the people don't stop," and, "The Revolution has begun/ Everything for everyone," enveloped me. There were news trucks every few yards, lining the street with their twenty-foot hydraulic satellite receivers mounted on top. Journalists sat inside these trucks—talking heads with screens glowing ghostly on their faces as they hunched over laptops. Fox, ABC, CBS, NBC—all the mainstream media were there. Countdowns were shouted intermittently, to warn us of the fast approaching curfew. Cops with batons, helmets, and face shields began to assemble on the periphery. It looked to me as if we were getting boxed in, which was an uncomfortable feeling. Trouble seemed imminent. I was nervous, but otherwise happy as a clam to be at an authentic Occupation.

I began interviewing people around me with my new cell phone, a Droid, that I could barely use or read because I'm too old to figure out new technology and I'm practically going blind—probably should have been wearing trifocals. Eleven thirty arrived with no uptick in police activity. I lingered until 11:45 when an Occupier offered to give me a ride back to my hotel. I was reluctant to depart the exhilarating scene, but duty called and I knew I'd have to be crisp in the morning. I went to bed that night believing we'd gotten bad information about the police crackdown and thinking, "Oh well, it sure was a great experience."

Two days later Holly emailed me with an Albany newspaper link reporting that the local cops had been poised to act, but looked out at the late arriving "sea of grannies," alongside families with kids in strollers, and the chief of police decided to defy orders to enforce the curfew, citing their presence as a major justification. He pointed out that his area of expertise was policing, and Mayor

Jennings's and Governor Cuomo's was not—"they know politics." So he overrode them, citing that "it wouldn't have looked too good on TV to have cops hauling grandmothers off to jail and tearing children from their parents' arms to prove a point about curfews." "Besides," he added, they didn't have the ability to adequately enforce the law anyway because of "downsizing and cutbacks in city spending." He also revealed that none of his officers wanted to babysit a bunch of crying kids while their parents got booked into the pokey. Wow, how sensible, I thought. This whole Occupy thing is going to be easy peasy. We should be able to get this justice thing done in a hurry. At this pace we should have the world totally turned around by Christmas.

By the end of my tour with Holly, I was obsessively googling Occupy stuff at every chance to get the latest news about Wall Street. I was intrigued by the notion that a handful of college kids had done a little sniffing around, saw what a raw deal they were getting from their government—(no good jobs, drowning in student debt, endless wars, a toxic food supply, global warming, relatives in foreclosure, gigantic oil spills, etc.), connected the dots, and traced the source of their predicament right back to exactly the place where I thought it should be—big corporations, big banks, and big fat rich people!

On October 23 my longtime manager, ex-partner, housemate, best friend, and co-parent (it's complicated), Mary McFaul, joined me in New York City to see the greatest show on earth—Occupy Wall Street. She and I felt festive as we walked the short distance from the subway stop to the Financial District. We passed the World Trade Center Memorial that had a huge line waiting in the unseasonably warm weather. It had been ten years since 9/11 and the Memorial planners themselves said they'd been overwhelmed by the amount of visitors they had received. There was still a lot of construction going on and between the jackhammers and the frantic New York City traffic, we were deafened and didn't hear the Occupy drums until we were almost on top of Zuccotti Park.

I squealed with delight when I laid eyes on the chaotic scene of tarps, tables, tents, and teepees obfuscating the landscape, obscuring the masses and anchoring scores of people, many who were absorbed in stimulating conversations about things that mattered to me, too. Signs that said things I'd been thinking for a long time were plastered everywhere. I was glad that I had been able to convince Mary to fly out the day before to join me in the "witnessing of history." "This is an extraordinary moment in time," I insisted. We were both wide-eyed and jubilant as we dove in and lead a sing-along beginning with "This Land is Your Land," then "We've Got the Whole World in Our Hands," followed by "Ain't Gonna Let Nobody Turn Me Around." It felt in those moments like the revolution was finally here, and I became wholly committed to the Occupy Movement on that day. There was a huge phalanx of cops on scooters all around the square; cops on foot, cops in a mobile cop tower, cops on horses, cops in vans, cops in cop cars, cops on bikes, cops in buildings, cops with assault rifles, cops with flash-bang grenades, and cops with tear gas overlooking the park. There were a lot of cops. Many colorful protest signs caught my eye and resonated deeply with me as I wandered about. WHY ARE YOU WATCHING THIS FROM YOUR LIVING ROOM? GIVE MY GRANDMA'S HOUSE BACK FOX NEWS: RICH PEOPLE PAYING RICH PEOPLE TO TELL MIDDLE CLASS PEOPLE TO BLAME POOR PEOPLE, I'LL BELIEVE CORPORATIONS ARE PEOPLE WHEN ONE HELPS ME MOVE FOR PIZZA, and my personal favorite, from an ordained minister, THE BEGINNING IS NEAR. Exciting discussions about topics like constitutional rights, corporate greed, war, environmental devastation, and the Glass Steagall Act abounded all around me. I hovered like a vulture on the edges of intense interactions, craning my neck to hear arguments about issues such as the military industrial complex, incarceration rates, GMOs, and capitalism. Sometimes I'd overhear people groping for a word or asking each other a question I knew the answer to, so I'd crowd in close, hoping to cadge an invitation to jump in and break the impasse. In addition to the intoxicating atmosphere, the mercantile setup was fantastic. Leave it to the scrappy resourceful people of New York City to hijack a trend in its infancy and turn it into a full-on merchandising shopportunity. There were micro vendors at every turn. The place was lousy with them. None of them could have been there for more than a few weeks max, but they all looked like they'd been shilling Occupy Wall Street souvenirs for generations. In fact, in order to gain access to the park, we'd been forced to squeeze past a stocky, impatient black woman, who'd located her sales stand directly in front of, and almost blocking, the main entrance to Zuccotti Park. She was aggressively hawking Occupy-themed buttons: WE ARE THE 99%, MAKE BANKS PAY, EAT THE RICH, STOP FORECLOSURES, THE PEOPLE ARE UNITED. I was drawn to one that said, I DON'T NEED SEX—WALL STREET F*CKS ME EVERY DAY. I bought it.

All too soon, Mary and I were packing to return home from our visit to Occupy Wall Street. By that time I'd learned a few basic functions on my phone, and before we took off, I was reading an online account of a police raid on Occupy Oakland demonstrators. I read that two-term Iraq War marine veteran, Scott Olsen, had sustained a severe head injury from a tear gas canister spitefully hurled by an overzealous Oakland police officer. The words on the page elevated my blood pressure and I could hear a rushing sound in my head as I digested them. The more I read, the more I could feel my activist button being pushed, and I announced that I was going immediately to Oakland. Mary's eyes rolled as she said, "Don't go there, it's dangerous. Here, let me show you something funny on your cell phone instead." She dialed up a series of "Honey Badger" YouTube videos on my new device to make me forget all about Scott and his broken skull. I leaned in to focus on the collection of bastardized, overdubbed, National Geographic–style nature videos which had recently gone viral and blown up all over the Internet. The unlikely subject was the formidable, obscure animal known as the honey badger. The narrative was delivered by a fussy, catty, gay man, who was demonstrably impressed with the Honey Badger's large bag of tricks. The flamboyant observer continually interrupted the original narration by shrieking things like,

"Oh my Gawd, Honey Badger's a *badass*. Did you *see* Honey Badger fuck up that whole pride of lions?! HONEY BADGER DON'T GIVE A SHIT. She's all like, 'Thanks for the dead zebra, stupid,' to those dumbass lions." We laughed ourselves incontinent before takeoff. We'd been flying for about five minutes before she looked at me and said, "I suppose I have to book your flight to Oakland since you're too dim to figure that out on your own." I rolled my eyes, dismissing the fact that she'd just insulted me. I shrieked, "Honey Badger don't care, she's a *badass*, she's going to Occupy Oakland!" God bless Mary.

Chapter 2

Occupy Oakland

The next day I took the Bay Area Rapid Transport (BART) train from Oakland Airport to City Hall at Fourteenth Street and Broadway, where I was told the Occupy Oakland Commune was located. There weren't many people there—maybe four or five tents, and I was disappointed. A young woman with freckles approached me and told me her name was Lindsey. There were a few news vans, but otherwise a fairly quiet Frank Ogawa Plaza. At the time I didn't know why, but every place the name Frank Ogawa was written, it was either scratched out or covered up by a sign that said OSCAR GRANT PLAZA, or, OGP. I soon learned that the Occupy Oakland Commune had renamed the building to honor a young black man that had been shot dead by a BART officer on New Year's Eve, two years prior, as he lay facedown—unarmed. I noticed how old and ornate City Hall was, as I began to unpack my Target tent. Lindsey asked me if I'd like help. I started to say, "No, I'm good," but she'd already begun before I could utter a word. As I reached to assist her, a horde of reporters descended on me like white on rice, thrusting logo-encrusted microphones in my face. I wasn't certain why, but I think it may have been because I looked so ordinary—even matronly, unlike what they may have expected. And there were very few of us—I was one of only about twenty people in the entire plaza. I was first questioned by KRONTV, then Al Jazeera, the *Chronicle*, ABC, and CBS. I granted five interviews within the twenty-five minutes it took Lindsey to assemble my tent and place my belongings inside it. Each one asked the same three questions, "What is your message," "Who is your leader," and "Why are you here?" None seemed particularly satisfied with my answers which were, "There are many messages and issues in the Occupy Movement, not the least of which are bank foreclosures, destruction of the environment, joblessness, corporate money in politics, homelessness, the military industrial complex, and Wall Street fraud. We are all the leaders, and I am here as part of the Occupy Movement, to demand social, economic, and environmental justice for the 99% from the 1%. We wish to hold corporations, the rich, Wall Street, and corrupt bankers accountable for compromising everything we hold dear. We want to establish a true democracy and wrest power away from those who now influence and control every aspect of our lives in the United States." My answers seemed to frustrate them, and I was getting the idea they didn't feel they were "sound-bitey" enough. I shortened them for each successive interview. I wanted to please and give them something brief that their viewers could understand. By the last interview my responses had been winnowed down to, "We're mad at everything. I'm here because it's too cold in New York," and, "I'm the leader." The minute those words left my mouth, I grimaced. I felt like Al Gore claiming he'd invented the Internet. I decided to either not do any more interviews, or figure out an accurate, but succinct answer (preferably three words or less) that encompassed the entirety of the movement. In my defense, I had been distracted at the end by a random passerby, who shoved a slice of vegan pizza into my outstretched hand, which was extended to emphasize a point I was making.

By Friday, we'd grown to well over a hundred tents. Everywhere I looked, people were putting up tents. I watched a young black man trying to figure it out for about two hours. I can attest to the well-known fact that black people don't camp—we call it "homeless."

The only reason I knew how to camp was because a white woman I was dating in the eighties dragged me out into the woods where I saw a lot of other white people in REI clothing, who also seemed to be enjoying themselves, though it was raining and windy. I was petrified of being in the wilderness with Caucasians, who may not have heard about antilynching laws, but by the second or third day I had relaxed and was even having an okay time. The woman I was with told me that I was so light-skinned no one could even tell I was African American, and I am not proud to admit that that brought me solace. I have since learned to love camping, but it was not an easy sell at first. Feeling my brother's pain, I offered assistance, which his ego did not allow him to accept. He struggled for another hour or so alone. I spent the better part of the day helping out in the encampment wherever I could. I bought ketchup, mustard, and margarine at a Smart and Final store from the wish list posted at the kitchen tent. I didn't know about the "smart," but I was certain it was "final." I never buy margarine for myself, so I randomly chose I Can't Believe It's Not Butter. When I got back to the camp I smeared some all over a hunk of artisan bread that a local bakery donated. I tasted the spread. It was awful. I thought, I can sooooo believe it's not butter. I can't believe it's not *illegal*. I can't believe I put that toxic shit in my mouth, I can't believe I ruined that perfectly great piece of bread with that horrible dreck. I can't believe someone's not in jail for inventing it.

Sometime in the late afternoon, filmmaker Michael Moore showed up, and said a lot of uplifting stuff like, "Something good will come of this movement," and, "This weekend will be a watershed moment in Oakland," and "the Occupy Movement has killed apathy in this country," as evidenced by the fact that some folks had actually "turned off *Dancing with the Stars*." He laughed about having dropped some weight and gone vegan. Then he complained good-naturedly that the news media would glom onto that as the most salient feature of his speech and say nothing about the rest. He recounted how he'd tried to contact mayor Jean Quan (loud boos) with his concerns about recent police actions and tell her how horrified people had been to see what the cops did to Scott Olsen last Tuesday night (October 25, 2011). She'd had a member of her staff notify him that she was unavailable to meet with him, even though he was a movie star and everything. He asked that we give thirty seconds of silence for Scott, and then he congratulated Occupy Oakland for having the courage to come back after what happened. He said millions had been inspired by our return. I felt honored and mentally took the credit, even though I'd not arrived till the twenty-seventh. The fact that I hadn't seen one police officer since I arrived the day before was both exhilarating and eerie. I prayed they learned their lesson after the global backlash and the media spanking they got from that bad behavior.

On Saturday, October 29, many more tents arrived and there was no room to move or walk between them. We were up to 185 by my count. Heavy discourse by people from all walks of life and every skin color surrounded me throughout the day, giving me the sense that we were doing something worthwhile and momentous, however, as our tent city expanded, nights got louder and stranger. Halloween party tourists coursed through Oscar Grant Plaza after the bars closed. One young woman was wrapped completely in white cotton, painted red at the bottom with a white rope dangling from it. She said she was a tampon. A full brass ensemble with drums, trumpets, trombones, and tubas marched through the encampment around 2:00 a.m., but by that time things had become so surreal, I didn't even bother getting out of my tent to take a look. I couldn't sleep. Some young men were sharing a joint just outside my tent and laughing that halting, stuttery stoned laugh we're all familiar with, as they wondered at the size of the rats scurrying around inches from my door flap. "Whoa dude, that fucker was bigger than my mom's dog . . . tchuh huh huh huh." There were arguments breaking out in every habitable space. "Crack Head Corner" was populated by jumpy, agitated black folks who came and went all night. Tragically, men, women, and even mothers with small children came to smoke rock cocaine. A darling, bright, three-year-old, still awake at 2:30 a.m., played with trash as her mom scored. A twitchy black man with Chia Pet hair and glowing road map eyes was blurting out Tourette's-y sentences, "Fuck you, bitch. Die motherfucker," and "Pop Pop," as the child's mother hit the opaque glass pipe, oblivious to the incredible barking man with the Cujo snarl. I began talking to the little girl as her mom eyed me warily. We were playing high five and patty-cake, when she rasped, "Get yo' ass over here," to her daughter. My heart ached. At the opposite end of the encampment, a pale, straw-headed, pasty-skinned man in caked overalls began to argue loudly with an emaciated thatch-haired woman—his significant other. Another unshaven methed up guy with rotten gums and a Charles Manson vibe started threatening to slice the first guy up if he didn't stop abusing his "goddamn old lady, man." I dubbed the area, "Pit Bull Park," as the amped up, muscle bound beasts heaved, barked, and lunged at everything with a pulse. I strolled casually past their owners, hoping my cameo appearance in this Quentin Tarantino film would intrude enough to make them forget about their petty argument. On my way past them, I noticed a handmade flag affixed to one of their tents, which said, WARNING—DOG IS VERY PROTECTIVE. "Protective" . . . that's a nice way to put it. In the background some free spirit started loudly strumming his guitar and singing made up Occupy songs, in unrecognizable keys. A light sleeper nearby offered to bash his guitar, "over his fucking head," if he didn't stop playing. The complainer was upset because he'd been "volunteering in the kitchen and working security" all day and it was "fuckin' *quiet* time, dude." This was a night from hell. I walked toward another group of crack-addled black kids who were making a lot of noise and on the verge of coming to blows. I tiptoed gingerly over beer cans and food waste to tell them I'd really appreciate it if they'd take it down a notch and try not to bring police attention to our revolution. I pointed out to them that nothing kills a party like the riot squad. One of them with neon *Children of the Corn* eyes got in my face to tell me that if he "wanted to meet the goddamn Virgin Mary, he'd go to a moth-erfuckin' church." Another of his skeletal friends with *Night of the*

Living Dead mannerisms and Don King hair, laughed sharply as he asserted that, "We ain't even the *real* motherfuckin' problem anyway. It's all them goddamn loudass crackers over there and they mothahfuckin' outta control dogs."

After spending so much time with potty mouths like that, I am over curse words. Their impact is totally lost when overused, and should be reserved for the most extreme circumstances, and then only to emphasize an important point, such as, "I have had it with these *motherfuckin'* snakes on this *motherfuckin'* plane!" I sighed wearily, and returned to my tent. On the way I spotted copious volumes of urine pooled in the corners of surrounding buildings and running over cracks in the pavement. I also noted that some more motivated, less high Occupants had strung extension cords from light poles to recharge their cell phones and other electronic devices. Looking back, I question how I ever could have survived without a mobile phone. Just to think that a mere three weeks earlier I'd never even held, much less operated, a "smart" phone. I'd wholeheartedly rejected the expensive technology that required its own "data plan." I resented the unavoidable intrusion into my life. I feared I'd become umbilically tethered to it—almost unable to function without it—which is exactly what had occurred. On two occasions, I called Mary that night, anxiously detailing the drama playing itself out in every corner of Oscar Grant Plaza. The second call was at 2:30 a.m. "What the actual hell was I thinking coming out here and pitching a tent in downtown *OAKLAND! I* must have been on crack to think I could pull this off," I wailed into the receiver.

Mary sounded groggy and irritated on the other end. "Yeah, well Laura, what *were* you thinking? Why in the world would you expect it to be anything *other* than this? Is it a surprise to you that homeless people in Oakland smoke crack, publicly urinate, shoot heroin, and sometimes kill each other? Is it a surprise that drug-addicted dog owners in Oakland prefer pitbulls to shih tzus? Gee, who could have predicted that folks might want to stay up later than you, and maybe some of them would get into spats with each other. What, do you suppose, are the odds that the police officers who raided the place last week and broke that Marine's skull are going to let you stay there for as long as you like? Let me answer that for you, since you don't seem to have done your research. The odds are zero, idiot. You shouldn't even be there. And don't even *think* about getting arrested in Oakland, Laura. They will throw you into a stinking rathole where everyone you meet is going to be toothless and ruthless. What part of the equation did you fail to consider before pitching your tent there? Either pack your stuff up right now, get on the BART, and come home, or stop calling me, unless you've been shot or stabbed, because there's nothing I can do about it from here. I've got to get up, take care of Kristy, and work tomorrow. Remember Kristy? She's your daughter."

"Okay, okay . . . look, I won't call you anymore unless I'm dying," I returned, wounded, before hanging up. "She'll be sorry if I do get stabbed tonight," I grumbled to myself before reinserting my foam earplugs.

After that terse exchange, I lay there tightly clutching my phone as if it was the only thing keeping my heart beating. That I even possessed such a clever invention was pure coincidence. Just before leaving for the East Coast to tour with Holly I had been fishing on the Okanogan River at the Chilliwist Hole when I'd felt a tug on my line that meant business. Excited that it might be a fine bass, I reeled in as far as it could go, only to discover that my hook was snagged on someone else's abandoned line. Perplexed, I reached to free my hook when it jerked away from me and began snapping back and forth crazily. It dawned on me that the line I'd ensnared already had a fish on it. *Okay, well . . . no problem—now all I have to do is pull it in.* But just as I pondered that, it lurched out of my grasp into much deeper water. I could still see the filament though, and reckoned if I didn't jump in at that very moment, all would be lost. I plunged into the river with all my clothes on, grabbed the line, and dog paddled back with my prize. I quickly clubbed the fish, dropped to my knees and began to clean it on the warm muddy river bank, just as I imagined Indian women had done for

centuries. I was hurling the entrails into the river for other wild-
life to consume when I heard something that reminded me of the
hissy static my transistor radio used to emit when I tried to dial in
a new station as a kid. Puzzled, I patted myself down and looked
all over trying to identify the source of the sound. The answer
eventually presented itself as my fingers curled around the rectangular outline of my two-year-old, dumb, cell phone. Staring
woefully at the dripping, crackling remains, I was forced to admit
it was a goner. I gently laid my costly fish in a cooler full of ice,
drove myself home, logged onto my computer, and ordered the
"ruggedized," most water-resisting-est phone on the market. And
late at night, in my hour of darkness, that magnificent Droid was
the only thing standing between me and the abyss. By the end of
the week I'd mastered most of the functions my new phone could
perform as a matter of sheer survival. It amazed me how facile I
had suddenly become at learning the once daunting technology
when faced with the alternatives at OGP.

By 5:00 a.m. the ground was thick with tents that blanketed
every inch of the dank, wet earth. More people arrived overnight,
even as I clung to my electronic lifeline and hoped for the best.
My plastic Halloween pumpkin chamber pot with "Trick or Treat
Wall Street" sharpied on it was nearly full, and I hoped I wouldn't
accidently kick it over, if I ever did fall asleep. I finally lost con-
sciousness just before dawn, as things quieted down in our busy
little corner of the world.

Sunday, October 30. I woke up at around 10:30 a.m. The sun
was streaming generously into my tent and radiating its warmth
throughout my achy joints. I rose to see that there were rows of
clean porta-potties in Frank Ogawa/Oscar Grant Plaza—maybe
fifteen in all. I was overjoyed. I gratefully took my orange pumpkin into one and emptied it—so convenient. Going number two
would be a holiday in this inviting atmosphere. I smiled to see that
someone had scribbled, "99% Occupied" on the door. Last night
seemed like a distant nightmare. I overheard a fellow camper saying he'd heard Bette Midler had donated the facilities to us. I didn't

know or care if this was true. Whether or not, God bless Bette
Midler. By four o'clock in the afternoon the johns were all full to
overflowing. There was diarrhea and vomit on the seats, floors,
and walls. I yearned for the Michigan Womyn's Music Festival and
all its man-free space. I vowed to either join or form a committee whose sole job was to designate some of the portable units as
women only. I was disgusted at the men who did this. They peed
everywhere—on the floor, on the walls, on the toilet paper, in the
corners, in the bushes, on their shoes. They even peed on car tires,
just like a scurvy dog. I was growing a little tired of the revolution.

That night I ordered a ninety-eight dollar meal of calamari,
porterhouse steak, and two Bombay Sapphire dry gin martinis—
neat, with three olives each—at Flora's Restaurant. I finished with
Tiramisu and coffee. I ate like a sow as I Occupied Flora's and
looked insane in the process. My homemade cardboard sign saying, TAX THE RICH was taped on my backpack that I wore throughout my feast, since I had to carry my valuables with me wherever
I went, for fear of losing them if left unguarded in the tent. After I
gorged, I felt invigorated and ready for lots more Occupying.

Later that night during the General Assembly (GA) there were
speakers of color who'd been invited to share their stories about
ongoing police brutality and the targeting of ethnic minorities that
were hallmarks of the Oakland Police Department long before
Occupy arrived. I found myself tearing up as one person after
another testified how they had been systematically mistreated
by the OPD. Many had been funneled into the prison industrial
complex after their arrest and deprived of liberty for some period
of time. Some of the OPD misconduct they detailed had caused
either permanent injury or death to the speaker or a loved one. I
gazed up at the beautifully designed City Hall Building, with its
two brilliantly lit carved eagles flanking the American flag, and I
wondered how we could ever have allowed ourselves to get to this
point. A moonless night fell on the long line of black and brown
people who were patiently queued up to speak. Each grievous tale
saddened me more than the last, until the line finally dwindled

down to one remaining speaker—an older, prosperous looking white woman who seemed out of place in the gathering. She toddled unsteadily up to the microphone with the aid of a young black man, who gave her his arm to lean on. The lighting was such that I strained to make out her delicate features as she spoke quietly and earnestly in the soft voice of a well-bred woman. She described, matter-of-factly, how her marriage to a black man had produced three lovely brown children, who often came home from school with troubling stories of racial profiling and unwarranted run-ins with law enforcement personnel who, they contended, had singled them out based solely on their race. She remembered listening to these stories with some degree of skepticism and wondering sometimes if, in fact, her children weren't exaggerating the details of the incidents simply to shock or alarm her. She even admitted to, once or twice, having dismissed her kids' perceptions of harassment by the police as an oversensitivity to well-meaning officers who, she confessed, she'd always seen as allies and protectors. She went on to classify herself as "not exactly the 1%, but at least in the top 10% of wealthy individuals in this country." Then she said that, on the few occasions in her life that she'd had reason to call the police, they'd always treated her courteously and respectfully. Her genteel, refined presence clearly defined her as an educated member of the upper class as she explained how unfailingly she had always relied on them to protect her and serve her needs. She revealed that she never fully bought her interracial children's assertions that their realities were far removed from hers, as a privileged white woman. That is, until she found herself helpless to defend her son from a grossly unjust, manufactured allegation leveled against him by the Oakland Police Department. The charge had landed him a considerable prison sentence, which only permitted her to visit once a month, for a short time, and then only through a bulletproof, plexiglass window. She was trembling visibly and on the verge of tears when she paused for a moment to gather herself. By that time I was weeping openly for her pain, as I waited for her to regain composure. She resumed her dissertation by saying that she would never again dismiss the stories of any minority person after the travesty her own family had endured at the hands of the police. Nor could she ever trust a country that trains and arms its officers to attack and jail its brown citizens in such disproportionate numbers to whites. She paused again and breathed in slowly as she prepared to deliver her closing remarks, which began with a weary admission that the painful lesson had almost destroyed her. As her voice trailed to a whisper she professed, "I am now intimately aware of how deeply flawed our criminal justice system is. And on this evening, I say to you, my dear brown and black brothers and sisters of Oakland . . ." She paused briefly, and in that split second, the disembodied spirit of Huey Newton leapt, unbidden, into her diminutive body and took full control of her faculties as she roared, "FUCK THE POH-LICE, FUCK THE POH-LICE, FUCK THE POH-LICE!" Over and again she repeated the phrase, like a boss, with the accent on the "POH." She thrust her fists wildly into the air, apparently not ever intending to stop, until she was finally ushered, still screaming, away from the microphone. All of us, in the shock-paralyzed audience, sat in stunned silence for several unsure moments, before jumping to our feet and erupting into riotous applause. Mama brought the house down.

Later, during that same week, I found my tolerance for bad behavior being challenged relentlessly. I had gotten my days and nights totally turned around as a result of being constantly awakened by drug fueled disturbances of one kind or another at Oscar Grant Plaza. The outbreaks of yelling and threats were not just annoying, they were scary as hell, as I wondered if anyone was going to pull out a gun or knife and kill somebody—hopefully not me. Somewhere toward the end of my stay, at the height of my irritation, I began to wonder if I might be viewing my brethren, in the encampment, with a jaundiced eye. What if I opened myself up to the possibility that I'd become inured to the daily injustices that had produced such miscreants? What if my intolerance was based on my own altered perceptions as a newly comfortable, middle-class, light-skinned African American woman living in the Pacific Northwest. Could it be that I had somehow turned into a *republican?* The very thought repulsed me. Certainly I had been born into poverty and had suffered greatly as a child, but my adult years had been relatively unblemished by the degrading occurrences that had been part of my daily life growing up in Nebraska. At that point I began to examine the unique set of circumstances that had allowed me to get where I am today. I thought about all the social programs that were in place when I was young, which served as my safety net, that no longer exist today. I thought about the fact that I am so light-complected that many people mistake me for white wherever I go, and treat me accordingly. More than once, I've been told racist jokes by people who had no idea I was black. In years past, a neighbor in my middle-class Seattle suburb said, "Hi Laura, I hope I wasn't making too much noise. I was in my Back yard with my beebee gun shooting at cans . . . Af ri-cans . . . Mexi-cans, and Puerto Ri-cans." I recoiled at the punchline and harkened back to times I'd seen my darker, kinky-haired sister being mistreated and called "Nigger" by other kids at the all-white school we attended in Lincoln, Nebraska until 1969. When I was in the fourth grade, we moved mid-year to an all-black school, sixty miles away, in a rough part of Omaha, where I suddenly wore a bullseye as, "the only honky in the whole school." Then I recalled the day my sister and I rented our first apartment in 1976. I'd picked up the phone and made a call to the landlord, who'd listed it in the newspaper. She and her husband had been so charmed by our phone conversation, that she'd rented the apartment to us on the spot—sight unseen. I had told her truthfully that Lisa and I were students— that we were both employed, and that we got good grades. Mrs. Fahlberg had been kind and sympathetic—even motherly over the phone, and I knew that we'd be happy in our new home. When my sister and I took the necessary buses to her house to pick up the apartment key, she'd let out a horrified gasp. "Oh my goodness," she had said, looking first at my sister, then me, "Why didn't you tell us your were *colored?* We've never rented to coloreds before." I remember her hastily excusing herself and leaving me and my sister standing on the porch while she disappeared inside the house to caucus with her husband. She reappeared at length, to frostily announce, "My husband and I have decided to rent to you *only* because we told you that we would, and we *never* go back on our word, but it was extremely dishonest of you not to tell us that you were colored. We just don't know how this will work out with our other tenants." I remember my embarrassment and shame that day, and the feeling that my sister and I had done something deceitful and immoral, when it was in fact, her own prejudices that had allowed her to reach such faulty conclusions about our ethnicity. In her world, intelligence and proper speech were incongruous with being black.

A few months later the Fahlbergs found the excuse they were looking for and gave us thirty days to leave after they said another tenant in the four-plex had complained about seeing a black man with a gun lurking around the property. My sister's sixteen-year-old boyfriend had been playing with a plastic toy gun that belonged to one of his little brothers as he sat on the porch swing, in broad daylight, and waited for Lisa to come home from her after school job. She said her other tenants had been frightened, which jeopardized her rental income, so we had to go. I seriously doubted the veracity of the statement, since all of my brief encounters with the other renters had been pleasant and uneventful.

My sister and I scrambled to find a new place to live, which we eventually accomplished, but the apartment was more expensive, less nice, and much farther away from school and work. We did get back on our feet, but the experience devastated both of us and left a lasting impression. We lived at "The Floral Court" until 1978 when I began to attend the University of Nebraska, free of charge because of the readily available Basic Educational Opportunity Grant, (BEOG) offered by the Carter Administration to minority and underprivileged high school graduates. Today's college hopefuls can only dream about the ease and accessibility of this program, whose only requirement was to be a good citizen

and maintain a grade point average above a C. That year, because
of the grant and a work study job, I was able to work reasonable
hours for decent pay, which created the environment for me to
earn a 4.0 GPA and live in my own apartment for the duration,
with relatively few financial worries. The self-sufficiency I was
afforded paved the way for me to throw myself fully into my studies and eventually graduate with honors. Once I'd achieved this
goal, I gave myself permission to delve more deeply into my artis-
tic interests—songwriting and music. And in 1996, I signed on to
a major label, which kickstarted my career as a singer/songwriter
and recording artist for Mercury Records.

When I look back, it's undeniable that I was able to take tre-
mendous advantage of a wealth of opportunities and safety nets
which, for the most part, don't exist any more. When I gave it
some thought, I understood that these marginalized, disenfranchised people who caused so much commotion at night, didn't
have a ghost of a chance to "pull themselves up by their bootstraps." They didn't even have boots, let alone straps. The BEOG
and work study programs had been my "boots" and my hard work
had been the "straps." How was someone born in poverty, to a
poorly educated single mother, whose own opportunities were
severely curtailed by her blackness, femaleness, and geographical
location, ever going to provide her children with the tools needed
to thrive in the modern era? How could she ever instill the virtues
of hard work and dedication to her progeny, when she couldn't
pinpoint a single example of success in her own zip code? Yet here
I was, all pissed off because folks weren't "behaving" like I wanted
them to, when such conduct would have virtually guaranteed
banishment and ignominy in their home communities. Excelling
in prostitution and drug careers were the only realistic pursuits
in much of Oakland. Even if these ne'er-do-wells had somehow
found it within themselves to remain unswayed by the pressure,
they'd likely be pulled over, or stopped and frisked anyway, at the
whim of big city police departments who'd populated mega-prison

complexes with scores of young bloods who looked and sounded just like them.

And yet, given all these strikes against them, almost every one of the bereft, wounded, disenfranchised people, joined, at one time or another, in conversations about the import of the Occupy Movement and its significance to them. Even the drunkest and druggiest among them were beginning to educate themselves on the issues, and provide glorious insights to the sources of their misery. Each day I allotted some time to eavesdropping on political discussions between stoned people, which yielded a wealth of precious memories.

A hard-bodied black man with saggy jeans belted at the knees, and colorful red paisley cotton boxer shorts blooming from the top blew cigarette smoke from the side of his mouth to be polite, as he led a conversation with four other men. "Dawg, we need to *end* corporate personhood, 'cause these corporations are turnin' hella profits from all them negroes they be sendin' off to the joint. I'm serious man, fuck the *privatization* of *incarceration*."

"Um hmmm . . . yup . . . you're right," agreed the others, one of whom stood out for being bony, slouchy, and white—wearing a dingy wife beater shirt that gripped his toneless torso as he hung out with them, completing the tight circle.

The leader continued, "Man, that whole goddamn financial crisis was messed up from the git go. They was playin' us. That shit was tore up from the floor up. You know them banks and investment companies, like Lehman Brothers and Enron and them— they *caused* all that bullshit by gambling with our money and *losin'* it. And then we gave them thievin' motherfuckers a bunch *more* money to bail *them* out, even though they *still* throwin' *us* out on the street, like it ain't nothin'.'"

The white man interjected, "Whoa, you just touched on somethin' there. 'Cause shit is seriously jacked up when I was gettin' nine bucks an hour to work full-time, in the same factory my old man worked at for *eighteen*—twenty years ago. *And* I got *no* health care, while some joker at the top's haulin' in thirty-seven million to run it into the ground. Hey man, hook me up with a cigarette will ya?" he concluded, eyeing the first speaker's fingers hungrily.

Paisley shorts reached into his back pants pocket, which was at his calf, and produced one, extending it warmly to him.

"Shit man, why you guys always gotta smoke these goddamn menthol cigarettes?" complained the pale receiver, smiling as he accepted it.

"Cuz that's what Newports is, fool!" shot back the giver, sending them all, including the beggar, into torrents of laughter.

Pearls like these were dropping out of the air around me and landing in my tent every night as I sipped on whiskey, peeked occasionally through the flap, held my journal pen aloft, and waited for quotable moments. I even heard one man named Greg, who used a walker and lived on a bench in front of City Hall year round, say that he'd been a Black Panther back in the sixties and that "shit has gotten so fucked up since then that black folks are worse off now than ever." "But," he conjectured, "the Occupy is fo' real, and we gonna git shit done now. This a revolution baby." There were drunks talking about the Glass-Steagall act, hookers talking about the Prison Industrial Complex, meth addicts debating Citizen's United, Cal professors and gangbangers discussing Keynesian economics, and famous people like Danny Glover and Yoko Ono dropping in to express their support for Occupiers. Remarkable things were happening all around me, and all I had to do was open my mind up a tiny bit to appreciate the enormity of the event.

The improbability of surviving completely unharmed, amidst a population of hard-core frequent fliers in the criminal justice system, started to hit me and I began to understand the richness and rarity of the experience, as well as the grandness of scope. Not only had no one attempted to harm me, I even got a sense that people were looking out for me while I was there. A jagged looking white man, who was a dead ringer for Jack Nicholson in *The Shining*, gently tapped my elbow to tell me I'd inadvertently dropped a wad of bills out of my pocket when I reached for a tissue to blow my nose on a sleepless night at 3:30 a.m. After I thanked him, he'd said, "No, problem. We gotta look out for each other, sister." On that Saturday night before Halloween, when arguments and physical fights were breaking out in every nook and cranny, someone or other had always intervened to reason with the combatants and remind them how vital the revolution was to all of us. During every single outbreak, the arguers had chosen to de-escalate for the good of all, and not draw the attention of the police to us. Everyone seemed to intuit that we were making history. Many said as much, and no one—no matter how compromised or damaged—wanted to be the one that ruined the dream. No one wanted to kill the hope and promise that we all felt during that heady time. I have now had some time to read different statistics about what transpired during the weeks of the encampment, and it was reported by the Bay Area's KTVU TV that, according to official correspondence between Police Chief Howard Jordan and Mayor Jean Quan, the crime rate in Oakland actually dropped by 19% during the first weeks of Occupy Oakland's tent village.

Between the celebrity drop-ins, scholarly teach-ins, and the night time drama, I also volunteered to help plan the entertainment for the day of the General Strike, November 2. The evening before was mercifully conflict free, thanks in large part to the delivery of a sound system that pumped out the jams until the wee small hours, on the steps in front of City Hall. The sound engineer was a young guy named Brian, who made it his job to provide us with free PA equipment at the nightly GAs. He chose the hours between 11:00 p.m. and 3:00 a.m. to troubleshoot his larger system, so that he'd be up and running by dawn for the next day's events. It had served an unintentional purpose of soothing the savage breasts that yearned to break each other's faces late at night.

All night long Occupiers had danced to Rick James, The Jackson Five, James Brown, Earth, Wind & Fire, and a host of other hit makers, which had lowered the threat level from red to beige instantly. Though I still didn't get much sleep, I enjoyed dancing, and then sleeping, to the joyous sounds that pierced the night. Just after sunrise, I lay awake in my tent for a few luxurious moments before getting up on my haunches to squat and pee into the festive container that served as my indoor commode. After transferring its contents to a widemouth water bottle, I unzipped my tentflap and walked over to the porta potties (thank you Bette Midler) to dump it. I thought myself cunning for having devised such a stealthy way to avoid sitting directly on the vile toilet seats while voiding my bladder in the morning. After tidying up my tent a bit, I headed on over to the amphitheater stage, which I was scheduled to manage throughout the day. Performers were beginning to arrive and check in with me, and from the stage I could see my neighbors, some with children and pets, forming a line at the kitchen area, which had expanded and improved throughout the week. I'd put out a Facebook SOS the day before, and we'd been gifted several large bags of premium dog food, which had been met with elation by our animal-loving residents. Two large solar panels powered the refrigerator that kept the perishables cold. Mounds of fresh donated bread and produce lay on one of the five stainless steel tables we now owned, and propane tanks fueled the burners which heated steam trays of scrambled eggs, tofu, oatmeal, sausages, and turkey bacon.

The inviting smell of brewing coffee wafted to the stage and made our crazy quilt village feel like home. Many of the people in the breakfast line had been homeless for ages and had taken shelter in downtown Oakland long before we got there, but were now welcoming the community and protection our presence lent them. As out of hand as nighttimes sometimes got at #OO, the old-timers assured us things had gotten much better after we arrived. They regaled us with stories of really horrific incidents that had ended in serious bloodshed and even death. Even though I was certain there were at least one or two murderers and rapists in our midst, it filled me with gladness to be a part of this fabulous melting pot—everyone engaging in that yawny, sleepy morning small talk that binds us together and makes us family.

I introduced myself quickly before registering performers arriving to the stage, always keeping an eye out for last-minute additions, when I looked over toward the kitchen and saw a tall, regal woman, with a marvelous bushy coiffure, walking toward me from the kitchen area, accompanied by another mocha-skinned beauty. I immediately recognized her as one of my childhood heroes from the Civil Rights Movement—Angela Davis. I confess, I was instantaneously immobilized and rendered daft by the very sight of her unmistakable face and hair. In the late 1960s, this woman had transformed me, my mother, and my sister, in the blink of an eye, from obedient, pressed hair Negroes, to twelve-inch Afro–flaunting, fist-pumping, "Black Power" shouting Soul Sisters as we watched her, agape, from our first colored television set. Her scathing, unapologetic analyses of racism and injustice in America floored us, and then redefined us. That very night, my mom cut off our long plaits and reshaped our hair into superb "naturals" that felt so liberating, I tossed my head back like a stallion as I strutted into my all-white, third grade Catholic school classroom the next morning. I remember that as the first time in my life I felt lucky, instead of cursed, to be black. That feeling has remained with me all my life, and I was forever beholden to her for creating it. So much so that I wanted to tackle her to the ground and smother her with gratitude when I laid eyes on her. I suddenly understood how those hysterical, seizing, Beatle, fans could debase themselves so, watching John, Paul, George, and Ringo stride onto the stage to perform on the Ed Sullivan show in 1964. I forgot all about my job, as I dashed my clipboard to the pavement and accosted her like a crazed stalker—gushing like a madwoman as I shadowed her to the Fourteenth and Broadway stage. She was tolerant of the intrusion, but averted her eyes from me when ushered onto the stage to impart a brief, but memorable speech. Her parting pronouncement, "We are the ones we've been waiting for," reverberated through my core as I rushed back to the duties I'd so thoroughly abdicated after her arrival.

The sun shone brightly on us all day as rappers rapped, dancers danced, singers sang, poets recited, and actors acted. My own short set with Bluegrass legend Laurie Lewis and stellar guitarist, Shelley Doty, went well and by three thirty so many thousands of people had amassed in the Plaza, we had to shut our stage down half an hour early to send marchers out in waves to the Port of Oakland. There were six buses ferrying the elderly and disabled along the route, while large union contingents milled around, waiting for their turn to go forward. Entire families, brass bands, dogs with bandanas, drummers, unaffiliated marchers, and all kinds of professionals adorned the route, in perfect step with teachers, doctors, truck drivers, and health-care workers. I could see neither the beginning nor the end of the two-mile route, as it snaked westward down Fourteenth Street. Our lengthy processional concluded at the Port, where we hoped to shut down the evening shift. It was our aim to disrupt commerce and disallow business as usual—to demonstrate to the owners, investment firm Goldman Sachs, that we meant to cost them money and flex our collective muscle. We wanted to compel them to treat the longshoremen and truckers better. We also wanted to prove that we the people have the power, and their livelihoods depended on our disposition toward them. In recent years they busted unions by dishonoring contracts with them and hiring non-union laborers to drive down wages and benefits. Things had gotten so bad that the Port workers had gone on strike, insisting that they were routinely working dangerously long hours, with overloaded vehicles and unsafe conditions—sometimes making less than minimum wage, often with no benefits. The day's agenda had wiped me out, but I enthusiastically walked the dozens of flat surface streets in solidarity with the large crowd. It wasn't until sunset, when I perched on a hilltop overlooking the march, that I saw how many people were actually there. I was dumbfounded to realize there were tens of thousands of us in an almost endless stream of humanity. The Oakland Police Chief, Howard Jordan, went on the news that night with a preposterous crowd estimate of between three and five thousand. Months later, aerial footage released by news helicopters, confirmed the number to be nearly one hundred thousand. Upon entry to the Port, most of us broke off into groups, to block individual terminals and prevent trucks from coming through the gates for the night shift. The drivers were obviously expecting us, and many chose to park adjacent to the roadway, honking and waving their appreciation for us. A small minority displayed minor irritation with our invasion, but the overwhelming majority gave us peace signs, high fives, and thumbs up. Some even got out of their trucks and hugged us, as they expressed how good it made them feel to see that someone cared about what they were going through. A handful of them told me that they'd been in a dispute with the operators for years, trying to advocate for better wages and working conditions from the owners. It meant a lot to most that someone outside their profession cared enough to organize in support of their efforts. We did open our human gate to allow the retiring shift to leave, but no workers were permitted to enter. Within a couple of hours the Port was declared unsafe to operate and the evening shift was declared cancelled. Someone grabbed a bullhorn and relayed the news to us which was met with deafening whoops and cheers. After our victory, I stayed to dance and sing with others before finally returning to Oscar Grant Plaza, where a few thousand of us lingered to talk and groove to the recorded music Brian was treating us to from the back of his sound truck. It was some time after midnight when I fell into my cozy tent home, took a long pull on my bottle, and fell triumphantly asleep.

Chapter 3

Oakland General Strike—N2

There we sat, peace signs extended, nine or ten feet in front of three hundred uniformed, fully armed police officers in riot gear. Three rows of fifty in front of me and three rows of fifty beside me on the right. Three different agencies in all were represented. The Oakland cops were in the lead, followed by Santa Rita County cops, and a SWAT team. An hour earlier, I had been comfortably bedded down in my tent, after a life changing day of revolutionary miracles. Wednesday, November 2, 2011, had been the day of the massively attended, hugely successful Oakland General Strike. It was the realization of a long held dream—of people rising up and demanding their right to the America we were promised—"land of the free and the home of the brave." I understood that this beautiful ideal required diligence, bravery, and sacrifice on each citizen's part. I treasured the noble doctrine put forth by our forefathers along with Thomas Jefferson's vision of a nation where, "Dissent is patriotic," and "One has a moral responsibility to disobey unjust laws." In many places around the globe, the trajectory of a life was determined by the accident of birth, but not so in these United States. I counted myself lucky to be born into a country where, theoretically, anyone could improve their station, graduate college, own a house, or even become president one day—where immigrants were introduced to their new home by a kind, compassionate Lady Liberty, who welcomed them with open arms, and assured them that the indignities they'd suffered thus far were now over.

Though, in reality, my native land had always fallen somewhere short of this idyllic wonderland, I always believed that it was possible, with some adjustments, to come much closer than this. I knew that my country was a unique and grand experiment. It once relegated my mother and her blackness to the back of the bus—then awakened to the barbarity of its actions, and went on to have an epiphany, culminating in the election of a man with that same original sin to the presidency. Could this magical oasis also suddenly have an awakening about the assaults that corporations, banks, and the richest people on earth were committing against us—the masses, the proletariat in the twenty-first century? And so, given my undying devotion to the stars and stripes, how had I come to be sitting there, on a cordoned-off downtown street in Oakland, faced and flanked by severe looking men with guns and tear gas bombs, that were trained directly at me. Physically, I knew how I'd gotten there. I heard the concussions shaking the ground under my body, and then heard the screams, "**Poh**—lice, **Poh**—lice! Y'all motherfuckers get up outta your tents—they fixin' to blow this motherfucker up again!" I crammed all my stuff into a suitcase and considered running, not walking, to the nearest airport. To my way of thinking, there was no dishonor in hightailing my fifty-one-year old, comfortable, plump behind back to my mountain home, nestled inside 160 acres of verdant forestland. What would be the harm in retreating back to my gardens and the horses—reacquainting myself with my fourth grade daughter and the rest of my dear family, whom I'd left three weeks earlier to participate in first, Occupy Albany, then Occupy Wall Street, and finally this, Occupy Oakland? But instead, angered by the intrusion into my perfect day, I stumbled to my feet and staggered toward the commotion just outside the camp on San Pablo Street.

There I found hundreds of shocked celebrants—leftovers from the successful port action—standing around in disbelief at what had just transpired. Seconds before, they were talking, dancing, and listening to music—digging the after-party—when along came a handful of Black Bloc anarchists, who swooped in, dragged over a green metal dumpster, and set its contents ablaze. They'd also broken a couple of plate glass windows on the downtown OPD criminal investigation/recruiting office, which was, unfortunately, located adjacent to our tent village in the plaza. There were ten or eleven of them, all dressed in black, with homemade shields and face masks, whooping and hollering like errant teenagers when I walked onto the scene. I sidestepped them with ease, as I looked north up the street and saw a multitiered row of about a hundred and fifty riot police officers facing us from about half a block away. They had just assembled and fired tear gas canisters and flashbang grenades into the crowd before I got there. A thick cloud of gas hung in the air and burned my nose, eyes, and throat. *Wow, my first taste of tear gas,* I thought, almost proudly, as I surveyed the scene. Some cops had their guns up and trained on us, while others merely stood there—eyes locked forward. I ran the distance to them, leaving about ten feet of pavement between us, and began imploring them to stop firing. Seeing them, expressionless, armed to the teeth, and looking on the verge of shooting everyone into swiss cheese knocked something loose inside me, and I felt an unexpected sob leap into my throat as I began pleading, "Please don't hurt them—they're just kids. They have a right to their anger. Don't you hope your sons and daughters will get to go to college someday? Most of these kids did everything right. They stayed out of trouble and got good grades, and now they're in debt up to their ears. They're living at home with their parents—working for minimum wage at Starbucks. That's not going to pay the bills. They're mad because they know they're screwed. Some of them are really smart and still won't ever be able to afford college. Wouldn't you be mad? Aren't you mad? Are any of you having a hard time coming up with the money for your kid's education? Are you feeling a little bit squeezed? How's that going for you? Is that going well? Do any of you have grown kids at home, occupying your couches, because there aren't enough decent jobs out there? If you need to arrest someone, go after the ones that broke the windows and torched the dumpster. Most of them are still right over there. Right there in the black jeans, with the shields and masks and leather jackets. That big 'A' on their backs stands for, "arrest me." They're the only ones that caused any damage, so maybe you should go after them. They're easy to spot. They're not even running. In fact, they're over there waving at you. But these kids over here, they're not thugs—they're not even doing anything illegal. Why would you hurt these kids when they're being peaceful?"

One officer said, "Look lady, these ain't kids, they're over eighteen." Nonetheless, the whole row of cops seemed to hesitate, as if they might be mulling over my words. Some registered uncertainty while others appeared to be flummoxed about what to do next. Even though none resembled the friendly "peace officers" Catholic nuns advised me to seek out if I was in trouble, it was encouraging that no one had shot me yet. I did see a few of them on my right begin to advance slightly, so I ran over to them, gesticulating madly, imploring them to think about what they were about to do. I remembered my grade school teachers saying that calling "the authorities" could get you out of a bad situation in a hurry. These guys looked much more likely to put me in a bad situation than to get me out of one. Nonetheless, I tried to stay on track, beseeching them again and again to think about their own children and how slim their chances of getting ahead were becoming. I riffed as long as I could, often reaching for what I hoped would be compelling imagery to give things a chance to simmer down. Some of the words coming out of my mouth actually seemed to be having an effect for a while—judging by the fact that I was still alive. I kept filibustering, but was running out of material, and now resorting to blurting out anything that came to mind. "Yeah, soooo, don't you want your kids to have like, clean water and fresh air and healthy food and shiny new textbooks and weekend trips to the petting zoo and stuff like that when they grow up? Yeah, wouldn't it be nicer if the mayor had asked you all to come down here and *talk* with us, or help us plant flowers and plant vegetables, instead of tear gassing us and shooting us with bean bags? 'Cause I mean I've never actually been hit by a rubber bullet or a beanbag, but I bet it smarts right? They gotta be goin' pretty fast when they hit you, huh." I asked them to chew on how the mayor threw them under the bus and then distanced herself from their actions, after *she* told them it was all right to fire on protesters. And then, after they wounded Scott Olsen, she said they'd acted on their own. She told the media that she was out of town at the time (which was true) and unaware that her police department might resort to aggressive tactics and chemical agents to disperse the crowd (which was not true). It was later determined that the OPD acted on her direct orders, and had not, in fact, gone all rogue on the Occupy demonstrators. I tried to make the point that they, too, were getting a raw deal, and asked them to understand that we weren't just out for kicks. We were assembled there because we hoped to make things better for all of us, including them.

At that point I began to sense the guys' attentions waning and impatience setting in, so I tried a new tack and asked the dark, muscular cop who seemed to be in charge, if he'd consider not harming us if everyone agreed to sit down and be silent. He looked at me scornfully through his shield, but, to his credit, didn't outright reject the plan, saying, "Yeah, right, that's gonna work." I told him I thought it just might, and instantly ran back toward the group before he had a chance to stop me. "Sit down! Sit down!" I shouted. Then I put my finger to my lips and motioned, "Shh-hhhhhhh! Everybody, please just sit down and they won't fire at us." I hoped that I was right about that. Many didn't sit down, but, thankfully, over half of them did. Lots of them sat with peace signs extended, and almost everyone ceased talking. The contrast in behavior was wholly impressive and I hoped it would be enough to satisfy the army of police in front of us and get them to turn around and head out, which would leave us free to do the same.

I ran back to the squad that had since closed in and decreased the distance between us to only twenty yards. I positioned myself directly opposite the guy who seemed to be in charge. "Okay, so . . . lots of us are sitting down and we're all quiet and peaceful. Can we just call it good and you guys go home now?"

"Hey, you seem like a nice lady, just get out of here and don't get yourself hurt tonight," he replied. And, with that, he pushed past me, and signalled to the whole row to move forward, which they did—nightsticks raised. Upon seeing the police charge, the last of the remaining Black Bloc troupe bolted and ran into the shadows, leaving the rest of us, who were seated, to pay for their deeds. The explosive surge of uniformed gunmen rattled us into paralysis, as we closed our eyes and flinched in expectation.

I had come here to Oakland to witness history, to be a part of a peaceful revolution—a social media facilitated groundswell, populated by other frustrated, hopeful, determined people who, like me, aimed to demand and create the America we wanted to live in. So then, why was I, all of a sudden, sitting in a tense standoff with all these pissed off, armed to the teeth, cranky cops, who looked as if they'd like nothing more than to separate my head from my neck? Furthermore, why was a sloppy, wasted chick sitting inches away from me, sounding like she'd only come out to the revolution because she heard there was going to be free booze? God, we were just about to be slaughtered by a bunch of hopped up automatons, and here she was, rambling on and on about some of the dumbest shit I'd ever heard. After they pushed me aside, the cops had applied the brakes and stopped on a dime a few feet in front of us. They dug in and planted themselves, as if someone had just yelled, "Simon says stop!" It was creepy to see how stiffly they could stand—completely immobile—eyes cold and dead, not saying or doing anything. I shot a sideways glance at the sodden goddess, and wondered who the hell had invited her to our party.

Physically, she was beautiful, I could see that. She looked like she could be in a Super Bowl commercial, selling . . . anything. She was the perfect combination of slutty and wholesome—sassy

and submissive—hair like spun gold, teeth like pearls, drunk like a
skunk—a heedless tumbleweed, party hearty womanchild, of perhaps twenty or twenty-two years of age, sucking fellatially on a
gigantic brown beer bottle, and writhing around on the ground
like a cat in heat. She seemed to have no idea whatsoever how
she came to be there, or even why we were all there. Apparently
unable to contain all her deep thoughts in one pouty, sexy, little
mouth, she kept blurting out things like, "I'm *horny*," and, "Will
somebody just fucking *kiss* me," as she reached out and drew both
black and white men down to the ground to grind on and French
kiss. After a time, another attractive young woman strolled by,
unaware, only to be grabbed and pulled earthward by the insatiable coquette. Her victim seemed genuinely shocked, yet unable to
resist the impossible urge to kiss and grind back. One cop, observing, looked like he was going to pass out. Not one among us could
look away. She, with her brown forty-ounce bottle of beer resting between her sometimes crossed, sometimes splayed wide open
like Olga Korbut, legs. She with the hoarse, childlike voice, rend-
ing the night air with illuminating pronouncements like, "I'm not
political, I don't even give a shit about any of this crap, the 69%
or whatever—I just wanna *fuck* somebody *hot* tonight. Is that too
much to ask?"

I watched some of the cops begin to tremble, hardly able to
contain the physiological responses they were having to her. I
saw riot shields move to cover sensitive areas. I saw men looking
down at those areas, some breaking out in a cold sweat. Hell, I
was having some sort of physiological response to her, though I
was way past menopause. Not only that, I loathed her. I wanted
her gone, and the fact that the entire revolution was turning into
a farce because of her stupid, compromised, randy ass was pissing
me all the way off. Here we all were, about to meet our maker at
the hands of a bunch of frothing-at-the-mouth cyborgs who were
armed to the eyelashes, and all she could think of to say was, "I just
wanna fuck somebody *hot* tonight." Please God, make the sniper
shoot her first, I thought wickedly. I hadn't spent every night of

the last week in a tent with maniacal crack heads and toothless tweakers to go out like this. I didn't sacrifice all my creature comforts while placating murderers, and rapping with rapists for this. It might have been worth losing a few nights' sleep trying to talk down meth addicts, hell bent on "beatin' the shit outta their ol' ladies," if we'd made a little progress on foreclosures and income inequality, but not so this chick could party like it was 1999. I wanted to be charitable toward her, after all, she too was part of the 99% and probably could have benefitted greatly from services that didn't exist anymore. I mean, it had been a life-altering journey and I had been brought to my knees watching damaged, ravaged people, even at their psychotic, paranoid, drugged out worst, attempting to have meaningful dialogues about social ills and the problems plaguing the planet. Overhearing their hazy, fucked up, jagged, and sometimes indecipherable conversations about democracy and out-of-control corporatization had made me love them all the more—but I hadn't gone on that epic journey, only to have Drunky Drunkerson get us all shot up into confetti .

Drunky Drunkatelli had the potential to whip these cops into an overstimulated, trigger-happy frenzy if she didn't watch out. And to be sure, she wasn't watching out. I may have had a little more patience for the girl if she hadn't been turning the entire body of our labor and devotion into some sort of bizarre, third-rate spectacle. But, because I *had* spent that intensive week with all those whacked out, scary people, I was not predisposed to tolerate nonsense. Being jarred awake after marching with tens of thousands of like-minded, passionate, unstoppable dreamers, who dared to demand the impossible, made me disinclined to suffer fools. I did not think I could bear her running monologue of physical needs ("I need a cigarette, I need to get my nails done, I need a bigger bra, I need another beer, I need to get *FUCK*ed") one second longer. That's when she launched into the chant that made springs shoot out of my head. She spun around to face the police, who now stood rigidly, ten feet before us, as she pointed at them with her premoistened fingers, which she had swirled suggestively in her sensual little mouth. "You're sexy—You're cute, Take off your riot suit," she began, giggling nymphishly, obviously tickled pink with her clever little rhyme. She continued for some time. I wanted to stab her.

I, along with several other terrified, anxious demonstrators, had begun our day wanting to change the world for the better, and somehow instead found ourselves sitting here in a tense stalemate with a mob of agitated police officers, who didn't seem to know right then whether to shit or go blind. Somewhere in the crowd, a ragged violinist began to play and softly sing, "I'd rather die on my feet than live on my knees." I felt as though I'd fallen into a Dostoyevsky novel as he continued his mournful tune. Drunkenfrau resumed her writhing, looking as if she'd rather make a living on her back than anywhere else. How had our social justice movement become a personal opportunity for her to score with three hundred guys all at once? Some among us had even begun telling her to stop. A young man somewhere behind me yelled, "Shut the fuck up drunk bitch!" Another, growing bored with the impasse, stupidly skipped a votive candle over the brick street, where it rolled, broke, and came to rest just short of the line of police, who had nearly panicked and jerked their guns toward the harmless object. I too had almost mistaken it for a molotov cocktail. The close call prompted all of us to launch into a made up on the spot, chant, "Don't Throw Shit, Don't Throw Shit." Then, sensing their ongoing ire, we amended the chant to, "Don't Throw Shit—AT THE COPS." We repeated the refrain until the tension eased and once more we resumed our uneasy standoff.

Nearly two interminable hours dragged by in semi silence. Some stayed because we wanted to assert our right to peacefully assemble, while others stayed because they didn't know if we had permission to leave. Some people lying down had even gone to sleep. Others, like me, kept a wary eye on the weaponry before us, as the holders began to shift from foot to foot in restless irritation. They too looked tired, and anxious to get on with it. Drunk girl even dozed for a few moments, but jerked wide awake to resume her favorite chant anew. "You're sexy, You're cute—Take off your riot suit." The surreal atmosphere crossed the line into absurdity when all the young men in our group began to take up the chant. Growing stiff and weary, I got to my feet and stood about a yard in front of the black officer with a bullhorn, who seemed to be the main guy in charge. I asked him if there was any possibility, since it was so late and we were all tired and frazzled, that he could just order his guys to turn around and head back to the precinct while we all returned to our respective corners. Without question, none of us harbored any secret plans to break windows or light fires—we simply didn't want to be ordered to give up our constitutional right. And the cops did not want us to feel like we'd gotten away with something. Just then, a woman's voice began to flood the airspace around us.

"Attention! You must leave the area immediately. Please be advised that this area has been declared closed and you are unlawfully assembled. Failure to disperse may result in arrest or injury." The policewoman recited this same sentence, with little or no inflection, so many times, that it almost became soothing to me. Eventually she tagged the phrase, "Return to the Plaza and you will not be arrested," to her mantra. It was well after my normal bedtime, and I wanted to go back to my tent. I asked the commanding officer again if we might call it even, and sort of mutually disperse. I told him that I understood how annoying it must be to have all these youngsters out here refusing to go home, but that it was not violent or unstable really, and none of them were breaking anything or acting a fool. He shot back with, "They're all actin' a fool," after which he snatched up his walkie-talkie and spoke gruffly into the receiver, "Okay, uh . . ..You gotta tell me *somethin'* about what you want me to do out here now."

The disembodied voice on the other end said, "Well, what's going on out there? Is anybody rioting or breaking anything . . . or . . . are there any more fires?"

"Well, no. Nothing much is happening here right now and nothing's *been* happening for a long time," he answered, abruptly.

Whoever was talking to him on the other end asked, "Well, what do you wanna do with them? Can you flank 'em and push

'em back into the camp, or what . . . how far are you away from
the tents out there?" That's when I realized the person who had
the power to order us all blasted into microchips wasn't anywhere
near the Plaza, and probably hadn't been all night. For all I knew,
the voice was coming from an office downtown somewhere. It was
unfathomable to me that someone wielding so much power and
influence over our immediate well-being could give life-threatening commands without even being on scene to assess the threat
level for himself.

"Hell . . . I don't know man, just tell me whatchyu want me to
do. We been out here all night and ain't nothin' goin' on. Whatchyu
want me to do, man?" returned the cop in front of me, gesturing
impatiently into the handset as if it were a live human being.

"Well, get on it—arrest somebody and get it over with if that's
what yer gonna do," was the final edict. I wasn't sure what that
meant, but it all became clear when I felt someone's hands grab
the straps of my backpack, pull me into the row of cops, shove me
onto the ground, and put a knee in my back. I hit the pavement
hard, despite having put my hands out to break my fall. Someone pinned my face to the ground, and I felt my right hand being
grabbed and yanked behind my back, and then, the left one. A
set of rigid plastic zip-tie cuffs were then placed around my wrists
and pulled savagely to their tightest possible setting. "Ahhhhhhh-
hhhhhhhh!" I screamed, "please, it hurts. It's too tight. It's cutting
into me. Please, I know you're just doing your job, but please, I'm
not going to give you any trouble, sir, can you just loosen it a little
. . . *please*," I beseeched. He didn't acknowledge my request in any
way. After awhile, I stopped asking and tried to endure the pain,
as the police officer reached into my pockets and searched for
weapons and sharps. Tears ran down my face and onto the street. I
was completely isolated from my group. Most everyone fled either
back to the Plaza encampment or home, and that meant no one on
my team was around to see what happened to me or film them, as
I was violently arrested behind the curtain of cops. I was afraid—
very afraid. A powerful hand grabbed my wrists from behind and

jerked me up, by my handcuffs, to a standing position. I yelped in pain just before the officer scowled, "You got a little gas tonight?" At first I was confused, saying, "Excuse me?" But then, understood exactly what he meant. "I said, you got a little gas tonight?" He repeated disdainfully. "You just farted in my face." I felt my own face flush, as I remembered the air that escaped from my rear end as he wrenched me, painfully, to my feet. "Um, yeah, I guess so. Sorry . . . I wasn't expecting that," I said, instantly furious with myself for letting him embarrass me. I stood there in abject fear, until another police officer, whose name was "Alvarez," came over and asked my tormentor whether he should "cut my backpack off, or just loosen the straps."

"Whatever—it's your call," was the flat response from the first cop. I remained silent, knowing instinctively that my opinion mattered little here. I expected Alvarez to make a show of selecting the biggest knife in his arsenal and hacking away at my newer backpack, but instead, he opted to loosen the straps until they were undone, and gently lift it from my shoulders. The unexpected kindness made more tears flow down my face as I ventured to quietly ask him if he could loosen the cuffs just a little bit. There was genuine concern in his eyes when he asked a colleague if there was a way to decrease the pressure. The answer didn't surprise me, but Alvarez's bothering to check did. He walked me slowly to the van and then helped me up into it, as I struggled with the high paddy-wagon entry. Three men were already in the divided cages of the van, as was a woman who looked distressed. "You shouldn't have to wait too long. You'll just get processed downtown and released . . . probably won't be more than two, three hours, tops," Alvarez said, helpfully, as he left us to get back to his job.

Three hours later we arrived in a large, enclosed concrete bay at a downtown Oakland jail and were asked to stand up outside the van to await processing. By that time the fetters had cut off the blood supply to my hands, which had swelled like sausages, and my wrists were throbbing in pain. It was nearing four o'clock in the morning and I was calling out pathetically, to have the shackles removed. A woman officer came over to me and snapped, "You see that?" pointing to the inside of the building, where a madhouse scene of protesters were being dragged here and there by mean looking cops. "Yes," I said wincing.

"If I stop everything I'm doing here and pay attention to you, then all those guys over there gotta wait even longer. And then they take it out on *you* for making *them* wait. You don't want that. You got it?"

"Yes," I said.

Though she'd indicated otherwise, she did return quickly to free my hands, which put me in a much better mood. After the manacles came off, I felt downright giddy and decided to make the best of what I hoped would be a once-in-a-lifetime experience. Three anxious young women and I were soon placed in a holding cell, where I was pleased to have company, so I began to chat them up. None were thrilled to be there, but we did have a few laughs while we waited for something to happen. Hours went by before one of my cellmates, Andrea, who held two master's degrees from Cal, noticed that there was a phone hanging on the wall. She picked up the receiver and minutes later was placing a collect call to the National Lawyer's Guild Hotline. We all had a chance to give the lawyer details of our arrests and tell her how badly we wanted out before hanging up, which made us feel better. Another hour passed before a severe officer came to free us from the cell. I was ecstatic to be leaving and said so, only to have the officer laugh at me, "Oh no, you're not done. You're going over to Santa Rita at Alameda, County. You're gonna love it there. Your party's just starting."

We were combined with a dozen or so other female Occupiers and lined up in the concrete bay we arrived at to board a prison bus to Santa Rita jail. I smiled conspiratorially at the other women, who were all much younger than I, and in no mood for joviality. Ignoring their standoffishness, I congratulated them for surviving our first night in jail. I hoped my friskiness would rub off on them as I imagined the fun of telling my friends about the whole ordeal. The ride reminded me of a sixth grade bus trip I'd taken to a YMCA summer camp. I broke the ice with other riders, just as I had then, by telling funny stories along the way. Everyone seemed to perk up somewhat, after a fashion, and the morning sunshine felt good to me through the dirty bus windows. I struck up a dialogue with our transport driver through the metal cage mesh between us, which seemed to amuse him some. I guessed that didn't happen too often in his line of work.

The Santa Rita "Campus" was manicured and green—almost inviting from the outside, which I glimpsed briefly before being unloaded inside another enclosed bay. I was swiftly disabused of this notion as we were paraded past a cramped holding cell full of mostly black men on the way to our destination. They jumped to their feet, grabbing themselves and ogling us hungrily as they pressed up against the bulletproof glass windows. The young women with me were obviously humiliated and some came visibly unglued, clutching their clothing and covering their faces while we walked the gantlet. I, on the other hand, felt like a tourist at Disneyland and began waving deliriously at them—flashing the peace sign in solidarity with my fellow incarcerees. Because most of the men were less than half my age, I felt more protective toward them than threatened. It pained me to see such numbers of dark-skinned people caged up and serving time, rather than studying for exams and launching careers. Many of the hard-bodied inmates abandoned their rough exteriors, returning my grins and signs exuberantly. Thirteen of us were escorted to a sterile white cell meant to hold no more than six. It did boast a tiny cut-out shower, which had a tile bench and a single drain in the middle of the floor. Unfortunately, the tile bench was already occupied when we arrived, by a tiny young black woman with a buzz cut, who looked more like a twelve-year-old boy than a nineteen-year-old girl. She was curled into a fetal position on the bench from which she hung her head every few minutes to vomit what appeared to be fruit flavored vodka onto the floor. She did not look up at any of us. I tried to keep my nose closed while selecting a bench seat as far away from her as possible. She kept her eyes closed and did not acknowledge any of us who tried our best to give her space and privacy. A few of the girls joined in my jocularity, but others stayed sullen and inward. I learned from them that they had all been arrested inside the Plaza, where the tent village was, and where we had all been ordered to retreat to by the OPD if we wanted to "avoid being injured or arrested." According to my cellmates, the police went back on their word and immediately began arresting everyone who returned to the encampment after the final dispersal order was given. Though they were promised safe haven there, they'd been chased, trapped, and teargassed anyway, even while compliant and cooperative.

We were all tired but there wasn't enough area for everyone to lie down on the cold floor with the metal toilet in the center of the room. Then of course was the inevitable need to pee, or worse yet, poop into a toilet that was inches away from someone else's head. We all found elimination difficult to accomplish, yet talking about it beforehand made it more bearable. Most girls took advantage of the phone on the wall (which I was jokingly referring to as our "cell phone") and made awkward collect calls to their parents, who ran the gamut from indifference to hysteria upon learning of their child's whereabouts. Some of the teenagers among us had furrowed brows as they listened to what their parents had to say. After observing a few painful exchanges, I cajoled my cellies into shouting, "Hi Mom!" gaily, in unison, to each parent that got the late night call, which broke some tension and helped reduce the number of interactions that didn't go well. After that was done, a cheery type named Kate made a proposal. "Hey, since there's not much room and some of us are feeling a little down right now—you're all welcome to join me in a cuddle puddle on the floor." Lots of the girls took her up on it and soon they lay entwined like kittens on the concrete surface.

A short nap was had by some before a uniformed woman, whose badge said "Fox," rousted us by loudly barking, "Hustle your asses out onto the floor before I lose all of your paperwork." We did as we were told and hurried to exit the cell, only to be commanded to stand with our faces to the wall with our arms extended outward. Another female officer joined Fox and walked up and down the line. I felt her hands reach under my breasts and lift them up. Then she worked her way down my body, over my buttocks, outside my thighs and down to the floor. After that she placed her hand inside my thigh and cupped my crotch. Some felt violated and had a hard time complying with this, as they flinched and shied away to avoid the contact—all to no avail. I didn't suffer unduly through the procedure though, as I was mentally cataloging everything that happened and enjoying the idea of holding court with the lively tale at Thanksgiving dinner. When we'd all been searched, Fox told us to turn around and run our hands back and forth through our hair, which we did. Then she told us to lift up our breasts for her, which we also did. Apparently she wasn't satisfied with our performance because she frowned exaggeratedly at us and brayed, "Come on girls, you can do a lot better than that. *SHIMMY*. Come on! Shimmy for me," she insisted. One young woman in the lineup, a journalist, who had her official press badge prominently displayed when detained, rolled her eyes theatrically and clenched her jaws, gritting her teeth as if she were about to explode. I hoped for her sake that she wouldn't. Then, Andrea with the two master's degrees, decided to break bad with Fox, who earlier had refused to bring her her medication, for an acute bladder infection, from her confiscated bag. "*You* are violating *my* rights and I'm having a *medical emergency*. I need my prescription NOW!" Andrea shouted.

"You ain't havin' no goddamn medical emergency. You know how I can tell? 'Cuz you ain't havin' no seizure and you're still breathin'," Fox roared back. Then, she began to laugh, viciously, at Andrea who glowered back at her. Then she added, "*And* you *ain't* got no rights in here. Just in case you hadn't noticed, you're in *jail*, sweetheart. Now, it's gonna be a hell of a long time before you get outta here, cuz I just lost your paperwork, Andrea."

After shimmying, we headed off for mug shots and fingerprints, where I was torn between smiling and looking dejected for the camera. I wanted to relax and be myself, but I was so tired, I wasn't sure how I felt or which look accurately depicted my state of mind. I chose the latter and walked the few steps to the finger print line, where five or six women preceded me. One of the women was a small, quiet teenager from Germany, who spoke very little English, but who'd told me earlier her name was Nadine, pronounced, "Nah-deen." A tall, muscular, slow-witted male officer was leaning close to her face, shouting at her. "I said, *What's your name?* I'm not going to ask you again." Nadine looked terrified as tears streamed down her cheeks. "Nah-deen! Nah-deen!" she cried. We were all watching in horror, when I realized the policeman thought she was being uncooperative. He thought she was saying, "Nothing! Nothing!" instead of furnishing him with her name. I interjected, "Sir, she's German, she doesn't understand much English! Her name is 'Nay-deen,' but it's pronounced, 'Nah-deen' over there. It sounds like she's saying, 'nothing,' but she's not. She has an accent . . ." I was trying not to sound like a big fat know-it-all college graduate when addressing him. The last thing I wanted was for him to think I was reprimanding him, or felt superior in some way. But in the end, none of that made any difference. The dolt cop took his pen out and jammed it between her wrist and the silver bracelet she wore. He jerked upward, breaking the chain and sending it crashing to the floor beneath her. Then, he reached down, picked it up, and hurled it into the trash can before I could finish my sentence. The brutality of the act was so unwarranted, we were stunned into silence. Even Fox lifted her head momentarily, raising her eyebrows as she sat on a stool next to him, completing her paperwork. I wanted to rush to the child's aid—we all did, but knew that it would only make things worse for everyone, most of all Nadine. So I stood impotently behind her and felt every ounce of mirth drain from my body. The girl, who had labored to explain to me in English that she was eighteen years old, also told me that, in her personal philosophy, it made no difference what country she protested in, because she cared about all people, not just Germans. She was crying hard now—frightened nearly out of her wits. Just then I was beckoned by Fox to come forward and state my name, which I did promptly. I articulated it clearly to her and then said, as humbly as I could muster, "Um, look, I was talking with that girl, Nadine, back at the cell and she doesn't know much English, so I don't really think she was trying to give him any trouble or anything. I covered the same ground with Fox that I had with her male counterpart, this time hoping for a better result. "Yeah like, I think she pronounces her name like' Nah-Deen,' because she's from somewhere in Europe or something. I guess that's how they say it in Germany or wherever." Then, for effect, I shrugged and rolled my eyes as if pronouncing it any other way than "NAY-deen" was the most idiotic thing I could ever imagine. Her co-worker's behavior was so uncalled for, that I could tell it even bothered Fox a little bit. She cast some of the nastiness aside and looked me square in the eye, saying, "Yeah, you know, cops are just like protesters or anyone else out there—it just takes a few bad ones to make us all look like assholes." She tossed her head over to the bully officer next to us that had just finished with Nadine when she said the word, "assholes" and I felt like we were having an incredible breakthrough. "You know we're not getting that great a deal these days either, right, Bill?" said Fox, throwing her words toward a uniformed man in his fifties who was sitting at a computer inside a nearby office. "Nope, not this year," he answered, affably. "They just hiked it up to five hundred bucks a month now that comes out of our paychecks for our benefits package and that's not all they took away," he went on. "Yep, it sucks," agreed Fox. "See, we're part of the 99% too, if you really think about it. To tell you the truth, I hope you guys get some things done." I fought to hold my facial muscles in check and resist the urge to let my jaw drop to the floor. Another teenager who was standing behind me, waiting her turn, overheard the entire conversation, and as I glanced back at her, she mouthed the word, "Wow." I decided to push a little further with Fox as she finished processing me, since the other big meanie had gone on break. I asked if she might be able to retrieve Nadine's bracelet from the trash and give it back, because it obviously meant a lot to her. She answered, "Yeah, I'll make sure she gets it back," sincerely. I thanked her and as I turned to leave she said, "Now why don't you convince Andrea over there to stop being such a cunt." I ignored the crassness of the diss to smile right back at my new BFF, Fox, then headed back to my cell.

It was just after 4:00 p.m. that afternoon when someone came to our cell, unlocked the door, and told us we were all getting out. I rose, arthritically, to my feet and began to stretch painfully. I was the last to walk out the metal door. We were deposited at a station where a clerk was responsible for releasing our confiscated personal effects. Nadine was ahead of me. We had all showered her with kindness and tried to console her back in our cell after the bracelet incident. She had been beside herself, saying that police in her country would never have mistreated her so. I felt ashamed when she said that she had no idea American police were so cruel compared to Germans. She'd never intended to be arrested that night. In fact she'd obeyed their commands and gone back to the tents in order to be safe and not jeopardize her travel visa. She worried now that it would be revoked and she would have to leave the United States prematurely.

When she got up to the clerk's window, Nadine gasped as she took an inventory of her stuff. The police had returned the brace-let, however had stolen all the cash from her backpack. The clerk shrugged his shoulders, telling her that if it wasn't written down at the time of her arrest, there was no record that she had ever had any money. I walked up and put my arm around her shoulder as she wept uncontrollably and pounded a frustrated fist on the counter, piteously lamenting, "How can they do this? All of my money is gone! This is not right! This is not fair! Why do you do this here?"

When that same clerk handed me my backpack, I surveyed its contents and found everything to be there, except for a handful of loose change and a few prescription ibuprofen pills. I remembered that fifteen hours earlier, when my personal property was being cataloged, the officer told me that she was going to do me a "big favor" because I was her "last customer that night." She said, "Tell me the four things in this bag that you'd really like to see again and I'll write them down so they don't (air quotes) 'disappear' in evidence." Without hesitation, I told her I'd like to see the hundred twenty dollars cash, my new cell phone, my Mp3 player, and my wristwatch. "Done," she said. "Now don't make me have to write down anything else because I'm not good at spelling and I'm tryin' to get out of here tonight." It was just a lucky break that I was last and got my possessions back, but I made a mental note never to carry anything I valued into a police standoff again. I thanked the clerk, who was behind a bulletproof enclosure, for my backpack, which was returned to me through a one way revolving drawer, and walked with the other women into freedom. There were a few news reporters outside the Santa Rita jail waiting to interview us, as well as a couple of National Lawyer's Guild volunteers, who had driven the distance to take us back to Oscar Grant Plaza. On the ride back I perused my release papers and read that I'd been charged with a violation of Penal Code 409, "Unlawful Assembly or Failure to Leave the Scene of a Riot."

Chapter 4

Quan Lake

Mid-November, 2011

After the unplanned night in Santa Rita jail, I flew back to Seattle, and drove 250 miles to Pagan Place, my North Cascades mountain home. I had no intention of returning to the Bay Area anytime soon. However fascinating and illuminating, I didn't think I'd ever need to experience that level of involvement with Occupy Oakland again. While still an ardent supporter of the movement, my brief but painful loss of liberty satisfied any curiosity I may have had about police brutality and incarceration in general. I slowed to a crawl on the dirt road to spot Buddy, Dancer, and Rosie, our fat quarter horses, looking up lazily from their hay bins, mouths full, as I passed the corral. Oh, to be home in rural Central Washington State again! No tear gas, no midnight fights, no flashbang grenades, no nightly disruptions, no crack, no meth, and best of all—no cops.

I burst into the door and embraced my family with the urgency of a returning soldier fresh from the battlefield. Our nine-year-old daughter, Kristy, leapt into my arms and didn't move a muscle, until I squeezed her so long she finally pushed away and asked if

I was okay. Later I tumbled into bed and peered out my curtainless window at the array of twinkling stars in the dark country sky, before falling deeply asleep for thirteen hours straight. The next day I rose slowly, took a good look around and contemplated how fortunate I was to be comfortable and secure—surrounded by life and beauty. Outside, the sun shone brightly on the Ponderosa pines across the way on Cook Mountain. The odor of trash and sewage gave way to the fragrant aroma of *Ceanothus* and fir. Honking geese and rustling leaves replaced the abrasive sounds of sirens and street hustles. Home was where we produced our own electricity, drank pure water from a spring, and grew ancient varieties of vegetables that we ate fresh out of the garden all summer and canned in the fall. Home was where I fished for trout all four seasons, then brined it up and smoked it for future consumption. I could ski from my back door all the way to Canada if I wanted, sometimes crossing paths with hungry moose foraging for food. The sun beating on my face was the alarm clock that told me when to get up and go to work. Some days the work was hunting mushrooms and wild asparagus for a savory soup while others it was repairing a section of downed fence or pulling weeds. When I got back from Oakland, I wanted to prostrate myself and kiss the fecund earth to give praise that nothing in my world was anything like the Alameda County jail. No more acutely aware of that was I than those first days back at Pagan Place in early November when I was eager to catch up on my duties. In my absence, the garden had been neglected and a banner crop of heirloom tomatoes had gone uncanned before the freeze and plump onions lay unharvested before they were buried in snow. I threw myself into my chores, enjoying even the most mundane tasks—be it washing dishes, cleaning the cat box, or gathering firewood. I became hyper aware of how strife-free and rewarding life on Buck Mountain was.

Appreciative as I was for the gifts fate had bestowed upon me, I still found myself logging on to the Internet every few hours to see what was happening with Occupy Oakland and elsewhere. As soon as my work day was done, I'd check to see who was live-streaming around the country, but especially in Oakland. The Oakland Occupation was like none other for rawness and unbridled passion. The insanity of Oscar Grant Plaza made an indelible impression on me with its unique culture of raging souls and quixotic warriors. Soon again, I was anxious to return to her streets and reunite with my comrades on the front lines, but I knew that shirking my responsibilities at home would be unpopular, so I tried to contain my restlessness.

Then, I stumbled onto a teach-in that Spencer (Oakfosho) was broadcasting live from OGP, a short distance from where I'd been arrested. I missed the beginning, but soon understood that I was watching a renowned scientist from Cal Berkeley, sitting on the steps of City Hall imparting her vast environmental knowledge to a group of Occupiers that encircled her. I'm sure that university students paid a handsome fee to attend her lectures on the same material she was doling out for free that day, to people ranging from homeless drug addicts to would-be scholars, who, for the want of tuition, may never have had a chance to hear her speak. What they all had in common though, was that they were listening intently, straining to hear every word being said. She was in the midst of discussing climate change and the dire necessity to act now in order to have any chance of saving our ailing planet from a terrifying, human-caused demise. She delivered a brilliant, unamplified, unrehearsed speech which asked that even those who didn't particularly support the Occupy Movement, or understand the message, please come out and protest what was being done to the earth by corporations and the fossil fuel industry. What really got to me though, was when she met the eyes of nearly every one of the fifty or sixty people sitting before her and said, "If you can't do it for yourselves, please do it for the Florida panther that is on the brink of extinction. The Florida panther needs you to come out here and Occupy. The evening grosbeak needs you. The Canadian lynx needs you. The honeybees need you. The manatee needs you. The whooping crane needs you. The monarch butterfly needs you and the gray wolf needs you. They can't buy lobbyists or Occupy for themselves so they need you to do it for them. The wild prairie grasses need you, the California condor needs you." She listed one endangered species after another that would not be here in another fifteen years if we didn't do something drastic right away to stop the wholesale destruction of habitat. She told her listeners that our insatiable appetite for more than we need was unsustainable and could not be allowed to continue. If unchecked, the damage our consumption had caused might be irreparable and fatal to nearly all living things. She ended on a positive note, however, by telling us that the technologies exist today that would allow us to thrive and prosper without depleting the Earth's natural resources. She cautioned though, that the window of opportunity was rapidly closing and "we must wean ourselves now from our addiction to oil in order to have any chance of reversing the cataclysmic path we are on." She divulged that there was systematic suppression of vital information by multinational corporations that controlled local, state, and national governments. These entities, she said, colluded to deny most of us access to simple, sustainable, sound practices that could feed, house, clothe, and provide electricity for every man, woman, and child on earth. Her last words were that if we did not immediately organize and radically oppose these powerful structures, life on earth was doomed. I booked my ticket back to Oakland that night and broke the unwelcome news to my family that I was leaving again.

My plane landed in the afternoon of November 13, and I was back in Oscar Grant Plaza by three o'clock. My friends Anne Irving, Laura Koch and her wife, Lori Delay met me with an old tent that they were willing to lend me for the cause, since I'd donated my previous one to a couple that needed it at the end of my last visit. They seemed uneasy about my staying there that night as we watched two young, visibly high women wildly screaming at each other over some chicken wings that had somehow been paid for by one of them and never delivered by the other. One was threatening to pull out her knife and cut the other, while their male companions alternated between laughing and half-heartedly pulling them apart. *"Bitch, I will cut yo' ass. You think I'm playin'? You think I'm gon' let you come in here and get all up in my grill, lyin' in my face after you done took my wing money and got yo' black ass high with it??"* Clearly the fellas were enjoying the entertainment the ladies were dishing up. When one woman tried clumsily and off balance to reach for something in her pocket, the men separated them in earnest and told them to "hush up and stop actin' crazy before the motherfuckin' po-pos come." Amazingly the girls obeyed the edict from they mens and almost instantly quieted down. Since it was my second time camping at OGP and still daylight, I wasn't overly concerned by the dust up, but my friends seemed reluctant to leave me there, offering me unlimited lodging in their homes and reminding me that it was okay to call any time of the night to ask for a ride out.

Shortly after we set up my tent, we were joined by more friends and Occupy supporters, Penny Rosenwasser, Lisa Vogel, and Terry Lynn Delk, who I knew from having performed at the Michigan Womyn's Festival. We decided to go out for a meal in the hood before the General Assembly got underway. Just as we were leaving for the restaurant we ran into a trio of police officers who were handing out eviction notices to us which said, NOTICE OF VIOLATIONS AND DEMAND TO CEASE VIOLATIONS. Underneath that headline it said that Occupy Oakland was creating a health hazard and obstructing free use of the park by others and that we were to discontinue camping there. I paid it little mind as I'd seen these warnings before and knew there was a good chance nothing at all would happen to us anytime soon. After dinner, my friends left and I got in on the tail end of the General Assembly, or "GA," which was to conclude with an address from an Ohlone Elder. She was standing regally before me on the City Hall Plaza stage in her ceremonial dress. I felt the weight of her distinguished bearing which commanded attention and respect. Her beautifully decorated robes conveyed her status within the Ohlone Indian community. I stood in awe of her—the sheer otherworldliness of her ageless, timeless voice undulating like ryegrass on the wind-blown plain. She had come, she said, to "deliver a message from [her] people," whose land was stolen over a hundred years ago by whites who had colonized it and occupied it ever since. The gravity of the moment gripped me as she raised an eagle feather before beginning her speech. I waited in breathless anticipation, enduring an interminable pause as the eldress leaned away from the microphone and into the shoulder of another Ohlone at her side, who whispered gravely into her ear. An eternity elapsed before she returned her focus to us and uttered, "A silver Toyota Rav 4 with Oregon license plates left its lights on in the Plaza and is also illegally parked and about to get towed." Uproarious laughter rippled throughout the crowd before the speaker realized we had mistaken the car announcement for the solemn message we were expecting. Even though she recovered quickly and returned to her original script about how her "long-suffering people stood in solidarity with Occupy Oakland and wished to bless us on this perilous journey," I took it as a sign to retreat early to my chamber and try to get through the night unscathed. Sleep came easily as it was relatively still in the Plaza and I thought of the Florida panther as I drifted off into slumber.

"*They comin' y'all. It's a raid! Git up. Grab yer shit—go! They on their way,*" came the frenzied call around four o'clock in the morning. I heard groans and swearing issuing from tents as groggy campers tried to come to their senses quickly and wrestle gear into nylon sacks and plastic bags. Bleary-eyed, I switched on my LED light and started stuffing my sleeping bag and other possessions into a rolling travel suitcase. Some Occupiers began preparing for the onslaught by beating out tribal rhythms on makeshift drums and metal cookware. Some women were ululating and whistles were being blown in addition to all the yelling. Within ten minutes I was ready to go and unzipped my tent flap as I emerged, with suitcase, into the foggy Bay Area night. The sound of cursing voices intertwined with rasping zippers began to fill the air as I dragged my suitcase on the damp earth toward Fourteenth and Broadway where others were already gathering. I propped my tired frame against a streetlight across from a Rite Aid and waited for the riot squad to arrive. Forty-five minutes later they got there and surrounded us as we marched in circles chanting, "The System Has Got to Die/Hella Hella Occupy", and "One, We are The People, Two, We Are United, Three, This Occupation Is Not Leaving."

Just before dawn the police began projecting their monotonous order to disperse. This time I phoned my local community radio station back home—KTRT, in tiny Winthrop, Washington, hoping to be put on the air live as part of the morning commute. Technically, I guess it could be called, "drive time radio," but in our town of two thousand residents, it was not a big enough deal to warrant such a title. I called them on the chance that Deputy Don, my friend, DJ, and station manager, might get a kick out of exposing the Methow Valley (which is comprised of rednecks and progressives alike) to the real-life drama of a police raid on a political protest while it was happening. I tried to deliver pithy observations about the Occupy Movement itself, while the cops were surrounding us on all sides and pressing against us with interlocking metal barricades.

The temporary structures served not only to compact us, but also to keep us out of Oscar Grant Plaza as they slashed tents and made off with our stuff. Not only was it reassuring to know that as long as I stayed on the air with Don, there would be audio witnesses if the cops went berserk, it was also interesting to imagine what my friends and neighbors were thinking as one of their own stood in a pre-dawn confrontation with the law, a thousand miles away, in a big metropolitan city with actual traffic lights. It amused me to consider that some of my homies may have been actively hoping I'd be thrashed for taking a political stance they disagreed with. On this occasion, in contrast to others, the Oakland Police Department orchestrated an orderly, nonviolent operation with no arrests. There had certainly been moments of anxiety, but on the whole, the OPD had shown professionalism and restraint while they dismantled the place where we had eaten, taught, provided daycare, clothed, and housed hundreds of Oakland's poorest citizens for nearly three weeks. And just like that, it was over. The magical, miserable, wonderful, terrifying, Occupy Oakland Commune ended. The fantastic grand experiment that had decreased crime in Oakland by nearly 20% was over.

Later that day, I toted my bags to the nearest library, where a GA was scheduled so that we could regroup and discuss our next moves. I slept on the grass in the sun for an hour before the assembly began. Over a thousand people showed up from all over Oakland to mourn the loss of our tent city and to voice their continuing support for Occupy Oakland. Speakers reiterated the ongoing urgency of stopping corporate greed and putting an end to bank abuses. Some of the displaced campers spoke of the need to retake OGP, or find another location to set up shop. Overall it was a nice pep rally and a good way to process what had just happened to us, but I felt in my heart that it was over at OGP and that the experience of a lifetime, that I will forever cherish, would never be replicated. On the advice of others who had scoped out a new spot, I relocated to Snow Park where others said they might be heading. The new location was close to OGP, but larger and grassier. Lake Merritt was close by too, which was another plus, but it lacked the sense of community and purpose we shared at City Hall. Lots of Occupy activists who had homes in town went back to them. They had been at OGP for political reasons, not for lack of options. The Snow Park encampment was much less populated and more strung out—mostly made up of people who were there by necessity, not choice. Some refugees were milling about aimlessly, while others checked to see if there were any plans afoot to build a kitchen or serve meals. This place was depressing and had none of the gritty, explosive, history-in-the-making feel that City Hall exuded. This time my lifesaver was Terry Lynn Delk, who showed up with another donated tent, (the third so far) but the rainfly was missing, so I replaced it with an enormous blue tarp someone else had abandoned at the park. The tarp was so large I had to double it up under my tent and extend it out over the top to make it work. It began raining as soon as I finished, so I was immensely grateful for the find that was keeping my new home dry. I lay there in the dark listening to the raindrops plip plop soothingly on my roof, as I tried to fall asleep and hoped other activists would arrive soon and set up house. I wasn't liking my new residence, but I didn't want to turn tail and run to a friend's house to sleep. My cell phone battery was dying which made me feel vulnerable, so I decided to leave the park for awhile and take the BART over to San Francisco, where I saw on Twitter that there was speculation about an impending predawn raid at the Occupy encampment there. I got off at the Embarcadero stop, a few hundred feet from Occupy San Francisco, where I saw that hundreds of activists had created a bustling community for themselves as well. It was fun to note the differences and similarities from across the bay in Oakland. There was much more of a hippie vibe in San Francisco and I noticed a greater variety of incense permeating the air, along with more types of dogs, mostly wearing bandanas. Also, a higher percentage of the Occupiers were white. The camp had become so crowded that the overflow spilled across the street and onto the wide sidewalk in front of the Federal Reserve Building, where some managed to cram their tents between the walkway and the newspaper vending machines. The place was abuzz with talk of last night's Oakland raid, as well as strategies for surviving the same plans for theirs. I had only been there a short while before OSF members monitoring police scanners began announcing that there would be no raid that night after all, which relieved me, since I was finally starting to get sleepy. Off I went, back to the BART station and back to the East Bay where my Snow Park home lay waiting.

After I lay down in my sleeping bag, I discovered that in my brief absence, a homeless man had pulled loose my excess tarp and rolled it over himself for shelter. He slept inches away from me, with nothing between us but the nylon fabric of the tent. Perhaps he thought I'd moved out when I left for San Francisco, but not being certain, he'd not completely moved in . . . just yet. He had, however, made it cozier for himself by pulling some cardboard over to cushion his underside, along with some abandoned bedding to keep him warm as he slept and probably wished I'd been gone for good. The only reason I noticed him there was because I thought I detected an odd, previously absent bulge in the back of the tent as I approached it in semidarkness. After I entered it, I lay there awkwardly, trying to decide what to do. It was too late for me to feel good about calling anybody to come get me, so I stayed, prostrate—stiff as a board—until I began to hear the man breathing softly, as if in deep slumber. I must have dozed off momentarily while pondering my dilemma, but awakened shortly to the sound of the guy flicking a nearly empty Bic lighter about six inches away from my head. Then I smelled something, unpleasant and toxic, burning very close to me. I didn't relish the idea of forcing the poor lout into the rain, but come on man—really? You can't just give it up for a few hours so we can get through this fucking nightmare without killing each other? I fumed silently beside the man (figuratively) while he fumed audibly beside me (literally)—our backs touching. He didn't imbibe for long, and soon returned to his soft breathing pattern. I began to wonder if it might not be heroin he was smoking, instead of crack, which I'd previously assumed was his weakness; but didn't crack make you jumpy and heroin make you sleepy? Then I began to lament the inefficiency and wastefulness of *smoking* the heroin, versus shooting it, if indeed that was what he'd been up to. Because from everything I'd ever read, the best way to enjoy it was to *inject* it, and since I assumed this man wasn't well-to-do, I began mentally berating him for being lazy and not making the effort to prepare it properly, in order to get the most bang for his buck. Then I started chastising myself for having such a callous attitude toward my destitute brother. After all, *I* had the luxury of being homeless by choice, him—not so much. I did not want to be insensitive to my fellow man, but neither did I like sleeping with an inconsiderate drug addict guy that I didn't even know. I'd given that up in the eighties, and I wasn't about to go back at fifty-one. Worse still, when the space invader drifted off this second time, he wedged himself even tighter against me, dead to the world, as he fell into squawk snoring—accompanied by long pauses that gave me concern for his health—followed by apneatic gasps which bolted me upright as they punctuated the night and scared me shitless.

Though I'd gotten precious little shuteye, I arose the next morning and walked over to OGP, hoping to join up with other demoralized Occupiers. I detected a small group and wandered over to stand among them and commiserate. There was a foul-smelling muddy pit where our vibrant revolutionary community had stood days before. We loitered, dolefully watching the sprinkler system drowning all remaining life in the plaza. We surmised that Mayor Quan had *really, really* not wanted us to come back, since she'd put tons of little flags and signs everywhere on the lawn saying, KEEP OFF THE GRASS, and RESTORATION IN PROGRESS. She also had twenty or more cops doing nothing but walking up and down the sidewalks, yelling at anyone who even looked like they were thinking about stepping off the concrete—much less pitching a tent. By the third day the sprinklers were still running full blast and the grounds in front of city hall were inundated with three inches of standing water. The historic oak tree, whose well-being the mayor had originally cited as the main reason she objected to the encampment, was now swimming in the pool she created. We named the new body of water, "Quan Lake."

On November 15, instead of spending another evening at Snow Park with the lazy, inefficient drug waster, I decided to support fellow Occupiers on the campus of Cal Berkeley. They too had their tent city violently dismantled by campus police, days before. The students of Occupy Cal were hopping mad at the excessive force campus cops had used on them during a November 9 protest. After that encounter, many of them uploaded YouTube videos showing police shoving, pushing, pepper spraying, baton thumping, tent-slashing, and kicking students as they linked arms and tried to resist them. Their campus Occupation was largely a response to planned tuition hikes, as well as growing anger and discontentment with their situation as college students in the new economy—unable to afford tuition without going tens and even hundreds of thousands of dollars in debt, unable to find adequate jobs, unable to move out of their parent's homes. Many complained that they now found themselves attending a university with little ethnic diversity and a decreasing quality of education. I went there that day hoping to support their Occupation as well as to ease my depression over the deteriorating state of Occupy Oakland.

I boarded a campus-bound city bus on that bright, sunny day, opting out of the miles long solidarity march I heard that Occupy Oaklanders had planned to make from OGP. The bus driver let me off three blocks before my scheduled stop because another driver had radioed to tell her the demonstration was much larger than expected and that if she drove all the way in she'd be trapped for hours. I liked hearing that so I hopped off and looked around for the parade.

Half an hour later I'd still not seen them and walked dejectedly to Sproul Hall, legendary home of the Free Speech Movement. In 1964, Mario Savio had caused a commotion by leaping atop a police car that held Jack Weinberg, a former UC student who'd moments earlier been sitting at a table he'd set up with materials from CORE (Congress on Racial Equality) to support the Civil Rights Movement. The cops had come to shut the table down and arrest Jack Weinberg and Mario had jumped up on top of the car and just sat there, in order to stop them from hauling Jack away. Then he'd made a rousing speech to the gathering crowd of Cal students which began a thirty-two-hour sit-in that began the Free Speech Movement. Later that same year, on the steps of Sproul Hall, Savio gave his now famous speech where he said, "We're human beings! There's a time when the operation of the machine becomes so odious—makes you so sick at heart—that you can't take part. You can't even passively take part. And you've got to put your bodies upon the gears and upon the wheels, upon the levers, upon all the apparatus, and you've got to make it stop. And you've got to indicate to the people who run it, to the people who own it,

that unless you're free, the machine will be prevented from working at all." Reading about Mario and the sacred ground I stood on
jumpstarted my heart, and even though I couldn't find any Occupiers to share it with, I was way into being there.

Ninety minutes later, just as I was turning to leave, I looked to
the left and saw a snaking line of thousands, chanting, waving flags,
and wielding signs as they poured into the plaza. People started
running out from the student union and surrounding buildings to
greet them by sending up a resounding cheer for the returning
heroes. I yelled myself hoarse as humanity kept streaming in until
there was someone occupying every nook and cranny as far as the
eye could see. The jubilant crowd swelled to over ten thousand
as a speaker's podium was erected at the top of the steps in front
of the door to Sproul Hall. Hope and expectation were palpable as former Secretary of Labor under President Clinton, Robert
Reich, approached the microphone. He'd already been scheduled
to speak in a campus auditorium for a paid event, but decided
that the overwhelming presence of the Occupiers afforded him a
unique opportunity to express his support for the Movement, so
he took it.

The audience gave him rapt attention as he delivered a startling
analysis of income inequality and co-opted government, which
struck a nerve with the crowd that hung on his every word. He
gave a clear, concise timeline that described the journey that lead
us to this point in history where banks and corporations run everything and ordinary people are left with nothing. His spontaneous
speech wasn't long, but hit a crescendo of boisterous, cheering,
applause as he concluded that we all needed to get out into the
streets and "raise a ruckus," to stop what's being done to us each
day we do nothing to oppose it.

A few seconds after his departure the sound of seventies disco
music blasted into the airspace and instantly we rose to our feet
for an impromptu disco party. "I Will Survive," was assaulting my
receptive eardrums when I saw the first fully erected dome tents
being lifted overhead onto the plaza in front of the Hall. "This is

AWESOME!!!!!" was all I could think as I decided right then and there to spend the night and help defend the resurrection of the village at Cal. Maybe fifteen or twenty structures went up as the music kept thumping and the party raged on.

About 1:00 a.m. the PA system got packed up, while those of us planning to stay began hunkering down for real to brave the cold, damp air and hold down the fort all night. I hoped to get in a few Z's before boarding a 9:00 a.m. bus with students, bound for a big demonstration against University Regents in the financial district of San Francisco. Not coincidentally, many of those regents, who regularly voted in recent years to increase tuition, also had offices there, where they served on the boards of major financial institutions such as Wells Fargo, Chase, and Bank of America. Before then, I didn't know this obvious conflict of interest was common practice at state universities all over America. The largest banks in the world, which had caused the collapse of the American financial system by gambling with the bad loans they made, were now enjoying even greater profits by manipulating the exploding cost of getting a college degree. I already held considerable dislike for big banks, but this additional bit of information pushed me over the edge and I was completely down for this action, which I hoped would reap some concrete benefits for the planners and participants. Because my own tent was still at Snow Park, I dragged over some loose cardboard I'd found in the soggy grass, curled up in a ball, closed my eyes against the drizzle, and tried to go to sleep.

I was still awake when a dozen campus officers sauntered over, palming their billy clubs, and parked themselves in front of our remaining group of thirty-eight Occupiers. I was the oldest person there, save for an elderly man, whose ready smile endeared him to me each time I noticed him chatting avuncularly with students or showing them card tricks he'd learned over the years. One of the policemen put a superfluous bullhorn to his lips to advise us that we were in violation of a campus law prohibiting camping, and would be subject to arrest if we didn't leave. In response, the students called an emergency GA, where it was determined that we should pull the tents closer together in case we needed to link arms and physically defend them later. Not wanting to be snatched from the fringes and again hauled off to jail, I relocated my cardboard home in the midst of the tents and shivered there for awhile, still listening to the repetitious drone of the dispersal order. I conjured up the privation endured by Lewis and Clark, along with (new mom) Sacagawea, her worthless husband, Charbonneau, and the rest of the Corp of Discovery, whose journals I'd read years ago, to put my own discomfort into perspective as I mentally whined for my down comforter and memory foam mattress. The impending raid did not allow me to drift off for even a moment as I checked the time, (4:30 a.m.) and waited.

Just as I thought I might freeze to death in the wet predawn air, the first streak of light finally pierced the sky, signalling that our defiance of orders had been successful. Stiff as a corpse, I clung to tent poles to stand upright. Limping the soreness away, I hobbled out from Sproul Hall and entered the closest coffee shop, across the street from the square. I don't think I've ever appreciated a heated building quite so much as I did then. Since I was the first customer of the day, I selected a warm spot, plugged my phone in, and ordered a latte with a pastry. Moments later, one of my former Santa Rita cellmates, Andrea, a Cal student who had also spent the night outside, walked in and sat with me. She, a high-performing, hard-working postgraduate student, underemployed, living with her parents and drowning in debt, was a perfect example of why the student body of UC Berkeley was so upset in the first place. She had helped to organize the Cal Occupation and was as cold and sleep deprived as I was when she said, "Hey how 'bout Mister Pentagon Papers himself, Daniel Ellsberg, spending the night in a tent with us. Did you love the magic tricks or what?" That was my first inkling that the only person there older than me, was the historical figure who'd revealed this country's buildup to the Vietnam War to be an absolute sham, thereby making the case to end it. It was Dan Ellsberg who, in 1971, decided to sound the alarm by publishing nearly seven thousand pages of high-level, top secret documents detailing his work with the CIA during the Johnson Administration. By outing himself in this way, Ellsberg proved that he and his former employers, President Lyndon Johnson and the CIA, had deceived the American public by overstating (even manufacturing) the threat North Vietnam posed to our capitalist democracy in its plan to conquer South Vietnam and spread Communism throughout Southeast Asia. In those days the word "Communist" inspired the same sort of reaction that "Muslim" does in some circles today, and its very utterance often triggered irrational fears and jingoistic nationalism, especially from elected officials eager to attract new voters. By the time the Pentagon Papers were published, the United States and its Western allies had been in a longstanding "Cold War" with Russia and its Communist allies dating back to the end of World War II. The Cold War was characterized by a chilly ideological disdain for Communism which manifested itself in intensive efforts to contain its influence by the West, countered by a push to expand its reach in the East.

No shots were ever fired during the Cold War, due partially to the fact that both sides knew that each possessed enough nuclear weaponry to obliterate the entire planet, yet there still existed a good deal of mutual hostility and distrust. The West conducted a pitched campaign of fear mongering with its assertion that a "domino effect" would be brought about by the fall of even one seemingly insignificant country (like North Vietnam) to the doctrine. The conflict between North and South Vietnam has sometimes been viewed as a proxy war between the United States and the USSR. At the center of it all was Daniel Ellsberg, a single high-level official in the CIA, who ultimately did more perhaps than anyone to expose the false premise which resulted in the death of over fifty-eight thousand American soldiers. Daniel Ellsberg has since dedicated his life to encouraging whistleblowers everywhere to stand up and resist the pressure to be complicit in a system they know to be doing the wrong thing. In one famous quote he warned, "Don't do what I did and wait till the bombs start falling, to speak up and practice civil disobedience if necessary to advocate for what's right," even though doing so had made him a political pariah and caused a great deal of enmity between him and the Nixon administration.

So, how had the upper levels of authority handled the students' expression of anger and discontentment? Cal chancellor, Robert J. Birgeneau, defended the campus police choice to beat students with batons the week prior, by saying, "It's unfortunate students chose linking arms to protest . . . that is not nonviolent protest." In response to this, students printed and distributed leaflets on campus bearing an iconic image of Martin Luther King linking arms with Mario Savio and other justice workers in front of Sproul Hall in the 1960s, along with Chancellor Birgeneau's suddenly infamous quote. And the regents themselves dealt with the students' concerns by postponing a planned meeting, where it was expected that they would vote yes on the proposal to raise tuition by 81% to be phased in over the next four years. The students did not take kindly to the delay that was seen by them as a stalling tactic to let tempers cool before jacking up rates as initially planned. Not to be distracted, Occupy Cal organized a cooperative march with Occupy Oakland through the financial district of downtown San Francisco where the regents had chosen to lay low in their offices on the day that was originally scheduled for the tuition hikes vote. At 9:00 a.m., I boarded one of the waiting buses the students had hired to take us there and dozed most of the way, surrounded by union workers, students, and Occupiers from the night before.

We were let off right across the street from the Embarcadero BART stop, where Occupy San Francisco was still operating in the last remaining days of its tent commune. Lots of OSF members joined in the parade, which began at the Federal Reserve Building across the street after some speeches were made by experts on the topic. It was early afternoon and from the outset I gauged our numbers to be around six hundred. We promenaded past many of the greatest offenders in the financial collapse and paused in front of each one to chant slogans like, "Banks got bailed out—We got sold out." Some among us had megaphones and read the names of the regents with offices in each bank. The route took us deep into a canyon of tall buildings, where suited office workers pressed to the windows to record the spectacle, which had by this time grown to nearly three thousand demonstrators.

We were flanked on both sides by motorcycle cops who looked pissed as we clogged the streets for blocks brandishing our MAKE BANKS PAY signs and beckoning onlookers to join us. Our chants reverberated off skyscrapers as we raised our voices under the TransAmerica Tower, then Wells Fargo, Citibank, Chase, and others. We finally wound up facing the Bank of America, only this time, instead of pausing to chant outside, the vanguard of our procession marched us right into the foyer of the building, holding the entrance doors open while beckoning us to enter. The unscripted detour instigated a free-for-all romp inside the bank, whose manager chose, unwisely, to ignore our approach, perhaps hoping we'd go away. A teller finally noticed what was happening and ran to the door trying to pull it shut against the hundreds of us who were charging in.

Most of the startled employees ran back to their cubicles, grabbed their personal effects, and bolted out the back door, abandoning their posts. Gleefully I stood gaping in disbelief at the unfolding scene. Kids danced wildly atop desks that held computer monitors that stayed running the whole time, frozen onto the pages their operators had last opened. Bank documents were being grabbed and flung riotously into the air, landing like confetti wherever they may. Someone tilted back in an office chair, propping his feet on a plastic keyboard while he lit a cigar. Another Occupier busied himself resetting the system's screen saver and soon all the monitors began flashing, "MAKE BANKS PAY," in seventy-two-point bold red type. Another still, pushed the print command on a machine he'd commandeered, ordering it to produce hundreds of multicolored copies of the message onto the floor beneath the removed receiving tray. I knew it would be dangerous to linger since the cops weren't going to let this tomfoolery continue forever, but I did not want to take my leave. I turned my head toward a faint trickling sound to take in the silhouette of a bookish youth wearing a cardigan sweater, who was quietly urinating into the back corner of the room. I admired the carrying capacity of his bladder and the impressive stream volume as his urine splashed gaily from the wall onto the carpet, eventually seeking places to pool and call home.

Just as I was threading my way to the exit, a tiny, auburn-haired sprite, who looked to be twelve or thirteen, grabbed a dormant bullhorn, mounted a desk, and began to deliver a powerful address. She hoisted the speaker with trembling hands as she began, "My friends, colleagues, fellow students, and comrades in struggle." She went on to summarize the academic journey that brought her to this improbable present. Despite earning outstanding grades, devoting countless hours of free labor to internships, and receiving numerous accolades for community service, she'd been left virtually bankrupt, living at her parents house, trying to pay off student loans, and working at Starbucks for her effort. Throughout her speech I found myself fighting a gnawing sense of futility in trying to go up against these huge institutions and their fortresses. Even though her advanced intelligence and capabilities were obvious, how was this person ever going to dig out of the cavernous hole she was in? When she finished there was a reverent hush of sorrow and empathy that held us all for several seconds, even as I feared I'd tarried too long.

On my way out, I scurried past a glass-enclosed side office, where I noticed a lone employee who'd been trapped by the melee as we rushed in. She was hunched over her business phone, head down, talking anxiously into the receiver to someone, probably a police officer, on the other end. Our eyes met for an instant as she risked a furtive glance into the room where all hell was breaking loose. I guessed that this frazzled creature, who bore a passing resemblance to Mayor Jean Quan, was likely the branch manager. I'd love to have been privy to her conversation as she described her odd predicament to whoever was listening. I hoped she'd get a raise for her valor, even though she seemed in no particular danger from Occupy Cal, whose members paid her absolutely no mind as she did what she felt was her duty to the Bank of America. I also hoped the police would spare her, along with everyone else, when they stormed in, guns blazing.

Once on the outside, I pushed through the crowd of two hundred or so, and pressed myself against the window, to film the thirty or forty students who'd made a conscious decision to subject themselves to arrest. Inside I saw a boy of nineteen or twenty sitting at a computer, staring intently at the screen as he moved the mouse to scroll around. Minutes later he grabbed an empty sheet of paper and found a pen. He wrote the words: Monica Lovano/ BofA Regent to UC/213-622-8332. As he finished writing the last number, a young woman standing next to me fished her phone out of her purse to make a call. "Yes, I'd like to speak to Monica," she said assertively. "Who's calling? . . . Yes, tell her the people are calling." She waited a few minutes and then said, "Oh, she's unable to come to the phone at this time? Yes, well can you please tell her that there are Cal students here in San Francisco Occupying the Bank of America close to her office and we'd like to know why she thinks it's appropriate to raise tuition 81% on us while the bank is making record profits and education is unaffordable for most of the people in California. Thank you, oh and can you also tell her that we aren't going away anytime soon. Thank you."

After she hung up I began eavesdropping on another phone conversation from a copper-skinned, raven-haired boy with fine features, standing on the other side of me. He was talking to another boy with a similar profile, sitting cross-legged inside the building, just on the other side of the glass. "That's my little brother in there," he intimated to me. "I gotta make sure he's okay—or Mom's gonna worry." As I continued peering inside the bank, some enterprising individual began erecting a tent he had stuffed inside his backpack, between two teller windows up front. I admired the heck out of his preparedness for this moment. The police did arrive shortly after that, and used uncharacteristic restraint while making their arrests before dozens of filming onlookers.

That evening I headed back to Snow Park in the rain and spent another night sleeping uneasily against my tarpmate, who was proving himself to be harmless. Since this determination, I had decided to make peace with him, even though we'd never spoken a word or looked directly at each other. He was, in all likelihood, a hapless hobo, just trying to stay dry as he crowded my back, shifted occasionally, and snored from time to time. The next morning the sun shone brightly on me once more, as I roused myself and greeted the new day. Two policemen strode by in the warmth and began distributing newly minted eviction fliers telling us our days at Snow Park were numbered too. I wasn't sure what to do with my tent, but left it up for the time being while I tried to figure out how serious they were this time. I circulated around the sparsely populated park to learn that Occupy Oaklanders had identified a great big fenced vacant lot nearby at Nineteenth and Telegraph where there was ample room for us to re-establish our Oakland Commune. I walked over to OGP to see what was happening and on the way poked my head into a tiny art gallery on Fourteenth and Franklin. It was packed with people who were listening to Harvard graduate, and Princeton Professor, Dr. Cornel West, speaking. I had heard of him before but had to google him while standing outside in the overflow crowd, to get some background and find out that the body of his work had been on issues of race, gender, and class in this country. I could just make out the salt and pepper tip of his afro as he said, "I am not a supporter of the Occupy Movement, I am a part of it." He went on to assert the need for activists to, "stay focused on personal commitment to the movement rather than on creating consensus." I didn't stay because so many others wanted to get closer, but I did hear him advise that "we should use the diversity of the Occupy Movement to build and strengthen it instead of letting differences weaken it."

When I got to OGP I saw that Quan Lake, which was now also being referred to as Quantanamo Bay, had risen by a few inches and was threatening to flood the sidewalks of City Hall. I decided to sit down inside the Rising Loafer bakery whose owner supported Occupy Oakland and didn't mind if you took up a seat for awhile. I browsed the printed materials looking for news about Occupy. I learned that the tent village on the Berkeley campus had been torn down again, and that students vowed to put it back up as they could. Then I read a tweet that said Occupy Oakland would definitely be taking over the vacant lot at Nineteenth and Telegraph in front of the Oakland School for the Fine Arts on Saturday, the 19- of November. Another tweet said that OPD wasn't planning to raid Snow Park before then so, while I drank my latte, I decided to stay put the next two nights until the move to Telegraph. As I sipped, a woman of about sixty came in and sat at the table next to me. She searched the room as if she was meeting someone, so I took a chance and asked her if she was with Occupy. She said "yes," so I went over and sat with her. As we talked, I told her of my recent experiences with the OPD and Bank of America and she told me that she sang with a vocal group called Occupella, that went around performing topical songs for the Movement. Her name was Nancy Schimmel and she showed me lyrics for some of their parodies. I commented on one that was taken from a Malvina Reynolds song I've always loved called, "Little Boxes." "I'm so happy you're doing that tune," I said. "Malvina Reynolds rocks. What a great pioneer of feminist folk."

"I know," said Nancy. "She's my mother."

"Get out of here!" I exclaimed, before launching into, "Turn around and you're two—Turn around and you're four. Turn around and you're a young girl, going out my door." I, like many others, first heard "Turn Around" as a child when Kodak used it in a commercial for their cameras. Another title of Malvina's, "Little Boxes," was the theme song of a TV series called, *Weeds*, about a suburban mom who decides to grow and sell marijuana after her husband dies without life insurance, leaving her broke. It's about how people are put into boxes, socialized to conform, and discouraged from raising a fuss or questioning authority. "There are boxes, little boxes, little boxes made up of ticky tacky, little boxes on the hillside and they all look the same. There's a pink one and a green one and a blue one and a yellow one and they're all made up of ticky tacky and they all look just the same." Great lyrics, and great to be sitting there with her charming daughter. We talked some more and even sang together a little bit before exchanging contact information and heading back out into the world.

On the morning of the nineteenth, I packed up my third tent and waited for my friend Penny, who'd agreed to let me stash it in her car. As I crammed it in its stuffsack, I noticed there were several brand new burn holes in the tarp, right next to where my head was while I slept. Oy vey. Penny offered to bring the tent back to me later that night, after I checked out the situation at Nineteenth and Telegraph. First there was a rally to support labor unions scheduled for 2:00 p.m., followed by a long march which was supposed to end up near the new #OO campsite. It started out small, maybe five hundred people, but by the time we got to Lake Merritt there were a lot of us—thousands. We were several blocks long and took up the entire width of the street when we paused briefly to pay our respects to the Lakeside school that was closing in March because of cuts in educational funding. Along the route we also stopped to stare at the marquee of the Grand Lake Theater whose owner, another ardent support of Occupy, had written, YOU CAN'T EVICT AN IDEA WHOSE TIME HAS COME—SHAME ON YOU MAYOR QUAN. From there about five hundred of us turned back the way we came and began making our way to the Oakland School for the Arts at Nineteenth and Telegraph. Darkness was approaching as we reached our final destination, only to find that a chain-link fence had gone up since I'd last seen it days earlier. A group of motivated Occupiers came prepared with bolt cutters and began demolishing the fence as others pushed aside pier blocks and created openings. Soon we were all barging onto the lot, and tents began popping up everywhere. Brian brought the sound truck and from then on the party was in full swing. More bodies showed up to celebrate our new digs and in no time we were up to a thousand revellers as a light mist began to fall. The ground was rocky and wet, but twenty hardy campers set up nonetheless while we danced beneath the sculpture garden that would be our back yard once we were established.

Remember Them, Heroes for Humanity is the Mario Chiodo sculpture that we were all clustered around that night, after we tore down the barriers and tried to appropriate the space for Occupy Oakland. There are twenty-five historical figures in the piece, which was dedicated to the city exactly two months before our arrival. Among them are: Mother Teresa, Sojourner Truth, Mahatma Gandhi, Martin Luther King, Frederick Douglass, Maya Angelou, Malcolm X, and Rosa Parks. Remarkably, the nine million dollar artwork was funded almost entirely by private donations during a time of great economic instability, known as the "Great Recession." I was calmed by their presence, almost as if they were guardian angels overseeing and protecting us in our own fight for justice. Then I saw the cops. Lots and lots of them were amassing in every direction as it started raining hard on our celebration. I called Penny, who was already on her way, and reported, "Hey, it's looking kind of dicey, maybe we just keep the tent in your car tonight if that's okay." She was just pulling up to our location when she observed several dozen police officers in riot gear preparing to make a move.

"No problem, be safe tonight," she said, kindly, as I waved her away from the area. Brian was pleading through his sound system for us to stay put and keep our numbers up to defend the encampment as it got wetter and colder by the minute. I hunkered down under a canopy someone had brought and looked up at the balconies of the surrounding apartments. It seemed that every tenant had a cell phone camera capturing the excitement from above. Some also had small children and pets peering down at us from their decks. One young blond woman jogging with her Jack Russell Terrier glowered at me as she passed on the sidewalk to her residence. "Hey, thanks for totally fucking up my front yard with this *bullshit*," she sneered as I shivered.

After midnight the order to disperse was sounded, which some freezing, soaked comrades decided to heed. Hours later, we were down to roughly forty rain-soaked souls and a handful of tents. Those of us that remained were tired and miserable. Then, Brian announced that he had to take the sound truck back to the garage because it was too wet outside for the delicate gear, and he didn't want it confiscated again. He drove half a block, turned left, and was immediately pulled over by the cops who impounded the truck and towed it away, leaving Brian and his crew empty handed and without transportation. Morale took a nosedive when the music died and our misery seemed to compound itself. I saw the handwriting on the wall and opted to leave then, not wanting to be arrested again. I didn't know how I would make it back to Laura's house by myself, since she and Lori had flown out earlier in the day to spend Thanksgiving with family on the East Coast. They'd given me a house key and told me I could crash at their place anytime in their absence, which I'd almost refused as unnecessary. My, how things had changed. The BART train was still running, but not as often as in peak periods, so it was very late when I got off, exhausted, at the Fruitvale Station where Oscar Grant died, which was still miles from their home. I hadn't wanted to be without it, so I was forced to drag my cumbersome rolling suitcase behind me as I navigated the route to their address. Somehow I got turned around and found myself lost at 3:00 a.m., wandering through a graffiti plastered, payday-loan-mart-infested neighborhood featuring malt liquor billboards and Newport signs everywhere I looked. I could almost picture the pale ad executives in tall, glass buildings downtown, conjuring up the slick slogans they concocted to prey on every misbegotten occupant of these hellholes. Perhaps I could have respected them a little bit more if they'd just come out and said what they really thought: "Drink nigger, nobody gives a shit about you. Get goddamn good and drunk, broke motherfuckers— why the hell not? Cash your pathetic little check here dawg—it ain't enough to live on anyway, might as well give half of it to the man." The next day I figured I'd walked about a mile and a half out

of my way before I learned how to use MapQuest on my phone
and get where I was going. Dawn and my back were near breaking when I saw the familiar car in the driveway, signalling my safe
arrival to Laura's place.

On the short plane ride home the next day, I leaned my head
against the window, closed my eyes, and let gratitude flow that life
had provided me with a warm house, a loving family, and a tiny,
unsophisticated police force to return to for Thanksgiving. I'd had
enough drama to last forever hanging out in the dirty, desperate
city. No more forays into the dark side for me. I did my tour of
duty. I'd tried to make a difference by "throwing myself onto the
gears of the machinery" and "raising a ruckus." I had not "waited
until the bombs started falling" to blow the whistle on what was
being done to my country. I'd occupied for the Florida panther who
could not hire a lobbyist, and I'd been knocked around, tear gassed
and arrested by the cops for the evening grosbeak. While many
goals remained unreached, I was satisfied with the knowledge that
I'd at least gotten off the couch and tried to do something.

Chapter 5

Occupy Foreclosure—D6

Thanksgiving was lovely and relaxing. The turkey was tender and moist, my cornbread stuffing ruled, and the green bean casserole, nonpareil. In the days after my return from Oakland, my cat forgave my absence and things began to settle down to a normal routine. Not once had I missed my tarpmate, nor had I longed for the cloying odors accompanying the periodic flick of the Bic late at night. Christmas too passed happily with Currier and Ives landscapes outside my window and holiday sleigh bells affixed gaily to our horses' halters. We all went out as a family to select the perfect tree from hundreds of candidates among the young firs that were scarcely a stone's throw from the back door. The wild snowshoe hare reclaimed her annual residence in the barn, delighting us all when she darted between hay bales to show off a new, plush, white winter coat. From time to time, mice would spring unexpectedly from a bale, giving me a start and making me laugh as they narrowly avoided being scooped into the sled we dragged through the snow to feed the horses. Once in a while one of us would spy an owl, bobcat, or even a moose wandering about, reminding us what a wild and special place we live in.

When I was growing up in Lincoln, Nebraska, my family was very poor—at times we were homeless, which was one of the worst feelings I've ever known. On a few occasions, my mother, sister, and I would all share a bed in the homes of strangers, who'd answered the call to help from the Catholic Church. Once we stayed in the City Mission for weeks, picking our way past pedophiles and alcoholics, who asked horrifying questions of my eleven-year-old self, like, "Have you ever been kissed between the legs before?" I vividly remember ducking out on grammar school chums who were accustomed to walking me home after class, and making lame excuses to ditch them before we reached our old apartment, where we'd been evicted, unbeknownst to them, for failure to pay the rent. Once, I'd gotten all the way to our old unit with my best pal, who I was hiding my shameful secret from, and almost had to shove her to the ground to get her to leave before I had to reveal that we no longer lived there. It was humiliating beyond description, to have friends discover we were destitute and I've never forgotten the despair that overtook me when we lost our apartment. The recent foreclosure crisis reminded me of those hideous times and proved unbearable to watch on television, as a prosperous adult, from my own palatial abode. Story after story about families being cast into the streets by indifferent financial institutions filled me with a sense of helplessness and blinding rage every time I switched on the news. Bank CEO salaries and bonuses were going through the roof, while millions of people, who'd had the audacity to get sick, hurt, laid-off, fired, or divorced after the economic collapse of 2008 were, literally, left out in the cold. The banks themselves had been largely responsible for the national disaster, what with all the bundling and selling of bad loans to unsuspecting investors as secure investments, yet when the inevitable happened and those who were sold subprime loans found themselves unable to pay, it was all, "Out you go—see ya . . . buh bye." Slamming the dinner plate onto my TV tray was becoming a regular occurrence as I watched the nightly news and saw the carnage. For the sake of my own mental health, I knew I had to do something. I booked a commuter flight from Seattle to Oakland to put me in the East Bay on December 6 for an event called, *Occupy Foreclosure*, which I learned about on Twitter. There were three distinct actions that my friend Laura Koch and I wanted to attend, so we hit the ground running early that morning to get a good start.

The first was a foreclosure auction that was to be conducted on the steps of the County Courthouse, for properties whose owners had fallen into arrears on payments. We arrived on scene to see a couple dozen faces, all whom I recognized from past actions. During my weeks at home, I'd been asking questions of local realtors and county clerks, to be informed that it is often the case that those bidding on the parcels are unaware that the occupants are still residing in the home, having nowhere else to go and no one to turn to. How crappy would that be, I thought, to get a great deal on a foreclosure, and then find out it's your job to toss the previous owners, along with their furniture and pets, into the street? Some bargain. In most cases, the banks had already agreed in advance to take whatever money the auctioneers could raise, regardless of the balance due on the mortgages, in order to stem their losses. Ironically, this happened routinely in cases of bank foreclosure and it galled me to learn that most lenders steadfastly refused to extend victims the same terms as they readily accepted from buyers at auctions. I learned too, that homes in the East Bay had been particularly susceptible to being "underwater," as whole neighborhoods of minority buyers were sold subprime notes, then evicted—leaving those who stayed behind to fend for themselves in half-empty blocks of crime-ridden wastelands, where the few lucky ones that had been able to hang on discovered their dwellings were worth only a fraction of what they owed. In fact, banks had preyed disproportionately on people of color, funneling them into higher rates, and less-favorable terms, even when they qualified for much more desirable "prime" mortgages. Those who tried to wait it out until the market turned around were left holding the bag, while once-safe communities turned into havens for drugs and prostitution. A jolly black man emerged from the courthouse, smiling, clipboard in hand, and called out to ask if anyone on the steps was there for the auction. Five or six older white guys raised their hands, along with a young black man of about thirty-five. "Okay, then. Gather 'round so you can hear me and let's get started."

"Wait a minute," I interrupted. "Are you the auctioneer?" I asked.

"Yeah, what did you expect?" he chuckled. "A cowboy or something?"

I didn't admit it, but that's exactly what I'd expected—not some ordinary, run-of-the-mill guy wearing a navy blue utility jacket. He didn't even look like he could walk fast, let alone talk fast. At least that's what auctioneers looked like where I come from. Turquoise and silver bolo ties, fancy Resistol hats, shiny rodeo belt buckles, and polished pointy-toed, leather boots. I liked him, though. He was friendly and had a good attitude, so I almost regretted what we were about to put him through.

"Okay folks, we're gonna start with item number one on Jackson street . . . the opening minimum bid is fifty thousand . . . does anyone want to . . ."

And all of a sudden we brought out the signs, bells, klackers, whistles, kazoos, tambourines, shakers, and hand drums we'd been hiding beneath our clothing all morning. We began shouting nonsensical gibberish to create a cacophony that would prevent anyone from hearing the auctioneer. One apoplectic guy in a suit raised his hands in the air and began screaming at us to, "Shut the hell up and get the hell outta here!" I could see every capillary in his eyes and it pleased me that he had a dyed comb-over and sort of resembled Donald Trump. The auctioneer tried valiantly to be heard over our clatter, but to no avail. I began singing, "The hills are alive, with the sound of music," operatically, which actually got him smiling a bit after a brief period of grouchiness. Another guy in a Gore-Tex ski jacket, started kicking the brass plate of an exterior door to get the attention of a security guard inside. "Do something about this!" he screamed through the glass at the guard, who finally stepped outside, after shrugging a few times, apologetically. "Well sir, I can understand how frustrating this is—but they're actually not doing anything illegal, so . . ." he trailed off, looking as if he was suppressing laughter.

"What the fuck do you *MEAN* they're not doing anything illegal?" he shouted, gesticulating wildly. "They're stopping us from conducting business here!" I began to compose a song to his rant, "What the fuck do you mean—they're not doing anything illegal," I projected, in a vibrato infused soprano voice, to the tune of "Climb Every Mountain," from the *Sound of Music*. Soon my fellow protesters tapped in to the fun of singing, versus shouting, gibberish, and someone else began yodeling, while another sang, "High on a hill was a lonely bidder, lay ee odle lay ee odle lay hee hoo."

The decibel level reached earsplitting volumes as many of us tried not to roll on the floor laughing with the hilarity of the scene. I noticed the lone black bidder, slowly slipping away from us, shaking his head. One of the older white guys followed suit, leaving only three incensed buyers, who were now screaming hysterically for us to shut up and scram. The auctioneer, who never really did talk any faster than you or I, finally cupped his hands together and screamed, "This auction is cancelled!" and wrote, WE'RE DONE. GOODBYE, on a blank sheet of paper attached to his clipboard, which he held overhead for all of us to see. I caught up to him as he climbed the stairs to an office somewhere inside the building.

"Hey, you were really a good sport out there today, and I want to thank you for not going off on us. It really wasn't anything personal."

"No, I didn't take it like that," he replied, with the same good humor he'd demonstrated earlier. "I can respect what you all are trying to do. This job is just a temporary gig. It doesn't pay enough for me to kill myself trying to scream over you guys. I used to make good wages . . . had a good job. Then everything went downhill and my wife and I lost our house too. I got four kids and I wouldn't want to see anyone else go through what we went through. I really do hope you get some things done."

I thanked him and ran down the stairs and outside to meet back up with Laura, who had stopped to talk with the young black bidder that was still standing on the edges of the courtyard, probably hanging around to see what would happen. He listened intently to her as she tried to answer his main question, which had been, "Why did you all come down here and do this?"

Apparently her reply moved him, because when she was done, I saw him bend down and give her an appreciative hug. But I was already off and running up the block to where I could see people holding signs and gathering around an elderly woman who was standing behind a man in a wheelchair, who looked much too fragile to accompany us the three blocks we intended to walk to reach their Chase Bank branch. The man was reaching up from the back of the chair to clasp his wife's hand as she told us that she'd prayed for a miracle and gotten it when we answered the call. "My husband and I lived in that house for over fifty years and we didn't know what else to do but call the Occupy when they tried to put us out of it. We had that note paid off for fifteen years before he got sick. So we decided to go over to our bank that we've done business with all these years and take out a small mortgage to help us pay our bills. They told us the payments would be low and there wouldn't be any risk since we still had a lot of equity in the place, so we said okay, and they were low for awhile. But then it adjusted and they doubled, and we just weren't able to keep up. We didn't even know it was gonna go up till that happened. We found out later that we had qualified for a fixed rate that we could have afforded, but they didn't even offer that to us. We had good credit too. Well, then we asked them if they would give us the better rate that we should have gotten in the first place and they said they would. But after that, we could never get ahold of anyone to get the paperwork started. Finally we did find someone to help us fill out the forms, and now they say they can't find them. We just got an eviction notice in the mail and we're supposed to be out by next week. So that's why we got ahold of you."

After one of their adult children helped them navigate the Internet, they'd sent an email to Occupy Oakland asking for help. Occupy then contacted a woman from a home foreclosure advocacy group called Just Cause, and they teamed up to put together the day's action, which was to head over to the couple's bank and demand they find the missing paperwork and process it. We made our way slowly down the block, surrounding the frail duo on all sides. Both of them had silver white hair that framed their creased, ebony faces beautifully and gave them a leonine aura. When we got to the front doors we stopped briefly to caucus and review our strategy, which was basically to walk into the lobby of the small building and ask for an audience with the branch manager. As we strategized, I looked up for a split second—just in time to see a spry employee in a light blue shirt and tie sprinting from his desk with his hands clutching a ring of keys. Before I knew it, I heard the familiar sound of a metal bolt sliding into place, and we were locked out. The bank closed up shop so they wouldn't have to deal with us. Most of us were in our forties, fifties, and sixties, save for the couple we were assisting, who were both in their eighties. None of us were carrying anything more threatening than a handmade sign, nor were we dressed menacingly. At best, there were twenty of us, yet they'd felt the need to shut down, rather than discuss what happened to the paperwork and give us some idea how to get the ball rolling again. A few among our ranks tapped on the door and tried to get the attention of the employees who were studiously ignoring us, attending only to the handful of customers they were still waiting on. I watched one being walked behind a wall and realized the teller was ushering her to another exit around the side of the building. As I raced to that exit to intercept them, I dug for my Chase card that still occupied my wallet. The week before, I had planned to join the mass exodus of Americans who switched from corporate banks to credit unions, but hadn't gotten around to it yet. I managed to reach the door before the customer did, so I snatched off my hat and eyeglasses and stuffed them in my pocket, praying to be unrecognized by the teller. As the door started to swing open, I grabbed the handle and flashed my bank-card to the teller, who squinted suspiciously at it and then said, "Oh good, you're not with them."

"Huh uh, I just gotta make a deposit *now* before my checks start bouncing," I lied. I eased past the guy who'd locked the door on us and deftly slammed my body against it to admit my new friends. A tussle broke out between me and the male employee who pulled against the lever as I pushed to keep it open. He overpowered me quickly, but it was too late. Those of my posse who wanted to get inside were already in, while others shied away from the physical confrontation and chose to remain outside. Eight or nine of us from Occupy/Just Cause stood in a semicircle around the perturbed employee, who still clutched the metal key ring, and we asked him to please let us speak with the branch manager. "Look, she's upstairs in her office and she can't come down right now to meet with you," he said, displeased.

"Well how about you tell her we'd be happy to go on up to her office and talk with her there, then," countered a woman from Just Cause, who would not be dissuaded.

"Ummmm, okay, but I can't guarantee anything."

He wheeled around to disappear behind a wall while we awaited his return. We could hear him taking the stairs two by two before the room fell silent. More than ten minutes elapsed before we saw him again, this time with the faintest trace of a smile on his face. "Okay, well . . . she says she *will* speak with *one* of you, if you'd be willing to elect a representative, but she does ask that the others leave the building and wait outside first."

I bristled at the idea of surrendering the hard won real estate we were standing on, yet held my tongue as the Just Cause staffers considered the proposal. Soon all heads were nodding in agree-ment after they chose their lead negotiator. Reluctantly, I accom-panied the others back out the same door where I'd almost got my arm pulled out of the socket, and we began our vigil. Time slowed to a crawl as I sat beside the wheelchair and struck up a conversa-tion with the elderly married couple that were still on the sidewalk outside. They gave me more disturbing details of the impending sheriff's eviction, which made my blood boil, and I peered inside hoping not to lose my temper and throw a brick through the window. I didn't want them to be huddled outside shuddering in the wind with their creaky old bones pressing up against hard surfaces. They'd worked hard all their lives, survived the horrors of racism in America, saved their money, and finally retired after the kids were grown and the mortgage was paid. The greatest hardship they should have to endure in any single day should have been trying to dislodge purring cats from their laps so they could toddle into the kitchen to brew another pot of tea. Yet, here we were. Luckily our delegate returned before I lost my resolve to remain peaceful, and the words were encouraging. The branch manager had made a few phone calls and magically found the errant loan modification paperwork, after which she agreed to meet with the couple and their Just Cause advocates on Wednesday at 11:00 a.m. the following week. Laura Koch and I jumped up and down, hugged each other, and got in line to embrace the couple who were both crying and saying, "Praise God," over and over.

She and I had precious time to rest on our laurels because it was nearing four o'clock in the afternoon and we had to sprint to a home near the BART Fruitvale station in order to honor the last commitment of our day.

Sheila Newcome was an attractive, fit woman, with a hip, short Afro and an engaging personality. She also possessed a master's degree in Business Administration which had stood her in good stead until the corporation she worked for downsized and let her go, after fourteen years of exemplary service and positive relations with her coworkers and superiors. The timing could not have been worse, as she'd recently finalized a divorce from her husband, the father of both her children, ages twelve and fourteen. They had purchased a townhouse together over a decade earlier, which the courts awarded her in the parting of ways. Her salary was more than adequate to handle the payment on her own, and she maintained an excellent credit score, never being late on that, or any other financial obligation, even after she became a single mother. She was not unduly concerned about the dismissal—being confident about her qualifications and certain that she had an impressive skill set that would quickly land her into something new. Two years later her savings gone, her 401k plundered, she could no longer afford to make the payment on her townhouse, so she fell behind on her obligation. To make matters worse, the tanking economic climate had gobbled up the equity she'd labored to accrue and made the residence worth many thousands less than she'd originally paid for it, years ago. Undeterred, she maintained a dialogue with her lender who was working with her to modify the loan to reduce the principle balance owed, which would be more in keeping with its current value, as well as to secure a lower interest rate, given that those too had plunged in recent years. Throughout all her tribulations, she continued her tireless search for employment, finally landing a good job, which enabled her to begin catching up on missed payments. She was within two months of accomplishing that goal when she received a notice of foreclosure from the bank, saying she had thirty days to vacate the premises, or her possessions would be placed on the parking strip and eventually taken to the dump if she did not claim them. She made a petrified call to her account manager, who assured her there had been some miscommunication and there was no cause for alarm. He told her to disregard the erroneous message and do nothing. Weeks later, she left for work as usual, leaving both her children to get themselves up and off to the school bus in another hour. Sometime before noon she received a call from a neighbor, who said she was caring for Sheila's two panic stricken children who were still in their pajamas, having been escorted to the curb by a sheriff's deputy who'd arrived moments after she left for work, and had his men put everything they owned on the parking strip. As they pleaded with him to let them get dressed and call their mother, he had turned a cold shoulder, rebuffing them with the admonishment, "Your mom should've told you we were coming so you could've been ready." They'd looked on piteously as their belongings were piled up before them, unsure of what to do. A neighbor who had occasionally engaged in small talk with their mother, saw the scene, assessed the situation, and asked the children if they wanted to come inside her unit to call their mother at work. Upon hearing what happened, Sheila left her office early, gathered her sobbing children and paid an unannounced visit to her bank. They told her that the employee she'd been working with was no longer with them, and apologized for any inconvenience that may have caused her. Since that awful day, she'd been forced to relocate her family to her parents basement, which had been overwhelming, costly, and embarrassing. When she was at her wit's end, she called Occupy Oakland and asked if there was anything they might be able to do to help bring attention to her circumstances and perhaps even help get her house back. There were over two hundred of us who walked from the notorious Fruitvale Station, where Oscar Grant died, to the Newcome Townhouse. Someone unfurled a 10x10 banner that read, WELCOME HOME SHEILA, after which another Occupier produced a set of bolt cutters and removed the lockbox that was suspended from the doorknob. A U-Haul truck pulled up and the driver hopped out of the cab to pull out the long metal ramp stowed in back, and with the help of others, began unloading sturdy, attractive furniture. Sofas, beds, ottomans, tables, chairs—even a number of houseplants and framed paintings soon adorned the living space, which was instantly transformed to a cozy, inviting home that looked as if it had been lived in for years. Sheila, whose features reminded me of a young Gladys Knight, (without the Pips) stood in the front yard, struggling to staunch the tears that were cascading from her eyes. One of the event's organizers circulated a sign-up sheet asking for volunteers who would be willing to put in four-hour shifts, with a partner, to protect the house from a re-repossession. Police vehicles, inexplicably, maintained a half block distance as several law enforcement and media helicopters hovered over us to monitor our activity. Many of us were weeping as we watched her cross her threshold for the first time in a long while. I wanted badly to be able to stay in town long enough to put in a shift, or at least be on standby to receive an alert text, which would be our signal to get back there in a hurry to thwart another eviction attempt. An overjoyed Sheila agreed with us that it would be best to continue spending nights with her children at her parent's house, in the short term, until we made inroads with her lender to reverse the foreclosure and halt short sale proceedings.

When Laura and I returned to her home that evening, we were beaming with pride as we told her wife, Lori, what we'd accomplished. We got there just in time to catch the top story on Channel Two's eleven o'clock news, which happened to be the auction disruption we'd caused earlier. We jumped up and down with excitement as we picked ourselves out of the small group, and the anchor related how the sale would have to be rescheduled for a future date. Then they cut away to another short video clip of us standing outside bearing signs, which accompanied the story of how we'd shut down a local Chase Bank branch and demanded to have an elderly couple's loan modification processed. "Oh my God, there you are again!" Gasped Lori. The station then broke away for a commercial, followed by a zoomed-in videotape, taken from a helicopter, of us unloading furniture into Sheila Newcome's house, with the "WELCOME HOME Sheila" sign hanging in the front. "Look, we're in this one too!" I squealed, unable to wipe the silly grin off my face. Best day ever.

Chapter 6

Occupy the Rose Parade—J2

Occupy Congress—J17

Occupy the Supreme Court—J20

January 2012

January promised to be an action-packed month, chock-full of opportunities for arrest and incarceration. Reclaiming Sheila Newcome's home, getting a commitment from Chase Bank to begin the process of renegotiating the elderly couple's loan, and stopping the foreclosure auction were victories that lifted my spirits and energized me for the ambitious schedule I'd crafted for the next few weeks. After landing at the Burbank airport, I picked up my rental car and began to navigate my way southeast on the freeway to my host house. God bless Mapquest. I'd once more beaten the bushes of my social media accounts to find a home stay right in the heart of Pasadena, at the residence of a liberal couple who somehow, despite their political bent, had done well enough in life to own a beautiful stucco home in a safe, well manicured, upscale neighborhood. Their place wasn't far from the Rose Parade, which was where we intended to make a big splash this New Year. Dave and Louisa Fertig were Facebook friends of mine who had, years earlier, helped produce a fiftieth anniversary concert I played in Los Angeles, for the now defunct Ashgrove Concert Hall. The venue had earned its place in history by featuring legendary musicians who were also political activists during the Civil Rights Movement. Ed Pearl, owner of the old Ashgrove, was in his late seventies when he asked Dave for a hand with the details of the show. That's when he and I first met, and I'm guessing I was well behaved enough then, for him to offer me a room in his house, years later, during the city's high profile annual shindig, The Rose Parade. My purpose was to help orchestrate the Occupation of the nationally televised production, which was as American as apple pie, and to give viewers an alternative perspective to life in paradise.

When I first laid eyes on their place, I knew I would be comfortable and safe, which was in marked contrast to my challenging tenure at Occupy Oakland. And I owed it all to Dave, who had, some time in his youth, realized there wasn't much money to be made playing blues harmonica and smoking pot, so he decided to go back to college and become a lawyer, which was his day job. The restorative effects of country living had massaged my senses over the holidays and brought me back to reasonable health. The constant hoarseness, coughing, wheezing, asthma, and sore throat that plagued me ever since being gassed in Oakland, had mostly vanished and faded into the background as each day passed without incident. Invariably, pastoral quietude had given way to the niggling doubt that my country was never going to wake up, right itself, and get back to taking at least minimal care to feed, clothe, shelter, employ, and educate some of the non–rich people who also live here in the land of plenty. And that reprehensible fact was due, at least in part, to my own apathy. Down comforters, flannel sheets, all-wheel drive minivans, data plans, and vacations to Hawaii aren't what it takes to light a fire under soft, well-fed asses like mine.

So, this was Pasadena—palm trees, clean, bum-free storefronts, landscaped estates, and plenty of obedient, polite, hard-working

Mexicans to keep it that way. I was more than lucky to have found free lodging so close to Rose Bowl Stadium and the parade route. Bonus—Dave was a gourmet chef and loved nothing more than throwing together fabulous healthy meals, chock-full of fresh organic ingredients on a moment's notice, any day of the week, for anyone in his company. Added bonus; Dave liked to drink expensive, delicious booze—thinking nothing of uncorking stunning, complex, rich, peaty, sixty-year-old bottles of single malt scotch and pouring ample portions into a heavy highball glass, even for the likes of me, who would have been just as happy with a paper sack fifth of cherry Thunderbird and a pickled pigfoot. God Bless America. Dave was also a great, clever conversationalist, in addition to being kind and generous to a fault. Yay.

Louisa handed me an ornate antique house key before I left to meet with OTRP (Occupy The Rose Parade) planners, and said I could come and go as I pleased, even bemoaning the fact that I'd rented an economy car instead of allowing them to lend me their gorgeous 1962 baby blue Jaguar "that hardly ever got driven," and was parked "all by its lonesome" in the three-car garage behind the house. What a difference a month makes. They gave me the option of either, joining in whatever they were doing, or not engaging with them at all and giving my full attention to the cause. They even told me I could bring OTRP organizers over and have meetings at their house if I wanted. How in the world had such good-hearted people done so well in such a mercenary, dog-eat-dog world. Not only had they both landed squarely on their feet in this shi-shi habitat, they still gave a shit about those who hadn't fared so well. How rare is that. One night after I distributed leaflets for Occupy, Dave (who was the more gregarious of the two) told me of how he'd grown up poor, aimless, and without many extra groceries in his household, before he met the love of his life—Louisa. She had been his salvation, he confessed. She grew up an only child in a stable, well-to-do family and had somehow seen the hidden potential in her inauspicious classmate and fallen madly in love with this intelligent, but ambitionless boy from the wrong side of the tracks. I detected the trace of a smile on her face from the corner of my eye as she quietly knitted, listening to his story. Though lavish parties, extravagant gifts, riding lessons, and sailing trips to exotic places had never been his reality, she had seen beyond her own privilege and chosen him to be her life partner. She readily admitted that part of his allure was the exotic nature of his bohemian world. Her mother wanted, as all mothers do, only the best for her daughter, however, possessed the extraordinary wisdom to go with the flow of this unexpected curve ball and make lemonade out of the lemons that were Dave. Her parents had, in fact, cared so much about Louisa, that they graciously put Dave through law school, employed him in the family business, and gave their cherished daughter their blessing to marry him, only after he had proven his mettle through hard work, dedication, honesty, and sacrifice to the family. So visionary and forward thinking were her parents in predicting the unstoppability of this union, that they had gone to great lengths to groom and make something of this bright, but nowhere-bound lad before they passed into the hereafter, and left the couple the bulk of their estate and this rockin' crib.

So that's how Dave had come by his extraordinary understanding of, and compassion for, the other half—or, more accurately, the 99%. And that's why he didn't have a hint of the contempt most rich folks display in the first five minutes of assessing your bottom line. He'd grown up poor, and furthermore, his greatest heroes had been the black blues performers he'd revered since seeking out their recordings, as a youth, from the nearest library. Many of his idols had never achieved great wealth or even much fame. They were men and women with names like Tampa Red, Elmore James, Sonnyboy Williamson, Jellyroll Morton, Memphis Minnie, Blind Lemon Jefferson, Big Mama Thornton, and Sister Rosetta Tharp. He immersed himself in songs like, "Dust My Broom," "Shake Sugaree," "Black Snake Moan," "Keep it Clean," and "You Can Have My Husband, But Please Don't Take My Man." Not a great fan of the British Invasion or early American pop music, he'd skipped over Elvis, Cream, and the Rolling Stones and gone directly to the source, delighting at how those early lyrics, deconstructed, all seemed to refer to some kind of bumping grinding sexual encounter—just like the ones, I'm sure, he hoped to have someday with Louisa.

It soon became evident to me that the general assemblies and planning meetings for OTRP were little more than snarky, provincial, in-fighting sessions, often characterized by thinly-veiled contempt for co-members, frequent put-downs, petty squabbles, and territorial feuds between self-appointed leaders. I came to understand that Pasadena, with a population of 138,000, was little more than a small town, and compared to Oakland, had much less diversity within its borders. Almost everyone at the sparse gatherings was white and male, with a few notable exceptions. On this night, a young hiply attired black man drove from L.A.—walked into the GA—and generously offered OTRP use of his large, state-of-the-art PA system, along with high-quality video cameras, as well as his labor and expertise in operating them. Furthermore, he told the meeting that he had a group of highly skilled audio/video technicians who said they were eager to work alongside him—*for free*. I took an instant liking to him as he politely identified himself as Marcus Jackson, and briefly outlined his impressive credentials as a current part time resident of both L.A. and New York City. At that time, he was employed as a sound engineer and producer of MTV programming. He was immediately challenged by a slovenly man of about thirty-five, bearing a shock of greasy, black curly hair, partially enveloped in a grungy black scarf. The chubby challenger wore a stained Utilikilt and a dingy plaid shirt, There was a silver ring in his left nostril that was connected by a chain to an identical ring in his ear. "Um, yeah dude . . . what'dyu say your name was again?" questioned kilt-man.

"Marcus," others in the room answered, before Marcus could.

"Oh yeah, Marcus . . . Hey, pleased to meet you. My name's Stash and I got a shit ton of buddies I grew up with right here in the community, and we all got great gear and mad skills, so we pretty much have video and sound handled for all the pre- and post-parade events. All the details are already worked out and my mom's keeping the donated audio stuff in her garage, where I can keep an eye on it from my room, so nothin' happens to it between now and then, so . . . thanks anyway, buddy."

The soft-spoken visitor seemed slightly nonplussed, but made a gracious attempt to shift back onto the right foot with Stash in the meeting which was being held in a small room of a church basement. "Oh, I'm sure you're well prepared and everything—I'm sorry if I suggested otherwise. I love what you all are doing and I wanted to find a way to volunteer whatever skills I have to whatever needs you might have. I just feel like this is a great movement and I wanted to support your idea of bringing Occupy into the living rooms of America at such a high profile event. I've done some work with Occupy L.A. and maybe I can help you get some good footage at the parade. Perhaps I could pitch it to my bosses somewhere down the line if you're interested. At the very least, I could loan you my gear to flesh out your sound system if you're planning any large set ups on outdoor stages.

"Yeah . . . so . . . my best friend used to roadie for Dave Matthews when he was just startin' to go viral and he knows everything there is to know about outdoor venues so . . . again, thanks, Marcus. I'd hate to see you lose your rig by gettin' it stolen or something, what with all the out-of-towners that're gonna be stompin' around here this weekend," said Stash before turning his back to Marcus and walking over to a desk to retrieve his clipboard.

"Okay, now . . . let's see . . . what's next on the docket," resumed Stash after thumbing laboriously through what looked to me to be empty pages.

"Well, now wait just a minute . . ." piped up a hirsute, middle-aged woman, in a pair of denim overalls. She struggled to swallow quickly and free her mouth of the audibly crunchy trail mix she'd been grazing on ever since I walked in with Daniel, another OTRP volunteer I'd met online while sussing out the event from Pagan Place. " . . . I know we've got sound and video handled, but I bet we could find something useful for this young man to do in the group." She swept her head from side to side, glancing expectantly at the faces around her to solicit approval from the other eight or nine people in the room. As she did so, some of the trail mix crumbs that clung stubbornly to the light grey mustache on her upper lip dislodged and tumbled silently onto the tattered wool sweater she wore under her bib. Her glance was met with tepid shrugs and a few barely perceptible nods. "Can't we just give the new guy a chance to get in on the ground floor and make history with us?" Fewer nods, fewer shrugs. "Well look, Marcus, my name is Cindy, and I'm sort of the Jill of all Trades here. I've been helping to plan this thing right from the start back in November. We *have* been trying to figure out just how the heck we're gonna feed all the long-time volunteers after the parade and I was wondering . . . Well, can you barbecue? Are you any good with a grill?"

The words that fell out of her mouth sounded so condescending and demeaning that I felt my face flush with embarrassment. Could it possibly be that these well-meaning, but clearly clueless, white people had just asked the only black man in the room (who happened to be so accomplished and caring, I found myself wishing I'd done more with my own life) to cater a meal for the after-party?

"You know what—*no* . . . Not just no, but hell no! I'm not going to flip burgers and bust out the ribs to wait on your staff. You know, I was just running sound for a GA last night at Occupy L.A., and someone announced that Occupy the Rose Parade needed some sound volunteers, so I got in my car and came down here to see if I could help. But, hey, it doesn't look like it—so . . . I'm just going to carry my little self on out of here, and bid you all a wonderful night, people." With that Marcus got up and began to gather the printed business cards he'd left on a table, to put back into his wallet.

Alarmed at the unseemly turn of events, Cindy moved to intercept him before he could reach the door. "Hey, if grilling doesn't trip yer trigger, I'm sure there's other chores that need doing around here. You don't have to leave, you know. If that's not your bag I'm sure we could put you to work somewhere else." Marcus softened as his eyes met hers and saw her sincerity.

"You know, I didn't come down here just to upset your apple cart," Marcus said, addressing everyone in the room. "And, I honestly don't need to find things to do to fill my time. I'm plenty busy, but if you think you might be able to use some of my professional skills, I am happy to donate my time and energy here to help make your plan a success, if I can, because I believe in activism and trying to make things better for people who don't have many options."

"Look man, that's totally cool," chimed in an older man from across the room. "There's never too many volunteers for a big production like this. Even though we're 'Occupy *Pasadena*' and aren't technically affiliated with Occupy the Rose Parade, we put our feelers out to other Occupations to see if folks wanted to help us organize our *own* protest at the parade." This was the first I'd heard that I wasn't sitting in on an Occupy the Rose Parade meeting. "You see, we all took a vote here at *Occupy Pasadena* to not officially endorse OTRP, because we don't like the leadership over there, but we do appreciate what some of their members are trying to do. Even though we're sorta like, overlapping jurisdictions, [air quotes] in a way, we still wanted to do something similar ourselves at the Parade. Hey, Marcus, did you just say you're from Occupy L.A. . . . like the *official* Occupy L.A.?"

"Uh huh—yeah man, there's only one," answered Marcus.

"Wow, that's interesting, because I was almost thinking I might want to join up with those guys sometime, or maybe at least go to a GA, but I heard they were super racist up there, so I never did go." Jesus, how far is Oakland from here, I thought gloomily.

Monday, January 2, the day of the Rose Parade, dawned brilliantly with dazzling sunshine and a heady air of festivity. From all the meetings I'd attended the week before, (for who knows what organizations) I knew that the lead OTRP organizer, Jack Tatum's main objective was to bring attention to the fact that the Rose Parade's largest sponsor, Wells Fargo, was conducting staggering numbers of fraudulent, illegal bank foreclosures in California and nationwide. He had become a vocal opponent of the corporation's "robo-calling" tactics and wanted to expose other murky dealings with homeowners, which amounted to, what he considered, criminal behavior. He abhorred the discouraging, complex, convoluted, and usually downright unnavigable process the banks had put in place to modify distressed loans.

Banks routinely claimed ownership of homes they could produce no deeds for, nor could they even prove in some instances that borrowers were behind in their payments. Jack, and countless other Americans (like me) felt that something drastic had to be done. That something, in this case, was to gather thousands of foreclosure protesters together to create an arresting visual that the entire country would see. What better way to usher in a new year, than to shame wrongdoers into more just ways of doing business. To that end, Jack declared Occupy the Rose Parade as the start of "Occupy 2.0," which he touted as a more focused version of the much criticised Occupy Movement itself, which was often said to have no real direction or purpose. Jack envisioned a streamlining of the nascent uprising, which would now begin to hone in on on specific issues, such as this, and appoint recognized leaders, (like him) to implement direct actions which would address America's most pressing concerns. I knew this from conducting a battery of Internet searches over the holidays, trying to decide what my next big Occupy endeavor would be. I was beginning to understand, from persistent grumblings at the General Assemblies, that many people considered lead organizer, Jack Tatum, to be somewhat of a slimeball, but I wasn't sure exactly why. I'd read he was a lawyer of some sort, and that he shared my personal beliefs that America's big banks had become cold-blooded land thiefs, but I didn't know until the eve of the Parade, that Jack himself had been embroiled in a number of unsavory brushes with the law. On January 1, the day before the parade, a Pasadena newspaper published a scathing exposé of Jack's past that left me wondering who, and what, to believe about OTRP's mastermind. The article said that Jack had been busted at least twice, for shoplifting—once domestically and once in Mexico. I could forgive the shoplifting, especially if done in his youth, (who hasn't?) so I wasn't too put off by that, however, it baffled me how anyone who'd been caught and prosecuted could ever risk the humiliation and expense again. Still, the dirt I'd read on him wasn't a deal breaker yet. I could easily believe that the banks who stood to lose the most if the masses turned on them, had dug deep to uncover—even manufactured—the skeletons in Jack's distant past. The "scandal" might have been little more than adolescent bad judgment and immaturity. But I could also believe that these minor crimes were the portent of deeper character flaws, which had continued to grow and become more sophisticated over time. A more disquieting revelation to me, was that Jack had recently been involved in a nasty family dispute where he had sued his own brother for being a crooked investment banker that had bilked his customers out of much of their hard-earned money. He accused him of selling unwitting buyers some sort of creepy, Bernie Madoff-style Ponzi scheme investment fund. Now, I know that it's not exactly fair to assume that if your brother's a criminal and a jerk, you're a criminal and a jerk, but that's where my head naturally went, somehow. The news discouraged me, and I was just about to put the newspaper down without bothering to turn the page and read to the end, when I decided to forge ahead anyway, since I still had some time to kill. The last paragraph mentioned, almost as an afterthought, that Jack had lost his license to practice law in Nevada because of the second shoplifting conviction in that state. Oh, now that's much different, I thought. The guy shoplifted in his home state as a grown man, *after* he became a lawyer. Classy.

Since I was already there, Jack's being a weasel didn't detract from my original conviction that banks had committed egregious crimes against humanity, so I continued on with my plans to Occupy the Rose Parade. The negative press had made me wince, but I wasn't there to find a guru; I was here to protest corporate excesses. To that end, I woke up at six a.m, January 2, and walked

over to Singer Park to help make signs and join in the fun. I was
among the first to arrive on that glorious morning, so I got a rare
opportunity to watch the sunrise, which, as a musician and power
sleeper, I hardly ever do. Around eight o'clock people started filing
in from all corners of the park. Anti-War activist, Cindy Sheehan,
had been chosen to be the grand marshall of our parade, which
Jack was calling, "The Human Float." He told us, we'd been given
official permission by the Parade Commission to march at the very
end of the parade, which I thought was a major coup, given the
scope of the event and the surety that millions would be watching.
I had devised the perfect outfit for the festivities and couldn't wait
to show it off to my country. I'd purchased a "jailbird prison suit"
at an online costume maker for under thirty dollars (delivered)
and sewed the words "BANK CEO" on a large rectangular patch,
that I positioned prominently on the chest. To complete le tout
ensemble, I raided my nine-year-old's toy shelves to find a cash
register with large, fake dollar bills, which I stuffed all around the
neck, hat, and arm openings. It was marvelously effective as many
parade-goers stopped me to take pictures en route to the park.

By 9:00 a.m. I'd run into lots of Occupiers and Streamers I knew
from Oakland and elsewhere—some whose faces I recognized only
from seeing them on my computer screen. I estimated our crowd
to be around five thousand, which was adequate, but disappoint-
ing to me as I'd dreamed of millions showing up to overshadow
the whole affair. I found that my sentiments were shared by others
as I was approached by a woman who wanted to take my picture
before we got in line to march at the end of the parade. "Gosh, I
wish there were more people here," she whispered to me, after she
captured the shot. "I'm just a stay-at-home mom, but I came all
the way from Oregon to be here today. I guess most people just
don't care about what the banks are doing to us in this country. All
Americans seem to care about is football and celebrities like—hey
that's it!" she burst out, interrupting her own sentence. "I got it! I
totally know how we can make Americans give a shit about what's
going on. We need to Occupy a *Kardashian* and find out where that

one . . . uh, the super slutty one . . . *Kim*, goes all the time. We need
to follow her wherever she goes, with our signs about foreclosure
and stuff like that. That's what we need to do to get the word out!"
Her enthusiasm made me smile as I envisioned gangs of political
activists bird-dogging Kim Kardashian's every move.

By 9:30 a.m. there were around seven thousand of us standing
on a side street, watching the end of the parade behind temporary
wooden barricades. Our lead sign was a gigantic parchment-like
scroll, which read, WE THE PEOPLE, in reference to the Citizen's
United decision granting corporations personhood status. Dozens of us were upholding a giant red plastic octopus, which was
extending its eight long tentacles, labeled, WELLS FARGO, as they
reached out and snatched up single family homes with occupants
inside, hanging out of windows, screaming to be rescued. A large
contingent of police on the other side of the barricades informed
us we could file into the end of the parade line as soon as the last
float passed. I made sure to be in the lead group so I could be
among the first to see the reaction of thousands of spectators in
the bleachers lining the route. Three minutes after the last float
had passed, police still had not removed the barriers and people
were descending the bleachers in droves, leaving the scene. We the
members of "The Human Float" began complaining loudly, to the
cops, who still weren't letting us get onto the route before everyone
was gone. A full ten minutes after the last float passed, and more
than two-thirds of the spectators had left the scene, police officers
began to slowly draw back the barriers and let us come forward.
As we entered the route smiling, waving, and looking up into the
stands, I noticed platforms holding mainstream media cameras,
which were being hurriedly powered off and removed from the
area. As we advanced, the few talking heads still stationed ahead
of us, rushed to wrap things up before any of their viewers could
see us being disrespectful to their biggest sponsor, Wells Fargo,
who had bankrolled the whole event. Wells Fargo management
had been so fretful that OTRP would rain on their parade, that
they'd gone so far as to phone Jack-the-shoplifter up the Friday

before, and try to persuade him to scuttle the Human Float at the last minute, fearing a massive turnout, resulting in a public relations nightmare. The bank reps had promised to give OTRP an audience with Wells Fargo higher ups, who assured us they would "consider our complaints sometime in the New Year" if we agreed to abort our mission. Unwilling to do so, we now waltzed past hundreds of celebrants, who'd hung behind to let the crowd thin, wearing the colors of the football teams yet to play that afternoon. Half were in red and white to support the Wisconsin Badgers, while the other dressed in green and yellow, for the Oregon Ducks. "Boo! Boo! Go home freaks! Take a bath and get a job assholes!" came the jeers of hostile sports fans. Some even spat on us or flipped us off as we proceeded past them in our activist regalia. I reminded myself that if saving the world was easy, everyone would do it, and vowed to remain smiling, regardless of the insults. I was heartened by the small number of spectators who stood up and clapped—some even flashing the thumbs up sign and joining us.

We marched for blocks before finally running headlong into a moving channel of celebrants, whose numbers were so large and spread out, we were quickly separated and swallowed up by them. Unable to move forward, I chose to back up and shoot down a side street toward the city park where our own after-party was scheduled to begin soon. I had been apprised by OTRP "organizers" that some "major celebrity musicians" were planning to drop in and entertain us, following our historic hike.

Upon arrival I saw Marcus looking agonized as he leaned against a panel truck and observed the horror of Stash and his motley crew trying to cobble together a woefully inadequate PA system made up of odds and ends, unlikely to have seen active duty since before the Vietnam War. "Hey Stash," mumbled one of his staff, holding up a tangle of twisted cables and jacks. "Ummmmm, so . . . whut does this go to dude?"

"Fuck, man . . . Can't you see I'm *doin' shit*," growled a frayed Stash, his entire head stuck into a large guitar amplifier that seemed to be missing its speaker.

"Wull, yeah DUDE, like—no fuckin' duh, Sherlock . . ." retorted the crew member. "In case you hadn't noticed, we're *all* doin' important shit."

"Frickin' assclown," Stash muttered under his breath, while trying to locate parts for the amp. Marcus, standing on the sidelines, was unable to contain himself any longer as he interjected, "Hey man, I thought you could maybe use some extra gear to augment your system, so I brought a whole truck full of mics and cables and amps and stuff like that. I'd be happy to bring my board out and give you a hand with the set up if you want."

"I got it handled, Marcus," barked Stash. "No assistance necessary, man. I'm, like, fifteen minutes away from being ready to do a sound check. If you wanna help then, I'll call you . . . 'kay." A vein on Marcus's temple looked ready to rupture as he shook his head and climbed, into his truck, where he sat sullenly, still overlooking Stash's sound crew. As he did so I gazed past him through the windshield, to see a rail-thin woman with a guitar strapped to her back, stomping purposefully toward the sound equipment, haphazardly strewn about on the grass. Stash's crew, suddenly aware of its absence, had the "aftsight" to begin furiously attempting to construct a makeshift stage from two abandoned shopping carts and some plywood they'd found on site. As the guitar-bearing woman got closer and surveyed the scene, she ripped a pair of gimongous sunglasses from her eyes, and pasted an expression of sheer disgust over her entire face. I recognized her right away to be early-nineties folk/pop star Amy Startle, who I had neither seen nor heard about in at least fifteen years. She had written and recorded a minor hit called "Settled in Seattle," which became the single from her major label debut album, alliteratively entitled, *Brief Bold Brilliant*. The tune, which had been in medium rotation on MTV programming for the better part of a year, peaked at number twelve on the charts before landing in the cutout bins of record stores nationwide. Amy had managed to carve a fairly decent career for herself based on the strength of that one song, until it became widely known that she was a bit of a handful—on and off stage. Her last decade had seen a series of backstage tantrums and on stage rants, once or twice culminating in walk-offs, followed by threats of lawsuits from concert presenters. She had run through a series of booking agents and managers before deciding to train her current love interest, a woman she'd met at a women's music festival, to do the job for her.

I followed Amy with my eyes as she stepped on the brakes, seconds before reaching one of Stash's guys. She then pivoted alarmingly swiftly to glare accusatorially behind her. At that moment I spied another woman, roughly Amy's age and size, staggering toward her with sweat pouring from her brow—arms weighed down by boxes of compact discs, and a backpack the size of a tropical tortoise on her shoulders. As Amy's eyes locked on the other woman's, I saw rage replace disgust. "You better not tell me this is the fucking gig you booked, Sierra," Amy seethed. "And that better not be the fucking stage," she snarled pointing at the plywood/shopping cart contraption. Sierra grimaced at the scene and began babbling a disjointed, rapid-fire defense of her work. "They said you'd be on the bill with *Jackson Browne and Bonnie Raitt* . . . And there'd be a *totally tricked out sound system* . . . and they promised you wouldn't even have to soundcheck. They assured me every single one of the items on your rider would be provided, down to the last detail . . . and . . ."

All of a sudden, Stash was nowhere to be found, having hightailed it behind a brick building upon seeing ballistic Amy. He was, in all probability, hoping his crew would somehow deflect some of the blows Amy looked ready to rain down upon them. I sat on a marble statue base just out of the action, wondering what would happen next. Marcus is what happened. Witnessing the entire painful scenario, he had boldly evacuated his truck and leaned into Amy and Sierra's personal space to introduce himself. "Hi, I'm Marcus, and I apologize for the disorganization here. We've been unable to get the system fully operational because the police delayed our start time, but if you can hang on for about fifteen minutes, we should be able to get it together." Sierra looked as if she wanted to pass out, as Amy turned her wrath onto Marcus. "This is *bullshit*," she roared. "Complete bullshit. My manager and I are going to disappear for fifteen minutes, and when we come back, you're either ready to go, or you can go fuck yourselves."

With that she wheeled around and buried herself in the crowd, leaving an overburdened Sierra to try to catch up, as best she could. Marcus sprang into action the second she was out of sight, artfully directing Stash's handful of feckless foundlings in the unloading of his truck and the setup of equipment. Exactly fifteen minutes later Amy returned to a fully functioning system of amplifiers, microphones, and monitors, ready to deliver her dulcet tones to the crowd of three or four hundred onlookers, still in the area. Nothing could be done in such a short time to address the inadequacy of the stage, so Amy, still shooting scathing looks at Sierra, mounted the makeshift platform with the help of Stash, who had suddenly reappeared.

Since no one had had the foresight to introduce her, Amy did so herself, by announcing shrilly that she had been trying to support the Occupy Movement since its inception in September, but had been driven back at every turn by ugly detractors, who contended that she, a famous folkstar, was more a member of the "1%," than the "99%" and really shouldn't be seen trying to glom on to our struggle. "Well, fuck that," she brayed. "And fuck *anyone* who thinks that." She then launched into a spastic, angry progression of power chords, followed by a series of shouted rather than sung words, which comprised the verse and chorus of an Occupy anthem she'd penned, on the fly, the day before. I stood next to Marcus's sound board as he rushed to get a decent mix on her vocals and guitar. He and I had spoken briefly after the disastrous GA the week before, and he knew I'd done some singing, so he asked me for suggestions as he deftly dialed her sound in. She jabbed sharply at her guitar strings, while singing something about it being all of our faults the world had gotten so fucked up in the last few years. She then pounded a dissonant chord with her thick pick, before stopping the song altogether. "What is this, an *oil*

painting? Ya know what?" Amy shrieked. "I'm getting pretty god-
damned sick and tired of looking at you, looking at me, like you're
bored out of your fuckin' gourds, and like you got something else
better to do—so why don't *you* entertain *me* for a minute while
I smoke a fucking cigarette." With that, Amy bolted nimbly off
the stage, walked casually over to a nearby tree and lit up, to the
stunned silence of everyone in attendance. "How's this working
for ya?" She hollered pointedly at the audience, whose faces were
beginning to register the depth of their discomfort. Marcus looked
as if he wanted to throw up as his eyes met mine, and he pleaded,
"Can you just go up there and do a song or something?"

"Yeah, I can do that," I answered, wondering what else could
happen to make the day any more bizarre. I climbed, somewhat
less nimbly onto the "stage," and began singing a medley of civil
rights standards, "We Shall Not Be Moved," and, "Ain't Gonna Let
Nobody Turn Me Around," while clapping my hands. Once people joined in and began to loosen up, I started inventing verses to
lengthen the song and keep the groove going. Several verses in, I
felt the plywood shift beneath me as I realized Amy was attempting to reenter the tiny, unstable platform from behind. Fearing the
structure would collapse, I reached out to an audience member
to steady me as I turned around to lower myself, ungracefully, to
the ground—all the while still singing "Ain't Gonna Let Nobody
Turn Me Around." I felt hands reaching up to support me as I
landed, off balance, onto the pavement below. Somehow still on
my feet, I offered the microphone up to Amy, whose hand was
already extended toward me. She snapped her fingers impatiently
for me to hurry up. Just then, a vigilant Marcus lurched toward us
both, offering a wireless microphone to Amy who took it from
him roughly. Not wanting to further offend her, I then began giving my mic back to Marcus, as I saw Amy poised to address the
bewildered group standing before us.

"Stay there!" she ordered me, before returning to her audience.
"Oh, I get it . . . You guys are into sing alongs," she conjectured,
condescendingly. "Well, why didn't you say so. We can do that."

She resumed her complicated Occupy song from the same place she'd left off the first time around. "Okay, so that's the chorus," she explained, after running through a difficult assortment of syncopated rhythms accompanied by odd atonal chords and nonrhyming lyrics. "I hope you were paying attention. Now *you* try it," she demanded, in a strange tone that was meant to be either conciliatory or patronizing—I couldn't tell which. Wanting for this attempt to go well, I began beckoning people to sing along, as I echoed, to the best of my ability, the chorus she'd just sung. As we repeated her phrase, she cut us off, midsentence, screaming, "Shut up! That's *terrible!* You need to do much better than that," which we all struggled mightily to do. Still not satisfied, Amy speculated that we might not be "into doing the heavy lifting" that was required to rid the world of all the "fucked up shit that's happening right now." "If you're not even willing to sing the goddamn chorus right, then how are you ever going to stop bank foreclosures? I can't do *everything!*" was her parting statement, as she slammed the expensive microphone onto the ground, folded her guitar under her arm, and stalked past Sierra, who hurried to gather the rest of their things and follow.

Two weeks later I was making my way to the Hertz counter at Reagan International Airport to pick up the economy car I'd rented to Occupy both Congress and the Supreme Court in Washington, DC. I booked my trip well before Occupy the Rose Parade, but had been filled with reservations after that bust. Jack Tatum and Amy Startle had left a bad taste in my mouth and I hadn't wanted the disorganized, marginally successful event to be my last action with Occupy. "Be the change you want to see," had become my mantra in the days since the parade. If I didn't like the way the Movement was going, it was up to *me* to find the solution that would reinvigorate it. After all, not everyone could afford the luxury of jetting from place to place, following dissent and unrest around the nation in the hopes of unsettling the status quo. How could a twenty-something single mother ever be expected to travel more than a few feet away from the hungry mouths that depended on her to attend to their needs. It was incumbent upon those of us who still enjoyed some modicum of comfort and privilege to sound the alarm that would compel others to recognize the monster storm bearing down on us. If people like me didn't try to stop the onrushing social, environmental, and economic devastation, a fall of apocalyptic proportions would be unavoidable. Toppling the corporatocracy that had become the United States of America was as much in my hands as in those of every other thinking, feeling American—and it was high time I got to work doing something to combat the problem, even if it meant Occupying a Kardashian.

What in the world did I have to complain about? Sure the trip to Pasadena felt, overall, like a wasted effort, but I'd never eaten better food or drunk better alcohol in my life. On New Year's Eve, two nights before the Rose Parade, the Fertigs had thrown a raging, music-filled party to end all parties, replete with prime rib, lobster canapes, *Alice in Wonderland*–themed costumes, copious amounts of killer weed, and Dom Perignon champagne. That had been fantastic. I had walked into their fabulous soiree, fresh out of another interminable, unproductive, catty meeting with Occupy Pasadena, (or was it OTRP?). That epic gathering had set me straight again. Other than my time and travel costs, I was out nothing for my efforts. *And*, there had been some cursory, eleventh-hour attempts by Wells Fargo to acknowledge our anger at their ongoing bad behavior. A few mainstream media outlets and print newspapers had even given the event scant, albeit shallow coverage, which led me to believe there may be some hope for future actions, such as Occupy Congress and Occupy the Supreme Court, which I was bound for on January 15, 2012. Both of those actions were scheduled to take place between January seventeenth and the twentieth in our Nation's capital—the District of Columbia.

The first order of business was to navigate the way to my host house in Silver Springs, Maryland. Facebook had not let me down yet, and I was fortunate to receive another lodging offer from an easygoing lesbian couple who answered my query. Both of them were politically active and wanted to be more involved with Occupy, however, Beth, who was in her early thirties, was trying to maintain her employment as a full time labor union employee, while battling a rare form of leukemia that she had been diagnosed with the year before. She was still putting in forty hours a week at work, even though she felt like hell and was making frequent trips to the hospital to combat health problems that arose after multiple courses of chemotherapy. She told me she regretted that she couldn't physically attend Occupy Congress, so she was sending me as her "surrogate" to make sure I represented her interests. The room she and her partner, Jennifer, gave me in their cheery daylight basement was private and cozy, and even had its own bathroom which was swell by me. No doubt, the week was going to be much more plush and amenity-filled than OGP, yet I still missed the vibrant pulse of the Oakland Commune and had yet to replicate that exhilarating feeling.

Before coming to DC, I made an online connection with two focus groups that appealed to me. Both had originally formed to influence the political decisions made by the Obama administration during his first term in office. Frustrated with the 2010 Citizen's United ruling from the Supreme Court, (which stated that corporations are people and money is a form of free speech) the first group, Move to Amend, had been working for several months on overturning what many Americans thought of as the death knell to democracy. They believed that allowing corporations to spend as much as they want to get their candidates elected would do untold damage to the electoral process by granting them undue influence on who gets elected and what laws get passed. The other group, The Backbone Campaign, had formed specifically to embolden President Obama to find his spine and challenge the GOP by exercising the power of his office to get much tougher on corporate criminals as well as the scofflaw financial industry. Both organizations had collaborated to put together a series of political protests and events which they named, "Occupy the Supreme Court" that were slated to take place on January 20.

I volunteered myself, in whatever capacity, which soon developed into both singing and acting parts in two skits which they'd written to inform and entertain people about the worrisome aspects of the Citizen's United decision.

In no time, I was able to fill my calendar with acts of civil disobedience and rehearsals for the entire week. The morning of January 17, I got into my car and drove into the beltway to find the closest parking to the United States Capitol Building. It was early in the morning as I walked past several police officers guarding the building. I reached into my pocket to grab my cell phone and capture the moment on film. As I fumbled to activate my camera through gloved hands an officer walked up to me with an assault rifle displayed prominently across his chest. "What are you taking pictures of?" he asked, curtly. It bothered me that his dark, wraparound sunglasses did not allow me to look directly into his eyes as I answered, "Oh, I've never been to the Capitol Building and I wanted to get a shot or two."

"Then why are you filming me and not the building?" he continued, frowning.

"Oh, is it not legal to take pictures here?" I asked, genuinely perplexed.

"I'm asking you the questions right now, and you need to tell me why you're taking pictures of me and not the building." Another of the several officers within view strolled over to us and stood beside my interrogator.

"What's up?" he asked his colleague.

"This lady's taking pictures of me and I was just about to ask her if she was with the protesters we're supposed to have coming in today." My stomach churned as I watched a tiny smirk pass between the two of them.

"Well, are you going to answer him?" said the second officer, hostilely. I hadn't anticipated having two men cradling assault rifles putting me through a battery of questions concerning my political affiliations and intentions before even reaching the South Lawn of the Capitol. Part of me wanted to proudly proclaim my alliance with Occupy Congress, while the other envisioned being blown to bits on the spot and bundled into a vehicle which would whisk me away to swim with the fishes at the bottom of the Atlantic Ocean, if I admitted it. "Oh, is there a rally or something going on here today?" I asked, innocently. "Yeah, but you wouldn't know anything about that would you, Lady?" came the sarcastic response from number one, reminding me how much I hated to be called, "Lady," by anyone, for any reason. "Look, you can go, but we better not see you later with those Occupy protesters—got it?" I swallowed my fury and my pride as I answered, "Got it. Have a nice day fellas."

Once I put some distance between us and stopped shaking, I decided to go have a cup of coffee somewhere, before making another stab at congregating on the South Lawn. I vowed to break my habit of arriving early to big political protests. As a single person, I'd be a lot better off waiting until more people showed up before I made my entrance. It was 10:00 a.m. before Twitter and Facebook convinced me the crowd was large enough to venture out again. I'm sure the owners of the cafe were glad to see me go occupy something else besides the two-top I'd monopolized for the last two hours. I dropped some ones into the tip jar as I headed out for the South Lawn.

West Coast homies were a welcome sight as I drew near the congregation on the South Lawn of the Capitol Building. FUCK YOU MCCONGRESS was painted across the face of a sixteen-foot banner being hoisted by a rebellious brigade of youths. Many like sentiments were in abundance on the signage being carried around the grounds. By early afternoon a row of cops lined both sides of the concrete pavillion that led to the steps of Congress. Those who had "legitimate business"(as determined by the police) inside the building were permitted to walk the gauntlet between the protesters who lined both sides of the walk. Some brave souls made a stab at crashing through the human chain of officers in order to reach the wide set of stone steps leading to a long row of entry doors at the top.

Guy Fawkes mask–wearing demonstrators yelled at police to let us into the Capitol, which they argued, was "ours anyway." They were shouting that our business was just as legitimate as that of the lawmakers, whom we elected into office, and were not doing the job we appointed them to do. "*You* work for *us*, jerks," and, "Who do you protect- Who do you serve?" came the frequent taunts. A group of twenty or so agitators did manage to break through the phalanx of cops and they bounded up the stairs, only to be turned away by a row of admirably restrained, black shirt patrolman at the top, who brought all but the most combative back to the group unharmed. One of the local organizers of Occupy Congress took that opportunity to mic check the crowd and school us on regional differences in policing practices.

"I know that there are lots of people here from cities like Oakland and Chicago." (Repeat). "Who are used to getting the living shit beat out of them on a daily basis."(Repeat). "But please know that our cops in DC, have actually been pretty decent to Occupiers."(Repeat). "As a matter of fact, they've allowed us to have two encampments right here in the city."(Repeat). "For which we are very grateful." (Repeat). "So . . . let's not make this a personal vendetta against the cops today—"(Repeat). "But rather, an indictment on how fucked up our government has become." (Repeat). An outburst of applause, hoots, and twinkle fingers erupted all around me. "So let's remember—It's corporate greed and the co-optation of our elected officials that brought us here today."(Repeat). More riotous applause. After that, all three thousand of us downshifted to low gear and reined ourselves in throughout the rest of the day. I got up and sang some songs, while some folks went to the offices of their home state senators, only to find that most had either purposely bailed on Occupy, or were otherwise indisposed and unable to meet with their constituents. Although, one Republican Senator from a Southern state had been caught completely off guard by a group of Occupiers who had stormed past his quaking intern and asked him a barrage of questions about why he hadn't done more to stop foreclosures in his state and protect the environment, amidst a barrage of other accusations. "Who in God's name let you people in here?" he roared. "I'm not going to sit here and have a bunch of hoodlums break into my office and put *me* on trial—that's not how this works!" he fumed, before ordering his aide to call security. For the rest of the afternoon and on into dusk, the catch-phrase around the soggy Capitol lawn became, "Who in God's name let you people in here!" Which never failed to elicit peals of laughter from those hearing the tale, as told by the proud "hood-lums" who'd knocked the legislator off his game.

Still three thousand strong, we lingered on after darkness fell on that chilly, dreary day, relieved, only occasionally, by bursts of sun, before returning to the dense, wet air which clung to us all. We planned to circle the Capitol Building and disrupt traffic, when a group of mavericks broke off from us and began sprinting toward the Supreme Court, which lies just east of the Capitol. The officers who had hemmed us in on both sides were unprepared for the sudden detour, which forced them to chase after us, as we stormed past them and overwhelmed the thin row of guards who stood at the entrance to the Supreme Court steps. Clearly, no one had planned for this, as confirmed by the sudden breakdown in police communication. In no time, we swarmed every square inch of the stairs, right up to the classic marble Corinthian columns which held up the magnificent edifice. I admired the building's lovely lines, even as I hastened to avoid arrest or injury. It was Chief Justice William Howard Taft who had been given the task of selecting a designer for the nation's highest courthouse. Six-teen years earlier, he had served four uncomfortable years as the twenty-seventh president of the United States, from 1909 to 1913. It was his assertion that a governing body as large and important as the Supreme Court ought to have its own building, apart from others in Washington, so, in 1929, he hired noted architect Cass Gilbert, who'd already achieved accolades for designing New York City's Woolworth Building. I was aware that Taft's presidency had not gone particularly well and that he'd spent the majority of his time in office hiding from the cruel public eye and endur-

ing endless criticisms about his excessive weight and general lack
of competence or ambition, but I was glad he got this one thing
right. Even though he'd been hand selected by a wildly popular
president, Theodore Roosevelt, to be his successor, he was not
well-liked, and the stresses of his duties caused him to balloon to
epic proportions, finally topping out at nearly 350 pounds—no
doubt to the dismay of those who were once famously summoned
to liberate him from a White House bathtub, which he is said to
have become stuck in while in office. Sadly, neither Taft nor Gilbert lived to see the finished product, which was a shame, because
the building really was gorgeous.

As if scripted, a unison call arose from those on the landing at
the top of the stairs:

"MONEY IS . . . ," which was answered by, "NOT FREE
SPEECH."

And then: "COR—PORATIONS . . . ," answered by: "ARE
NOT PEOPLE."

The chant began echoing everywhere and my heart began to
beat wildly in my chest. A woman I didn't know placed her arm
around my waist to the right side, while a man's hand found my
own on the left. My eyes locked onto those of chanting strangers all around me and I felt tears rolling down my cheeks. Others around me were crying too as thousands of us held onto each
other and mourned the loss of our democracy.

By this time police were doing little to subdue us and merely
stood on the edges of the courthouse, settling for being bystand-
ers after losing their tactical advantage. Before long, another chant
began to replace the first one. "TAKE IT TO THE WHITE HOUSE.
TAKE IT TO THE WHITE HOUSE. TAKE IT TO THE WHITE
HOUSE." Small groups of protesters began descending the steps
to enter the streets below, carving out a route down Pennsylvania
Avenue which would lead us directly to the Obama White House.
Many more police vehicles and personnel arrived shortly on the
scene to escort us and direct traffic around us, since the rush hour
commute had not yet ended. A light drizzle began as we snarled

traffic for blocks, amid flashing lights, sirens, bullhorns, and commuter chaos. My position in the procession allowed me to see that
a bottleneck was forming about a block ahead.

As I got closer I saw large clusters of people pausing to face the
Newseum Building, at 555 Pennsylvania Avenue. Together they
were reading aloud the words of the First Amendment to the Con-
stitution, which were carved on the front. "Congress shall make
no law respecting an establishment of religion, or prohibiting the
free exercise thereof; or abridging the freedom of speech, or of
the press; or the right of the people peaceably to assemble, and to
petition the government for a redress of grievances." As my group
formed, we too began to read the powerful words before us.

Our ranks became much less boisterous, even somber after
the benediction of reading the First Amendment, and we continued to walk in near silence toward the White House. Our numbers had swelled by hundreds by the time we huddled in front
of the President's residence, and someone began to pass a megaphone around so that those who wanted to could tell us what had
brought them there that night. "My name is LeeAnn Bryce," said
a bedraggled woman with a pronounced drawl. "And I don't—
excuse my French—*fucking* understand why I had to come all the
way from Kentucky to ask this *bullshit*, do-nothing, Congress to
get off their ass and help me take care of my elderly, sick parents,
who got robbed of their pensions and their life savings, by the
banks." She passed the megaphone on as she stepped down from
her perch alongside the wrought iron gates that protect the occupants of 1600 Pennsylvania Avenue. Some voices were strident,
others matter of fact—but all were grievously wounded as they
enumerated their dissatisfaction with Washington that night. A
handful of people began distributing plain white folded cards with
hearts and strings attached along with little yellow pencils. "Fill
these out with your request to our President," came the instructions from one. "And after you're done, tie the card to the gate for
him to read, please." The river of people became strangely quiet
for awhile when we noticed a row of black cars entering the White

House from a side door that was just barely in our line of sight. Some began to speculate we might be granted a personal audience with the president as the atmosphere became abuzz with excitement at the prospect.

Again, as if preordained, one individual began a chant that caught on like wildfire and filled the air for blocks: OBAMA, COME OUT—WE'VE GOT SOME STUFF TO TALK ABOUT . . . OBAMA, COME OUT—WE'VE GOT SOME STUFF TO TALK ABOUT . . . " resounded all around me for a full ten minutes before beginning to die down. Then we all got silent, still holding out hope that the Commander-in-Chief might make an appearance. Moments later a slight young man with a booming voice took the megaphone and began to address us. "My sources tell me that . . ." he began, as others reflexively took up the human microphone system to get the message to the back. It struck me as odd to be hearing the words, "my sources tell me that," coming from a scruffy kid who looked neither old—nor connected—enough to have "sources" of any kind, save perhaps his mother. ". . . the president has just left the building," (disappointed "awwwws") " . . . because I guess it's like, Michelle's birthday today." A smattering of applause broke out from well-wishing Occupiers. "Okay . . . so, my sources *also* tell me that the President and the First Lady are, at this very minute, dining at a restaurant right down the street that way [pointing], which we happened to have passed on our way over here." This revelation, whether accurate or not, caused quite a stir, as we began chattering excitedly in response to the news. "So like, I guess we've all got a big decision to make here . . . ," he continued, almost playfully, " . . . about whether we take our protest over there . . ." he said, pointing again to the restaurant, "possibly ruining the First Lady's special dinner on her special day with her husband—or decide we've done enough for tonight and call it good for now." We debated the relative merits of each path amongst ourselves. Then, as if by decree, we began to quietly disperse ourselves into the darkness and back to the places we'd chosen to bed down. As far as I know, not one of us chose to disrupt the sanctity of their date on that frigid January 17 night. I hope the first couple had a wonderful romantic evening, and I wonder if she'll ever know how close she came to not getting to blow out all of her candles.

Three days later, I was again making my way toward the I-495 Beltway and Capitol Hill, to officially Occupy the Supreme Court of the United States. The daily rehearsals had gone well, and though I only had one spoken line in the skit, my big feature was to be the song I was scheduled to belt out at the end. During the previous day's practice session, five of us had crammed into my rental car to execute a thrilling guerilla "screening" on the side of the Courthouse. Armed with an industrial-strength film projector, two of the guys in our group somehow managed to put the materials together to project the words, WELCOME TO THE SUPREME KOCH, in giant neon green letters, all over the front of Cass Gilbert's masterpiece. Some homebound commuters got a kick out of the sight, honking and waving as they drove past. We tittered like teenagers from inside the car while watching the reactions of Washingtonians observing our handiwork. A few tickled travelers went so far as to jump out of their cars and snap photos before peeling off, in stitches. Almost fifteen delirious minutes passed before two officers on foot walked purposefully toward our car from half a block away. We were prepared for that eventuality, and alerted our video men, who scrambled to pack up the works before giving me the go ahead to drive off. That next morning as I donned my black robe costume, I wondered if any official laws against projecting images onto government buildings existed on the books in that town.

As for my role in the first skit, I was to play the part of a good-natured, albeit gullible, middle-aged housewife, (think Edith Bunker if you go back that far) who is taking a guided tour through the Supreme Court as a first time visitor to our Nation's Capitol from somewhere in the Midwest. Our performance took place on a rented, portable, sixteen-by-sixteen, elevated, plywood stage.

"So, ladies and gentleman . . . here we are at the highest court in our land where the most important decisions we face as a nation are made by the men and women and corporations who represent us within these hallowed walls."

"Excuse me, Ma'am . . . ," a gentleman from our "tour group" asked our guide, "did you just say, 'corporations' who represent us within these walls?"

"Why yes, yes I did," she replied gaily, before continuing her narration. "Yes, as a matter of fact, in a recent five to four decision, by *this very court*, [pointing behind her to the actual Supreme Court which was in plain view across the street] major multinational corporations were granted *'personhood'* status, which allows them to contribute as much money as they like to any campaign they please, to influence the outcome of any election they have a 'personal' [wink, nudge] interest in."

"Wait a minute . . . ," my character interjected, "does that mean that corporations can actually *buy* elections now?" I asked incredulously.

"Why yes—yes it does," replied our tour guide, still gay as ever, as she continued her explanation of the Citizen's United decision. She then burst into a song which was deftly accompanied by a pianist who sat offstage. The tune was a parody rendition of Sesame Street's, "One of These Things is Not Like the Other" game.

"Three of these things belong together/Three of these things are one in the same. If you guess which things belong with the others/You'll know how to play our game. One of these things is not like the others, one of these things just doesn't belong. If you guess which thing is not like the others/you can help me sing this song."

Then a "postal employee" walked out in uniform, followed by a doctor wearing a stethoscope and white coat, next came a teacher with chalk and an eraser. The fourth character to enter the stage was a walking skyscraper, covered with corporate logos (Monsanto, BP, Chevron, BofA, Exxon, Wells Fargo, Smith and

Wesson), as it was rolled in on a flat cart. At the end of her song, the tour guide grabbed her wooden pointer and asked a man in the tour if he could guess which thing didn't belong with the other. He guessed wrong three times, making moronic comments all the while, before being stopped by the guide, who said, "Oh . . . I'm sorry contestants, but those were *great* answers. Give yourselves a big round of applause folks." She then placed the tip of her pointer on the top of the cardboard building saying, "I know this game is *really* hard—but here's your answer." She burst into another merry song. "*This* is the thing that's not like the others/ This is the thing that isn't the same. Maybe tomorrow we'll sing together/When it's time to play our game. We'll find the thing that's not like the others/We'll find the thing that doesn't belong. We can all play and try together/When it's time to sing this song."

Our audience of passersby and journalists provided us with plenty of laughs as we quickly exited the stage to put on our robes in preparation for the next performance. In that skit, I was one of nine Supreme Court Justice look-alikes who had formed a garage band called The Supremes. I tried to look Sotomayor-ish as I sang parody lyrics to a song originally recorded by Aretha Franklin called, "Chain of Fools." It began with a chorus of:

"Shame shame shame—Shame shame shame shame shame . . . Shay-ee-ay—ee-ay—ee-ay-ee—ame shame on you"

I pointed and stared back to the Supreme Court Building, which was the backdrop from the stage, before launching into the first verse which was:

> *For many a year/ A vote was one citizen*
> *But I found out just now/That it's a corporation*
> *They treated us bad/Oh, they treated us cruel*
> *They think they got us where they want us yeah*
> *And we ain't nothin' but their fools.*

From there I progressed to this chorus:

> *Occupy won't leave you alone/No we ain't a gonna go back*
> *home*
> *You thought you could take it easy/ Oh but our anger is much*
> *too strong*
> *We've had it with you! Shame shame shame/shame on you!"*

Just as I was finishing, I saw a long line of marchers who were arriving from the two encampments that were located in the vicinity. One group had begun marching from McPherson Square, which was often said to be the rougher, (and also more "real" in the sense that a higher percentage of its residents were actually homeless) of the two, and continued toward the other from nearby Freedom Plaza, which was said to be a slightly more upscale, "homeless by choice" community of purely political dissidents. I was happy to be done with my official commitments and free to scurry from the stage to join the protesters who were now idling in the street and spilling outward onto the wide sidewalk which lead to the same steps we'd swarmed on January 17. Many reporters who had been covering our show dashed off to film the developing story across the street. Primal drums accompanied the cries of, "Money is not free speech/Corporations are not people," only this time refrain dovetailed into, "Whose Court?/Our Court!" as police cruisers began pouring in from all directions.

Hundreds of us soon faced off with scores of police, who were cramming to unload aluminum barricades from a van parked right on the sidewalk. Their goal was to keep us from climbing the steps to the marble columns as we'd done a few days earlier, while ours was to gain entry into what we were contending was "Our Court." The standoff was fairly predictable, until one demonstrator produced a long, slender wooden pole with a glazed donut tied to one end and began dangling it in front of the faces of the officers, in a game he called, "Fishing for Cops," which drew thunderous laughter from our side, and even a few smiles from some men in uniform. All was going well and tensions were ebbing until one officer, failing to see the humor, suddenly yanked at the fisherman's pole, raging, "Get that fucking thing out of my face, faggot," which pitched the holder forward, almost landing him on the police side of the barricade. A furious tug of war with the body of the fisherman broke out—us trying hard to restore him to our side, as a battery of officers jerked him in the opposite direction, attempting to get him into their clutches. Donut boy was screaming out in pain as his torso got raked across the aluminum top rail and his clothes were being ripped off of him. Our side eventually won, and we were able to reclaim our scraped, bleeding prize from the maelstrom. A loud cheer went up, followed, bizarrely, by an eruption into "The Hokey Pokey," at the other end of the barriers, some twenty-five feet away. I turned to see a big, scruffy guy leading other Occupiers in reaching through the barriers at knee height to poke cops' legs while singing, "You put your right hand in, you take your right hand out." Apparently, the feeling of having their legs groped by demonstrators freaked the officers out, because each one of them immediately recoiled and climbed the stairs behind them to avoid the sensation. Then, someone among us noticed how extraordinarily easy it was to lift up the momentarily abandoned barricades and back the row of police up the stairs, as they jumped back to avoid contact. In short order, the entire front row joined the Hokey Pokey game, while those of us further back sang along and kept the mood light. As we frolicked, lots of cops were becoming furious as they realized their own unwitting participation in helping us advance to the top. As their frustration grew, a few began swinging batons indiscriminately, in all directions. "Hey guys, stop swinging the clubs, you're gonna hurt one of *us*," came the order from a top cop. "Yeah—hey—we're unarmed! This is a peaceful protest," shouted some agitated demonstrators. We were almost to the marble columns when suddenly confronted by a solid row of riot troops, who had assembled quickly into place and exploded from the inside of the courthouse. They were wearing bulletproof shields, kevlar body armor, and gas masks as they maintained tight grips on their highly visible military-style assault rifles. We could all plainly see that the jig was up, and, as suddenly as the scuffle began, it ended, within a few short yards of reaching the entrance to the Supreme Court.

Chapter 7

Advance—Retweet—J28

A week later, it was a beautiful, warm Saturday morning at Oscar Grant Plaza. I thanked my lucky stars that I was sitting on a concrete bench sipping a latte in California, and not in a concrete jail somewhere in Washington, DC. We christened the event, "Move-In Day," because we planned to take control of a large, long-shuttered commercial building near downtown, for the purpose of housing Occupy Oakland, which had not been the same since losing the encampment back in the November raid.

It was envisioned as a family affair, featuring jugglers, musicians, dancers, poets, speakers, and musicians. I'd signed up to be one of those providing entertainment in our new home as part of the January 28 Rise Up Festival, which we hoped would usher in a new era for Occupy Oakland. We were tired of being arrested and shot at, and wanted a home base, away from Jean Quan and the OPD, who had demonstrated over and again how little affection they held for our movement. None of us knew what the building looked like, or even where it was. It was a well-kept secret, known only to a select few Occupiers who had been directly involved in the planning and selection process. The formerly vacant building was supposed to be a safe haven—the new and improved headquarters for Occupy Oakland. Our dream was not only to occupy a physical space, but to embody an ideal—to stanch corporate greed, as well as to house, feed, and clothe some of Oakland's exploding homeless population. There was even an ambitious, yet marvelously designed plan to operate a daycare/preschool for the children of our growing community. Many Occupiers, who were present and former educators, had already volunteered to teach children and adults how to read and write. Doctors, nurses, and dentists had also committed to providing free treatment for folks who currently had no access to such services.

Visions of the wonderful world we were about to create danced in my head as I sat on the stairs squinting, bleary-eyed in the unseasonably warm January sunshine. This would be the day we would give birth to a model community, where others, mired in the dominant paradigm, had not. We knew the job would be difficult. It would be hard enough to secure the space itself, let alone restore its dormant systems, sewage, electricity, water, heat, etc., to working order. Even though these obstacles presented challenges, I was wildly optimistic about the possibilities, and prepared to do whatever it took to overcome them.

As much as I considered myself to be a veteran of the Movement, I was unprepared for what actually did transpire that day in Oakland, California. I'd originally planned to play my bass guitar and sing later in the day, but since I'd been plagued by a series of tear gas–induced asthma attacks and respiratory infections, resulting in the loss of my voice, I'd ditched my plans to perform and was without it that morning, which proved to be fortuitous. Right off the bat there was trouble, as we'd been there for scarcely an hour when a disturbance broke out in the southwest corner of the plaza. Arms were waving and voices were rising in what looked to be a mini brawl, which prompted many of us to jump up and run full steam to the source of the commotion. I, along with about sixty other people, could see a number of OPD officers surrounding a tall, handsome, clean-cut young black man, who had been handcuffed and was now being dragged across the street to isolate

him from potential liberators. Occupy Oakland had quickly mobi-
lized and closed in around the officers, shouting, "Let him go," in
unison, while jamming cameras into the faces of the dozen cops
that controlled their victim's every move. I immediately asked a
graying woman of about fifty what had happened. She told me
that she'd been standing next to the man while he was filming
the actions of the same police, who were now trying to arrest
him. The officers had been making a show of strutting through
the plaza every few minutes, hand picking people, mostly black
males, to run background checks on, to "see if they had criminal
records or outstanding warrants." The woman said the man had
been complaining loudly about their "intimidation tactics" while
cataloguing abuses, and matching faces with badge numbers for
possible defense later. The man was responding to a developing
trend at Occupy clashes, where the OPD had made a habit of covering their badges with tape before committing particularly egregious crimes, like hitting people in the face with nightsticks while
they were cuffed, or lobbing explosives into a crowd of peaceful protesters as they administered aid to the wounded. Lately a
plethora of damning videotape evidence had surfaced which led
to the dismissal (and even conviction) of some cops who were
shown to have committed such infractions on numerous occasions. A shocked and often naive public was being exposed daily,
through social media outlets like Facebook, YouTube, and Twitter, to rampant police overreach, such as using excessive force on
noncombatant demonstrators and planting drugs on detainees.
Because of the ubiquitous nature of cell phones, these and other
tricks of the policing trade had been shown to be, not only unrare,
but common practice on the force. In reaction, many law enforcement personnel began violently discouraging the practice of protesters filming them in action. Their objections began to surface in
various forms of legislation being introduced around the country,
which were attempting to make it illegal to take pictures of an
officer while he or she was on duty. The eyewitness told me that
the officers had teamed up and pounced on the guy, forcing him to

the ground as they yelled that he was under arrest for "outstanding warrants." The man kept insisting that he had no such warrants against him, and that he was being unlawfully arrested. We stuck to them like wheat paste, especially since many among us knew him to be an upstanding citizen with a clean record. It was gratifying to back the outnumbered cops away from us, for a change, and to realize we were denying them the opportunity to do what they really wanted to do, which usually included whacking the perp a few times with their truncheons. First they dragged him by the cuffs south across Fourteenth Street, then, unable to shake us, they hauled him back north onto the Plaza. With us hot on their heels, they pulled him all over OGP before finally managing to shove him into a large vehicle that looked like a mobile processing station for just such occasions. It made us anxious to see him disappear, but we had to get on with our day, as Brian's PA system fired up and began pouring out beatheavy grooves. Nothing soothes the troubled mind like, Prince's "When Doves Cry" or emboldens a timid spirit like a cut from Public Enemy or the Beastie Boys when you're about to go into a tense situation. Brian's mixes were becoming the soundtrack of the Oakland Occupation, and I liked his musical taste, so that was all right by me.

Forty-five minutes passed, dancing and listening to various political speakers as we girded our loins for Move In Day. The last speaker had just shouted, "Let's git this bitch on," when I looked up onto the stage and noticed that the man I'd seen being carted off nearly an hour before had resurfaced, and was wrestling the microphone out of its stand to address us before we took off. Visibly shook up, he admonished us to be very careful about what we did that day, and how we did it. "Stick together and *never* get caught alone, because the OPD is showing us just how they plan to roll today, and it ain't gonna to be pretty." He advised that it was "all right to celebrate and even have a good time," but to know that the police were probably going to be relentless in trying to stop us from completing our mission. He also told us that the police had been unable to keep him, because, just as he'd loudly insisted, there were no outstanding warrants, and they'd had no legal grounds to do what they had just done to him—but they did it anyway.

Well, maybe the worst was over, and we'd gotten that out of the way and could all just go out and have a fabulous, revolutionary day. At around one thirty, we began assembling on Fourteenth and Broadway, between Walgreens and the Rite Aid store. I had to smile as I saw a new brigade of Black Bloc protesters; this time comprised mostly of giggling females barely out of Junior High, assembling at the front to be our first line of defense. Some weren't much older than my own daughter, and it moved me to see them joking nervously and teasing each other like school girls, as they gripped their homemade shields. Some brandished tampons and other menstrual products which they said were meant to "protect them from police assaults," however, their main armament consisted of cotton bandanas across their mouths, coupled with black plastic garbage cans cut in half with peace signs spray painted in white all across the front. The handles of their shields were fashioned out of rubber hoses, which allowed the bearers to lift them high enough to protect vital organs, if need be.

It was a gorgeous day and sunshine streamed in from all sides. I felt happy and hopeful that we might get some immediate help to people for whom the system had totally failed. I couldn't wait to have a refuge to gather in and have discussions about how to get the world righted and set back on a course we could all live with. On the whole, I felt protective toward this endearing Black Bloc troupe, unlike previous ones that had so turned me so off in previous actions. These looked nothing like the handfuls of marauders who'd strapped on gas masks, brought out hammers, gasoline, and spray paint, and turned our peaceful protests into terrifying police encounters. These youngsters had none of the menacing vibe that their male counterparts had projected while breaking windows, spray painting buildings, and starting dumpsters on fire. I wasn't particularly prudish about their activities, never having equated minor property damage with the violence and criminal behavior that was being perpetrated on the masses by corporations and the 1%, however, I hated how they'd draw fire to us, then cut and run, leaving hundreds, or thousands of peaceful protesters to bear the brunt of Oakland Police Department wrath. They'd poked the dragon, then disappeared into the shadows, leaving us to deal with injured protesters and the tons of negative press that was then directed at the Occupy Movement, in their wake. I had often posted messages on social media, excoriating them for the damage they had done to our movement. It bothered me too, that they didn't usually discriminate between corporations and small, family-run businesses when selecting windows to break. In the past I'd seen lots of Occupiers gathering in public squares on the morning after a Black Bloc rampage carrying sponges, cleaning supplies, and paint remover to clean up the mess others had caused the night before. I'd seen Occupiers going door to door to small businesses that had been hit, apologizing for anarchist actions, and asking them to please make the distinction between those vandals and the vast majority of us, whose peaceful actions were intended only to quell corporate greed and secure social, economic, and environmental justice for all Americans. I came into Move In Day with a bias against the way Black Bloc did business, but seeing these babes frolicking about in the light of day was doing a lot for my disposition toward them. Just before we got underway, some of the girls began to dance around and cavort like puppies while reciting, naughtily, "We're here/We're queer bitch—If it's vacant let's take that shit." The Rise Up Festival was beginning to take glorious shape as we began marching jauntily toward our still unknown destination.

Upbeat music accompanied us as we marched, via Brian's bannered up, decked out rolling flatbed sound truck. What would we have done without Brian Glasscock, the quiet, chain smoking boy with the peach fuzz and cherubic face, that had been a permanent fixture at Occupy Oakland since its inception. He always took it upon himself to crank out the best musical sequences I'd ever heard from every imaginable genre. Somehow, every song he selected, whether from Michael Jackson, Rage Against the Machine, Sir

Mix-A-Lot, NWA, Tupac, or Nina Simone, was just right for the moment at every #OO action. We walked south on Broadway for a while and then turned east up one of the numbered streets, pausing at times to let everyone catch up. I stayed near the front as was my preference during large demonstrations, and caught sight of my Ustream friends, OccupyFreedomLa, Oakfosho, Sky (@ CrossXBones), and PunkBoyinSF, who were livestreaming along the way. The role they played in revealing truths and dispelling mainstream misrepresentations cannot be overstated. Time after time their footage had told the true tale and refuted OPD claims that protesters had instigated violence, or that the police had issued clear directives to disperse before they'd shot into crowds with explosives and chemical agents. These indie journalists were a different breed of human being—not like you or I. They regularly placed their bodies front and center during the most heated actions—positioning themselves inches from gun barrels, while taking close ups of officer's faces and demanding they uncover their badge numbers. Streamers did their homework. They armed themselves with knowledge and could often be heard citing specific codes and statutes that police officers were violating in dealing with Occupiers. Unlike their mainstream counterparts, alternative press members often interjected spicy language—contributing editorial comments throughout their coverage—all the while maintaining constant twitter interaction with their viewers while in the pitch of battle. "You're outta control man . . . Stop thumping on that guy with your stick . . . That ain't cool . . . That's totally unnecessary . . . You didn't have to do that, man. You just broke his leg, douche! He's being peaceful you motherfucking pig! What the hell are you pounding on him for? You're breaking the law, officer . . . There was no order to disperse, Sir, you're not allowing us to leave Sir." In recent months I'd almost completely abandoned network coverage, as I realized their accounts rarely matched up with what I'd seen firsthand on the streets that day. I said goodbye to David Gregory, Sean Hannity, and George Stephanopoulos and the other flapping tongues that rarely seemed to say anything that moved me, or addressed my deepest fear that corporations and the super rich have overtaken our government from within.

With the exception of Rachel Maddow, Jon Stewart, Stephen Colbert, and Amy Goodman, I now relied mainly on the no frills, unvarnished raw coverage that was being delivered to me daily by the growing cadre of citizen journalists, who, armed only with their cell phones, showed it and told it like it was—unedited, uncompensated, and free of charge for all who wanted to watch and chat.

These were the on air personalities I was putting my faith in as we headed south and eastward toward Laney College. Laura Koch called me, en route, about a tweet she read saying that the OPD was amassing and planning to block us from reaching our final destination. Occupiers monitoring police scanners confirmed that the cops knew where we were going, even as it remained a secret to me. As we approached the campus, I looked to the left and saw, for the first time that day, three dozen riot cops, conspicuously displaying weapons, as well as chemical dispersants and tightly bound reams of plastic handcuffs. The officers told our front line that we were being denied permission to go forward, so our leaders rerouted us over a narrow footbridge to get us wherever we were going. We walked to the far side of the campus and finally ended up on a street which led us alongside Lake Merritt and directly in front of a large ornate building on the left, which is where we stopped.

There, I saw a tall, temporary chain link fence anchored by sandbags, which surrounded the entire property and enclosed hundreds more riot cops, who looked dead serious about keeping us on the outside. It was extremely disheartening to realize that this, the once grand but long vacant Kaiser Convention Center, (formerly known as the Oakland Civic Center) was our destination.

We stared at them. They stared at us. About ten minutes passed before some among us began to cut lengths of fence as others pushed over eight-foot sections and simply walked through. I saw a few riot cops raise their rifles and aim them directly at us, which worried me and others, who began to shout, "We've got children, stand down. We are unarmed, and there are children here and old people—Stand Down!" over and over. Then, a smoking projectile landed to my right and exploded, sending frightened onlookers screaming and running down the street. I saw senior citizens in wheelchairs and babies in strollers being frantically removed from the area and down the street, away from the bursts of fire and clouds of smoke. I tried to drive the image from my mind, of one of those "non-lethal" weapons landing in a stroller or the lap of a disabled protester. Some demonstrators left for good after the explosions started, but many, perhaps a thousand or so, stayed to continue trying to enter the Kaiser Building. A chant began circulating that harkened back to the night of November 2, on San Pablo Street, just outside OGP, when I had been arrested. "You're not sexy/You're not cute—Take off your fuckin' Nazi suit." It seemed like a thousand years had passed since the night I heard the original version from the drunk girl. Since then, there had been a dramatic escalation in the way police dealt with us. Some analysts traced the evolution and pinpointed the change to New Year's Eve, when President Obama signed the National Defense Authorization Act. The NDAA permitted the government to interrogate, harass, and indefinitely detain American citizens who were suspected of being terrorists. Most of us activists had been greatly disappointed to learn that we, as practitioners of civil disobedience, could arguably be considered enemies of the state or domestic terrorists, and therefore have the law applied to us. Though Barack Obama had assured the American public that he had no intention of using the law indiscriminately or frivolously, most of us, myself included, felt betrayed, disillusioned, and let down by this president, who many of us had hung so much hope on before the election. Even if he didn't plan to use the legislation against us, what would happen when his term was over? Who would protect us then? One man pressed his body against the fence as I held my phone overhead to capture the scene. He began furiously imploring me to, "Get that cop, the one right over there. That officer's pointing his gun right at us. Get him on camera! Get his badge number! Get his name! Get all of 'em that have their guns up on us. They can't do that. Hey motherfuckers, we got people in wheelchairs here. We got kids here and old people too. I know you assholes can see 'em. They're right here . . . right in front of your face, pricks! You guys think you're mighty special don't you. Yeah, what . . . now you're gonna crack open grandma? Good job! Be proud of yourself, jerk!"

Ultimately the tear gas and flashbang grenades did their job and we began filing away from the area, eventually winding up at the Art Museum on Twelfth Street. A row of trees lined the right side, while the entrance to the museum stood on the left. Fifty yards ahead of us stood yet another squad of riot cops, with weapons trained on us. Everywhere we looked, guns were pointed in our faces, which led the schoolgirl Black Bloc Brigade to call an emergency strategy huddle, resulting in the formation of a defensive line directly opposite the army of cops, who were aiming lethal weaponry at us. The impossible courage and naivete of their actions tore me up, as I watched them all begin to kneel down behind the few mils of plastic that separated them from oblivion. Tiny midriffs and pale, exposed derrieres dominated the foreground as the girls crouched in a pathetic formation, a scant few yards in front of an impenetrable wall of kevlar helmets, assault rifles, tear gas shooters, and beanbag launchers that were trained on them. The young ladies had decided it was their duty to get us past the cops and back on track to attempt another approach to the Kaiser Center, from a different angle. Personally, I was scared witless at the very thought of these brutes and their obscene arsenal. Even though I was a good ten feet behind the kids, I judged myself to be in a life-threatening situation, and couldn't stand the thought of them getting hurt. I do not possess that kind of bravery—I didn't have a lot of combat experience, but I was making sure to keep a meaty tree trunk between me and the army at all times. What could these children be thinking as they stared down the barrels of all those big guns. A high-pitched voice that sounded like it came from a fifth grader ordered, "Okay . . . um . . . Go forward," to the others who shakily got to their feet and advanced a couple of yards toward the riot squad, who stood there in utter disbelief, as did I. Then, shockingly, the pitifully puny crew crouched down again, as they prepared a second charge, to close the remaining twenty-foot gap that separated them from the squad. I heard one of the girls' panicked voices crying to the others that they must not stop until they got us past the cops, so we could get back over to the Civic Center. Oh Jesus, I thought, no one here expects them to be taking on the entire police force—no one here is going to hold them personally responsible if we don't get inside the building. Please, just give up. We're good, kiddos. It's all good. Turn around and run. I felt my bowels loosen and my eyes widen to saucers, as I saw them ducking behind their shields one last time, to lunge forward and lead the final surge, straight into a wall of uniforms.

When the gap disappeared, guns and projectiles started going off everywhere as the cops began firing on them and us with everything they had. *Pow pow, pop pop pop, kaboom, bang, pow, kaboom, kaboom.* Ordnance of every shape and size landed in our midst in an array of sparks and debris, only to screed and whiffle out on the ground before burning our eyes and boxing our ears with painful, lightning bright concussions. A scream escaped my lungs as my knees went weak, and my nose filled with searing smoke. I held my cell phone aloft as I cursed and dodged smoking objects. "It's a fucking war zone out here. Fuck . . . Shit . . . Ahhhhhhhh. I'm scared out of my fucking mind," I wailed into the camera, as I tried to keep the tree trunk between me and the police. I heard people screaming, "Medic, medic," frantically, as I saw a young woman lying, unconscious, on the ground ten feet beside me. A group of three lads, who'd crafted a shield of corrugated metal roofing framed by two-by-fours, ran to the aid of the fallen woman, along with a self-appointed medic, who held her hands up to request a temporary ceasefire around the victim. Another half dozen Occupiers formed a protective circle around them, after the kneeling medic placed the shield in front of the girl's body and tried to assess her injuries. While they were administering aid, police fired tear gas and flash bang grenades directly at them, then started swinging their batons and pulling responders away from the unconscious girl to arrest them. Two of the rescuers ran off, reluctantly, barely missing the swings of the batons, as the rest of the cops sprinted past the remaining assistants, who were now trying to drag the girl away from the paved street and onto the parking strip. I turned and began to flee from the police who were now chasing us all—guns drawn, night sticks flying. They were connecting with as much flesh as possible, and I could hear the crack of wood meeting bone all around me. Those who could not run fast were surrounded, pepper sprayed, and pummeled mercilessly as they tried to block the blows with their arms and legs. I saw women being hit as well as men. I saw an elderly man with white hair staggering, dazed— trying to feel his way through a chemical fog. Medics were running from person to person, holding their faces back and pouring milk of magnesia into burning eyes. I saw young people fleeing, wild-eyed and crying, as they tried to stay one step ahead of the police. I too, was moving as fast as I could, to put as much real estate as possible between me and them. I could see that they were picking off the slow and the weak, and I said so into my camera as I ran. Two men with megaphones were urging calm. "Remain calm. People, please do not run. Running gives them more power," repeated the black man. The middle-aged white man kept his back turned on the police and his face toward us as he calmly advised, "If we don't run, they won't chase us," over his megaphone. "If we walk calmly ahead of them, they will walk behind us," he repeated. "They'll have no reason to arrest us if we don't . . ." and just then, a handful of cops burst from their ranks and enveloped him, wrestling him quickly to the ground as his megaphone clattered noisily to the pavement. I was reminded of the opening scene in *Space Odyssey, 2001,* as he disappeared into the cluster, and I could see nothing more than clubs being raised and lowered where he'd once stood.

They pushed us west on Twelfth Street, for what seemed like miles, but what was probably few more than a dozen blocks. We'd stop briefly for traffic at each intersection, which allowed cops to catch up, then faced off for a few minutes before they charged, beat, and arrested us again. The whole unsavory affair lasted for almost three hours before we were driven back to our point of origin, Oscar Grant/Frank Ogawa Plaza at City Hall on Fourteenth and Broadway.

By 5:30 p.m., I was reeling from the debacle, which had seemed so unlikely at the outset. Part of me wanted to go back to Laura and Lori's house, curl up in a ball and go to sleep, while the other wanted to redouble my efforts to revive our commune that had twice been forcibly dismantled, during the Fall. Waves of bedraggled warriors streamed in from Broadway, as Brian's PA system came into earshot, and a male voice began to congratulate us for surviving and remaining peaceful during the fiasco. "Okay Occupy Oakland . . . How do you feel? Make some noise out there, people. How do you feel?" An anemic cheer went up and covered the square like a drizzling rain. "I tell you what we're gonna do. We're gonna rest. We're gonna get something to eat. We're gonna chill for a while. And tonight, we're going to try it again. Whaddya think Oakland?" Somehow I reached down into the well and found a reserve that had eluded me just seconds before, and I, along with hundreds of others, raised my fist into the air, and yelled, *yeah!!!!!!!!!*"

Laura and I went to Rudy's Can't Fail Cafe, a few blocks away on Webster, to get some comfort food and a quick partial charge on our phones. Minutes of silence would pass before one of us would blurt out what we both were thinking. "Can you believe the shit they used on us today?" I said, every five minutes or so, shaking my head. "I'm gonna have to get a big ass hunk of coconut cream pie, with whip cream slathered all over it, to make some of that bullshit go away," I mused. "Um hum, you sure are girlfriend. I'm a fucking vegan and I'm gonna have to order me some bacon àla mode just to get the taste of tear gas out of my mouth," she shot back. We laughed, but I knew we were both apprehensive about what was in store for us. As it turns out our fears were well founded.

Just after we paid our bill, Laura checked her messages and saw that there was an #OO Twitter alert informing us that our party was leaving right then from OGP. We were going again, to try to Occupy another building that had been selected as Plan B. We walked a few blocks north on Broadway, and then turned west on Eighteenth, to pause for a moment in front of a medium sized building, as some of us tried to calculate our chances of getting in through the partially blocked front door. Inside were some painters, who, while exceptionally friendly, asked us not to come in. We didn't want to cause them any trouble or get them fired, especially since some looked as if they may have been undocumented workers, so we moved northwest toward the intersection of Nineteenth and Telegraph, adjacent to the *Heroes for Humanity* sculpture, where we'd previously tried to relocate the encampment back in November. As I looked in all four directions, I saw van loads of riot police unloading to cut us off. There were so many of them with different colored uniforms on, that I was sure that there had been a "mutual aid" arrangement made between them, where different law enforcement agencies collude to provide overwhelming force to put down insurrections, such as this. It was nearing seven o'clock when we got to the statues, and encountered police blockades from all sides. The only place I didn't see law enforcement stationed was on the east side, where a long chain-link fence already served to deny us egress. At that time there were probably six hundred of us, while there looked, to me, to be about two or three hundred cops. We had been spread out earlier, but now I could feel the police herding us closer together and trapping us in a tightening group among the statues. Déjà vu gripped me as an officer with a bullhorn began barking out the order to disperse. He gave the familiar spiel that we were unlawfully assembled in an area that had been declared illegal or off limits, and that we must leave or be subject to arrest. I hadn't seen Laura Koch in a while, and hoped she was okay as the ligature surrounding us got tighter.

As a condition of attending J28, I'd promised my family that I would be home the next day, and that I would not get arrested again, as I had on November 2. It was critical that I be there to help one of my co-moms, Pam, at the Wenatchee hospital for her third hip replacement in four years. The "metal on metal" artificial hips she'd received were poisoning her and causing her to be terribly ill. Fragments were sloughing off into her body every time she walked, causing her cobalt levels to spike to damaging levels that were killing the surrounding bone and muscle tissue, as well as making her heart beat irregularly and her thyroid malfunction. She'd complained of feeling deathly sick most of the time after the second operation, and I'd seen her quietly crying on the sofa some nights, after especially difficult days. I promised I would stay by her side during her latest hospital stay, so that I could make sure she was receiving proper care and her needs were being met. I couldn't leave her there alone, knowing how reluctant she was to disturb anyone and ask for help. And it was hard for me to completely trust surgeons after I learned that the corporations who manufactured the joints were still paying some medical professionals huge sums to install them, regardless of the fact that many recipients were experiencing a host of symptoms ranging from severe allergic reactions to complete rejection by the body, which manifested itself in the form of fluid and tissue buildup against the artificial joints which, as in Pam's case, eroded and generally ate away and dissolved the once healthy bones (femur, pelvis, trocanter) surrounding the implant. Her latest x-ray showed that she was in danger of breaking a hip doing something as innocuous as walking down the road. To make matters worse, I also read that a few extreme cases had required heart transplants to replace organs so damaged by the metal that they'd not have survived otherwise. It gave me pause to hear her surgeon confess that that he was baffled as to why the hip had failed, but believed the manufacturer "was a good corporation," and that, even though I voiced my doubts about their innocence, he didn't think that anyone would "knowingly put out a bad product," and that he'd often seen "good companies that made good products, like breast implant manufacturers," be brought down by "hysterical, misinformed consumers, who merely thought they were experiencing symptoms based on overblown rumors." I liked her doctor otherwise, but was unsettled by his opinions about breast implant patient claims. I didn't elaborate my concerns, but I'd actually read a *Seattle Times* story the week before that speculated that so many of these hips were failing and causing permanent disability and even possibly death, that the entire Medicare and Medicaid industries might be forced to radically restructure if the true enormity of the problem came to light. The story went on to describe the experience of a man who'd received a hip, begun to feel extreme discomfort, had it removed, and then found that his body was rejecting the new one as well. In order to save the man's life, the surgeons had had to remove the replacement hip, leaving him jointless, in constant pain, and permanently unable to walk or do virtually anything but lie in bed in agony. Needless to say, I was worried that things wouldn't go well, and I knew that my presence was critical during her hospitalization. To further complicate things, Pam had developed a severe allergy to all the standard opioid painkillers during her last surgery, and had even "coded," (her heart stopped) while a local anaesthetic was administered during her last round of diagnostic tests to figure out why she was so sick all the time. The only drug she could safely take to manage excruciating pain was ibuprofen. There was no question that I had to be there for this latest operation.

Aside from my concern for Pam, which was considerable, I had a second reason for not wishing to be arrested again. I had inhaled a lot of tear gas that afternoon, and on top of the recurring colds and respiratory distress I'd already been experiencing since all the way back in November, I could barely talk, and was also having difficulty breathing. A few weeks before the OPD had arrested a bunch of Occupiers and taken up to six hours to process them, leaving many in a van for a large portion of that time, with the motor running. The exhaust from the vehicle had wafted up from the pipe and into the interior, where some detainees had vomited, passed out, and even had seizures, to the total indifference of the officers, who ignored their pleas while confining them there. I clearly remembered that, during my stay at Alameda County's Santa Rita jail, some women in my cell had begged officers to release their confiscated prescription medication to them, only to be derided and laughed at. I remembered my cellmate Andrea, being told, "You ain't got any rights in here—you're in jail, honey. And you sure ain't havin' no medical emergency . . . 'cause you ain't havin' no seizure." Apparently, the OPD policy had changed in the ensuing months, to preclude arrestees who actually *were* having seizures, since they too were now being denied vital medical attention, and I was concerned that I might again land in the emergency room, as I had in December, if they did that to me. I was afraid that if I had an attack, I'd just be allowed to slowly suffocate.

For those reasons, I decided I'd had enough that day, and though I was loathe to leave my partners, I decided to make my way to the edge of our demonstration, and leave the area as I'd been directed by the OPD. I was about fifteen feet in front of them when I saw a handful of young people pleading with the police to let them disperse. "You just told us to leave, and that's what we want to do," one girl wailed. Some cops gazed over the heads of the pleaders, while others turned their faces sideways, but all of them looked elsewhere, refusing to speak, or make eye contact with any of us. In fact, they stood so close together, with their batons resting on their thighs, that passage was virtually impossible. Seeing this, and remembering the snatch-and-pummel technique of the afternoon, I knew not to get any closer, and retreated back into the fold of Occupiers, who were now tightly trapped and clustered amidst the statuary. Seconds later, I began hearing explosions and pops, and saw bright flares illuminating our faces. I was struck by the irony of seeking refuge in the shadows of twenty-five bronze figures, honoring famous civilly disobedient history makers, such as Martin Luther King, Gandhi, Malcom X, Harriet Tubman, and

Sojourner Truth. They were looking over me as I was being gassed, grenaded, and shot at by the OPD. This time I was more psycho-logically prepared for the attack, and wasn't tempted to scream even once. Instead I looked all around me to select which sculpted hero to hide myself behind. I couldn't really decide on just one, so I ended up dodging wildly between them, depending on the posi-tion of incoming fire.

I wondered if there wasn't some sort of law on the books against trapping people and lobbing explosives at them. Just then I heard cheering from the east, where the vacant lot fence that contained us was erected, and saw that someone had either cut or knocked down a large section of it, which allowed us to run through and escape the dragnet. I was somewhere near the middle of the pack, when I saw two people in front of me trip on the chain links and go down as they got entangled in the fence. Others, like me, reacted and tried to avoid crushing them in the stampede. I jumped over one of them and willed myself to stay upright, as I watched them struggle to regain verticality.

Somehow, we all made it out uninjured, onto the cop-free street, which caused a flurry of excitement as people clapped each other on the back and gave congratulatory hugs to celebrate our narrow escape from the explosions, beatings, and chemicals. I felt giddy to be walking north on a street which didn't contain a single bar-ricade, as far as the eye could see. We advanced all the way down to Twenty-Fourth Street, then made a right turn and headed east over to Broadway. By this time the cops were following half a block behind us, looking angry as they gestured sharply to one another, and again I felt uneasy. I kept a considerable distance ahead of them, and decided upon a strategy of staying close to Oakfosho, since he seemed to be the teflon don within the movement. Time after time I'd seen him streaming live, inches away from the OPD, filming blatant acts of professional misconduct, and they had, amazingly, never laid a hand on him—never so much as harmed a hair on his head. Spencer's intelligence and righteousness were undeniable. I'd personally witnessed many citizen journos being grabbed as their equipment was smashed or confiscated, but never had I seen a single officer even try to arrest him, such was the natural authority and charisma of Spencer Mills. I doubted that my proximity to him would save me, but I hoped someone might take note if they did snatch me, and tell my family what happened. More than once I'd watched his coverage from home, and seen Occupiers pushing their faces into his lens to issue warnings to the OPD, such as, "Look here cops, we know you're monitoring this feed, and we just want to make it clear that if you touch Spencer, it's on." This was the kind of admiration and love most of us had for Spencer, who'd become the de facto eyes, ears, and voice of Occupy Oakland. Even folks that expressed jealousy over his newfound fame, were in awe of him. He had a cult of personality that seemed to affect anyone in his sphere of influence, even when he made questionable calls. There was his controversial decision to cover an FTP (Fuck the Police) march, where he shouted, "Hey, stop throwing stuff at the cops from behind me. I believe in nonviolence, and if you throw water bottles at the cops from way in the back, you put all of us up here in jeopardy, *and* it's cowardly. If I find out who's doing it, I'm going to turn the camera on you, because I disagree with what you're doing." Some folks had grumbled and lit up the Twitter lines with cries of foul and aiding and abetting the enemy, but few actually turned on him, regardless of their disapproval of his methods in this particular incident. Oakfosho had a presence, on and off camera, that made me feel calmer and safer than when I was outside of his aura. He had over ten thousand Twitter followers (which is huge in Twitterdom) and before streaming the General Strike on November 2, he'd been a gentle, thoughtful, big guy, with a master's degree in Business Administration, who was underemployed at a twenty-four-hour fitness gym in Oakland, which had barely allowed him to make his nut and pay his bills after graduation. He often said that the gym, although not ideal employment, had allowed him to survive the financial crisis, as well as given him the much-needed impetus to shed a hundred pounds, which had also improved his health and overall outlook. It couldn't hurt that, in the last three months, since he'd begun covering the revolution, he'd become somewhat of a star—the standard by which all others were being judged. Even major mainstream news channels, CNN and Al Jazeera, had appropriated his publicly available footage in their own coverage of Occupy Oakland.

At Twenty-Fourth Street, near the YMCA, we made a right onto Broadway. About fifty yards in was a big gang of cops ready- ing for a confrontation. The gym ahead of me on the left was filled with sweaty patrons, working out on exercise machines, behind plate glass windows and entry doors. Straight ahead was a wall of police. On the right were many more buildings with little or no spaces in between. My heart sank as I noticed that police officers were beginning to close in behind us, where we'd just come from, on Broadway. Hundreds of us were being contained and con- stricted in a choreographed maneuver the Oakland Police Depart- ment called, "kettling."

Others too, began to diagnose the situation, causing some to crowd, frantically, to the front of the line, and rip open the glass doors before darting wildly through the Y, looking for a rear door to make their escape. From my viewpoint, outside at the bottom of the stairs, I could just make out the backlit form of a muscular black woman with a YMCA T-shirt, as she lunged to the entrance, clawed at her waistband, and yanked off her belt to hold the doors shut against the protesters. Panic broke out on the landing, as I noticed that some of the shut-outs were women with small chil- dren, who'd been with us all day, ever since the frolicsome, family- friendly festivities began that morning. Hundreds of police shields pushed against us on all sides, inciting screams and pleas of, "Let us in," which fractured the night air, as incredulous gym mem- bers took it all in. "You are now ordered to disperse. This street has been declared closed. Failure to comply may result in your arrest," was the mantra that echoed throughout the enclosure, as I questioned how they could close a street where gym patrons and residents needed to come and go. I stood behind the women and children who were begging to be admitted into the Y, as police officers began infiltrating the crowd, singling out random demonstrators to interfere with. Just as I'd seen a few hours earlier, I saw a baton rising and falling upon the legs of a protester, who was screaming out in pain as he clung to a railing. The sickening thud of the baton hitting his flesh, coupled with the occasional ringing of a missed swing hitting the metal railing, sent the crowd into a desperate, terror-fueled frenzy. People started yelling, "Allow us to disperse . . . Allow us to disperse," as those who'd decided to opt out realized they were being prevented by police from leaving the area, as previously ordered.

A number of sweaty gym members grabbed their towels and beat a hasty exit, while others, sympathetic to the frightened demonstrators, began to negotiate with the belt-wielding employee to allow them passage. I could tell she was getting tired of holding the door shut, and her resolve seemed to be lessening, as Occupiers continued trying to wrench the door open. In the end, exhaustion won out as she loosened her grip and let the belt slither to the ground, and the glass doors were flung violently open to admit us.

A wave of humanity surged through the doors, and I let myself be carried with the tide into the safety of the multistoried workout facility. People ahead of me ran, willy nilly, toward exits on the first floor, while I chose, randomly, to mount the stairs to the second floor, praying for some handy escape hatch to reveal itself to me. I slowed down at a mezzanine before entering an open space, which was not visible to the floors below. Above me was a jogging track, still being used by a handful of die-hard fitness freaks who were ignoring the mayhem unfolding downstairs— while a few feet in front of me were six or seven women riding exercise bicycles, looking mostly bored, some with magazines perched open on handle bars, as they peddled endlessly, trying to rack up enough calories to earn their freedom. *Christ, maybe they really don't know what's happening downstairs,* I mused, silently. I then gazed down at my own attire and evaluated my chances of passing for one of them. Black stretch pants—good. Athletic looking walking shoes—good. Long sleeved cotton T-shirt covered by a hoody, not so good. Quickly, I removed the hoody and tied it around my waist, preppy style, as I tried to stroll casually past the women to one of the unoccupied bikes. "Hi," I said warmly to one of them, trying to mirror the same indifference they were showing to the disorder downstairs. It seemed very unlikely that they could not know something was amiss below, even as I began to hear the words, "Submit to arrest" being carried by a bullhorn to my attentive ears. My "hi" was returned by a curt nod, which I feared might indicate that they were on to me. I tried to recall how to operate the electronic cycle from my own days of working out at the Y, back home in West Seattle in the late nineties. To complete the deception, I nonchalantly grabbed a used towel that had been cast aside earlier by a previous cycler, and draped it around my neck.

Seconds later three or four male protesters, clad in jeans, overcoats, and bandanas, burst into the room with a dozen cops hot on their tails. That got a rise out of the bored bikers, as they all stopped pedaling at once, climbed off the equipment, and wordlessly scurried to the mezzanine exit. I crowded in beside them, trying to affect the same disgusted, horrified glares they possessed as a burly cop intercepted us at the exit. I can't let you leave the building until we make sure you're not with them, he shouted, officiously. "Oh my God, we are so not with them," a petite, put-together blonde spat witheringly at the giant cop, just as his mountainous buddy caught up to us. The two officers stared at each other, momentarily flustered by the cute little impertinent mouth, filled with perfect white teeth that had delivered the sassy rebuke to their massive shaved heads. "Yeah, my husband and kids are probably starving by now," I added, snottily. My goal was to mimic their perfect blend of contempt and entitlement.

"Um . . . wull . . . um—maybe just walk 'em through the crowd and get a look at their gym IDs as they head out," said one. "Yeah, okay," replied the other, vacuously. Oh no, I thought, there's no way I can pass this test. Desperate for a miracle, I lined up with the other irritated women. I felt like a complete dick as as we paraded, with our police escort, past my fellow Occupiers, who were sitting on the ground in handcuffs on the mezzanine floor. For an instant, my eyes locked onto those of a protester I recognized, as he sat there, under arrest. This made me feel so rotten, I half hoped he would expose me for the traitor I really was. The officer led us to an emergency exit door, which opened into a landing on the second story. Four women walked ahead of me, into the darkness, with their plastic gym cards held high, so that the cop with the flashlight could take a look. Blondie was just in front of me, looking put out, as she tossed her mane impudently and brandished her membership card like a weapon. The cop's flashlight had low batteries, and was fairly dim as he stood back a few feet and shone it in our general direction. Though I was trembling inside, I thrust my Visa card out like a pro as I entered the cursed sphere of light, which was about to seal my fate.

Somehow—someway, the goddess smiled on me at that moment, and I realized I'd passed muster and was walking freely through the street behind the YMCA. I was still unsure of my friend Laura's whereabouts, so after I put some distance between myself and the scene of the crime, I grabbed my phone and dialed her number. She picked up right away and shrieked, "Hallelujah, you're *safe!*" into the phone.

"Yay, you are *too!*" I effused back.

"I guess, I should amend that to, 'I think you're safe,' I mean, are you? You're not calling me from jail . . . right?"

I was pleased as punch to report that I was fine, but got unpleased in a hurry when she described what she was seeing on Oakfosho's feed. She had wisely left the sculpture park after the entrapment and teargassing began in earnest—so I reunited with her at City Hall and we charged back to her house to get online and see what was going down.

Spencer had had the extreme good fortune of being plucked out of the kettle by one of his followers, who was monitoring the situation closely from his third-story apartment, which just happened to be a perfect vantage point for him to safely film the action. We watched, aghast, at the numbers of protesters who were being knocked around, shoved to the ground, zip-tied, and arrested at the scene. Oak was saying that he felt certain the arrestees had not been allowed to disperse after the order was given, which had been his, as well as my, experience. He broadcasted late into the night, giving his thoughts and opinions with grace and wit, as he helped us make sense of what was unfolding. When it was all over, more than four hundred marchers had been arrested—most of the crowd—while only a small percentage (myself included) had managed to escape. Of those who did evade capture, nearly all had done so by racing through the Y and bolting out emergency exit doors before the law could catch up to them. I spent the next morning basking in the luxury of being able to look out the window and push the recline button on my economy airline seat back to Seattle.

Chapter 8

Doxology

My first week at OGP had taught me never, ever to be unplugged or out of touch, for even a moment, if I wanted to live through the night, or quickly reach a spontaneous uprising. This was true for every location I Occupied around the country. I'd learned to have at least a 75% charge at bed time, should it be necessary to call someone late and/or apprise my loved ones of urgent developments. I had a love/hate relationship with it, sometimes calling it a "Dread," others a "'Roid." I loved it for the comfort it gave me, while resenting the intrusion into my privacy and the high-priced monthly data plan. I was alternately disgusted and amazed at all the things it could do. There was an app for *everything*. I'd even found and downloaded one called, "I've Been Arrested," which automatically notified everyone I pre-flagged on my contact list that I was being hauled off to jail, and to call my attorney ASAP and get me the heck out of there. A cashier at Target had informed me of it, as I bought a tent to live in. She'd shown it to me on her own phone, and I was immediately drawn to the silly bright red animated cartoon logo of handcuffed hands being thrust in the air by a man jumping crazily around as if he'd just been tased. Not only was my phone a safety measure, it also allowed me to keep my finger on the pulse of the Occupy news that was developing rapidly across the country—and the world. Seconds after Marine Scott Olsen uttered his first words following his severe head injury by the OPD, I heard about it, thanks to Twitter. The same with notifications that this encampment or that was scheduled to be demolished anywhere in the United States. By December, my newly acquired tweeting prowess had netted me hundreds of new friends that helped me add words to my vocabulary that I doubt even existed before the Occupy Movement was born. One of those words was *dox* which I'd not heard before, but was now thinking of constantly and using competently in many of my sentences of late. Now that standoffs with the police were becoming a commonplace experience, I heard the word daily. "Somebody dox that jerk—He's running down Occupiers and he just clubbed that girl over there with his baton." Or, "Whoa did you see that cop pepperspray the old dude—Dox his Ass." And, "I just got that pig on camera planting drugs on that black guy— get his frickin' badge number so Anonymous can dox him." The first doxing occurrence that came to my attention was that of UC Davis Campus Police Officer, John Pike. The now infamous story of John Pike leads me to another favorite new term, *meme*, which was a result of what Officer Pike did on November 22, which caused him not only to be doxed, but then given a starring role in the "meme seen round the world."

On November 22, the student body of UC Davis had decided to come together and Occupy the campus to protest the out-of-control spiraling of tuition rates in recent years, which, again, were found to be closely correlated to the fact that many regents of the California State College system also served as board members to the world's largest banks. Recent studies had shown that, of the various reasons Americans got into debt, higher education was deemed to be the most acceptable of all—especially when compared to car loans, vacations, home loans, illnesses, funerals, and wedding expenses. In other words, it was okay in the United States, to mortgage oneself to the eyeballs for school, which was viewed as "good debt," because of the conventional wisdom that almost no amount of money was too much to pay for an enriching, solid education. In fact, debt incurred in the pursuit of higher education was considered not only acceptable, but even wise. To add insult to injury, regents were seen to be using this and the concurrent reality that the state of California was pitching in less and less tax revenue to fund state colleges, to their advantage, as they steadily raised student fees nearly every time they convened. They were widely expected to vote for an 80% increase in tuition, which was to be instituted, following the next meeting. For many students, this had been the last straw, as they looked around and saw how dim their prospects were becoming. They were beginning to organize and align themselves with the Occupy Movement, in an attempt to channel some of their anger and frustration into direct action.

Thus it was that Officer John Pike found himself walking up and down a row of arm-linked UC Davis college students, who sat impenetrably before him, like a human levee. They were inhibiting the flow of obedient, uncomplaining, debt-accepting students into the buildings they sought to take instruction from, as he and his fellow officers ordered them to get up and leave the vicinity, immediately. As they stayed there, defiantly clinging to one another, Officer Pike had grown annoyed, resenting the hell out of the pampered, spoiled refuseniks, who sat there, smugly defying a direct order from an officer of the law. When his simmering pot began to boil over, Pike reached into his professional arsenal, grabbed a can of orange pepper spray, and began casually, even langorously drenching the faces of the seated students, with no more regard than one affords an infestation of cockroaches.

His strutting and posturing was reminiscent of a contemptuous drill sergeant, setting young recruits straight, who clearly didn't understand the chain of command in the US Armed Forces. So repugnant was the sight of this man committing these acts within plain view of his fellow officers, who did nothing, that the video, which had been captured on a cell phone by another student, had gone viral in a matter of weeks. In response to the affront, a new group of computer "hacktivists," calling themselves "Anonymous," had made certain that almost anyone who had eyes was likely to see this image somewhere, somehow, in a matter of days after it happened. Better still, the "AnonOps" crew had also *doxed* Officer Pike, which meant that they'd published every bit of data that had ever been collected on him, from the time he was a zygote to that moment—including his full legal name, social security number, cell phone number, and residential address, along with all sorts of other private information I'm sure he'd rather the world not know. In short, if this guy had ever gotten a bad report card, wet the bed, or sought treatment for acne or erectile dysfunction, Anonymous had found out, and what's more, they'd published it to the worldwide web. So complete had the market saturation of the John Pike video been, that he instantly graduated from being an obscure, badge drunk creep in the campus police system, to being an inescapable household word, cultural symbol, and Internet phenomenon . . . a *meme*. People began gleefully photoshopping pictures of Officer Pike into iconic images, such as *The Last Supper* painting by Leonardo Da Vinci, however in the new meme version, Jesus was not being betrayed by Judas Ischariot, but be-sprayed by none other than Officer Pike. I saw one where ET (from the classic movie about extra-terrestrials) was reaching out longingly to the cosmos in search of his tribe, only to be answered, viciously, with a plume of pepper spray. Smurfs were sprayed, along with chipmunks, Sesame Street characters, babies in cribs, Bambi—you name it, Officer Pike sprayed it. For a few weeks there, you couldn't get away from this meme, even if you tried.

A close friend of mine who is skilled with a computer, sends me an original Christmas card every year, and her handiwork never fails to bring me cheer. In holidays past, I'd waited with baited breath to see what she created. For the last few seasons, she'd been on a nativity scene kick, where she would juxtapose herself and her pets in different places around the infant's crèche—sort of a

Where's Waldo theme, only instead of calling it, "The Nativity," she, the ever cynical atheist, had entitled her cards, "The Naivete." This year the card looked completely normal in every way, except for the fact that Officer Pike was strolling past the baby Jesus in the manger, casually dousing the infant with orange pepper spray. So successful had this AnonOps stunt been, that it soon became the tactic of choice when acquiring film that showed officers engaging in outrageous, improper behavior, especially in their dealings with the Occupy Movement. The policeman's actions had so offended the collective conscience of America, that it had served to bolster public sentiment toward the Occupy Movement, and against police departments, nationwide. Before the year was over, Officer Pike had been suspended, along with another colleague, and people across the country were calling for UC Davis chancellor Linda Katehi, to resign. The Campus Police Chief had been put on leave and an investigation had been launched to determine what further actions needed to be taken to regulate University policing and prevent this sort of future misconduct. So feared was this tactic becoming, that police officers, who had formerly bragged and made jokes online about the common practice of taping over their badge numbers before committing especially violent (and often illegal) acts, had begun warning each other about the dangers doxing posed to their careers. Exclusive, "police only" chat room posts were being doxed too, for all of us non-police to see and get a better understanding of their true intentions.

Doxed officers were beginning to complain loudly about the practice, and advocate for legislation that would dole out harsh penalties to those who published such records. The family lives of cops were already known to be somewhat compromised by the very condition of being law enforcement personnel, whose members have been been disproportionately associated with incidents of domestic violence, substance abuse, divorce, and childhood bullying, among other social ills. Doxed cops were suddenly finding themselves fighting an uphill battle to control growing negative public perceptions of their characters. The beauty of doxing, in my opinion, was that it only targeted cops who were doing bad things to people who didn't deserve it. And, to top it all off, it was non-violent. Don't want to get doxed? Don't be an asshole. It was just that simple. At least that's how I, and we, saw it. The other thing I admire about doxing is that it is a collaborative effort between the legions of citizen journalists, and the less abundant numbers of talented, often brilliant, hackers located around the world—a team building exercise of sorts. Armed only with cell phones and cameras, these daring individuals captured the dastardly deeds of miscreant cops and other wrongdoers, on film, and then the Anons, acting as a guerilla tech team, compiled a wealth of damning documentation about the offenders, often when provided with only minimal bits of information. With this great new tool, Anonymous had single-handedly given the Occupy Movement a profoundly effective method of deterring horrendous assaults on political protesters in the United States. Doxing was our A-bomb—our first, last, and best line of defense in the street wars of Occupy.

I was already a fan of Anonymous by the time we gathered for Move-In Day on January 28, but I marveled at how much reassurance I took from the existence of a completely unknown entity—people whom I'd probably never meet or know the name of, could mete out justice for me in the likely event that I was ever abused again by a municipal police force. Having Anonymous out there was sort of like having crime fighting superheroes on hand, that would magically appear in your hour of greatest need, just when it seemed there was no hope of ever making it out of a harrowing predicament intact. On Move-In Day, when I stood outside the chain-link fence separating me from the army of cops aiming at us, I remember hearing the comforting sentence, "Somebody get those motherfuckers over there on camera—the ones pointing their guns at us—we gotta dox those assholes."

The exact inception of Anonymous is unclear, but it is known that with the Occupy Movement, they rapidly evolved from being thought of as a coalition of merry pranksters, to being a potent and

formidable force against corporate greed and government oppression worldwide. In the early days they did things like dogpile on
Tom Cruise for his comical involvement with the Church of Scientology. Tom's antics had already provided endless fodder for water
cooler conversations about his evolving nuttiness, particularly
after appearing to have lost his mind on the Oprah Winfrey show,
where he'd run around maniacally and jumped up on a sofa, crazy-
style, all the while babbling on about how he was in love with
Katie Holmes. Then, just after that bizarre episode, in January of
2008, a Scientology video featuring Tom was put up on YouTube,
by a journalist who somehow got ahold of it, and leaked it to the
general public. In the video, Cruise talks about how the Church
of Scientology has all the answers for everything. He even goes so
far as to divulge that, when driving past a car accident, he knows
that he, as a Scientologist, is the only person who can *really* help.
Needless to report, that video shot to the top of the social media
charts in a big hurry, giving millions of viewers plenty to discuss
for the entire four days that it was up. Then, it got snatched off the
air by the Church itself, who claimed they owned the copyright,
and could pull it whenever they damn well pleased. That's the part
that got Anonymous all riled up. They flat out hated seeing the
video disappear, and called it censorship. Then it was on. Scientology message boards started getting flooded with unwanted posts,
unordered pizzas got delivered to Scientology centers, unsolic-
ited, all-black faxes clogged machines and drained printers of ink
and paper. The robust backlash against Scientology was broad in
scope, and unprecedented for the amount of people it reached
through social media. Anonymous stated their goal in no uncertain
terms: "The extent of your malign influence over those who trust
you, who call you leader, has been made clear to us. Anonymous
has therefore decided that your organization should be destroyed.
For the good of your followers, for the good of mankind—for
the laughs. We shall expel you from the Internet and systematically dismantle the Church of Scientology in its present form. We
acknowledge you as a serious opponent, and we are prepared for

a long, long campaign. You will not prevail forever against the angry masses of the body politic. Your methods, hypocrisy, and the artlessness of your organization have sounded its death knell." In the four years since the Scientology caper, Anonymous had surfaced here and there, but never so visibly as during the beginning months of the Occupy Movement. During the 2011 holiday season, I remember stumbling upon a video link from my Twitter feed, that began with Apocalyptic music, punctuated by random explosive sounds, and super reverb-y, devil-worshippy choir vocals, that accompanied an eerie image of a metal globe, revolving continuously around a strangely lit, diaphanous blue/green haze. That got my attention right away for its *Twilight Zone* weirdness, but then there appeared a glowing orb, surrounding a black business suit with its arms folded. Where the head should be, there was only a dark question mark, suspended just above the tie. On either side of the suit were arches that resembled the sides of a wheat stalk penny. Then came the announcement—from a robotic, emotionless, computer-generated voice: "Attention, citizens of the world. We are Anonymous. We wish to get your attention hoping you'll heed the warnings as follows. Your medium of communication you all so dearly adore will be destroyed." It then went on to make the case for not just eliminating, but annihilating Facebook. "Facebook has been selling information to government agencies and giving clandestine access to information security firms so that they can spy on people from all around the world . . . Everything you do on Facebook stays on Facebook regardless of your privacy settings and deleting your account is impossible. Even if you delete your account all your personal info stays on Facebook and can be recovered at any time. Changing the privacy settings to make your Facebook account more private is also an illusion. Facebook knows more about you than your family . . . You are not safe from them nor from any government. One day you will look back on this and realize what we have done here is right . . . Prepare for a day that will go down in history, November 5, 2011. We are Anonymous. We are legion. We do not forgive. We do not forget. Expect us."

That last line, delivered without nuance, without inflection, sent a chill up my spine for raw, naked, cool creepiness.

I wasn't sure whether to be frightened out of my wits or deliriously happy with the declaration. Did this mean that Anonymous was in charge now? Were they really going to bring down Facebook? And if they could do that, what else could they do? Might this be the beginning of a new era, where we were actually being governed by a nameless, faceless avatar—an Orwellian Big Brother type, whose motivation was not greed, but rather, an infinite kindness and concern for my well-being. In those heady days, I was so taken with the masked avengers of Anonymous, I even probed deeper to learn why they wore those delightfully scary facemasks.

As it turns out, the mask on the Anonymous videos was a likeness of an historical figure named Guy Fawkes, and its significance soon became clear. Mr. Fawkes was born in York, England in the year 1570. He joined the Spanish army in 1593, after converting to Catholicism and becoming a religious zealot. His zeal manifested itself in a failed plot to blow up the British Parliament's House of Lords, (the original 1%) in 1605, where he was caught hiding in a cellar, guarding a cache of gunpowder that he intended to detonate, right under their noses. Sadly for Fawkes, his efforts resulted in him being tortured by the Brits to rat out his accomplices, after which he was tried, convicted, and executed on January 31, 1606, right across the street from the very building he tried so hard to blow up. So . . . nowadays, to prove there are no hard feelings and that they are good sports about the whole thing, on November 5, England celebrates Guy Fawkes day with fireworks (not under the House of Lords) and children donning masks while begging for pennies.

So that's where the love affair with Guy Fawkes started. And then, in 2006, a film called, *V is for Vendetta* came out in which "V," a solo anarchist living in a society ruled by a fictional fascist party in the UK, tries to blow up the Houses of Parliament, just like Guy did. V is wearing a mask designed by David Lloyd, the same one which has now come to be associated with the Anonymous move-

ment, as well as to stand for a fierce, courageous form of individu-
alism which boldly forges forth, despite great odds against it. The
mask itself was of a pointy-chinned, sharp-cheeked man sporting a
skinny mustache and a narrow goatee. The likeness bears a strange,
Mona Lisa smile which can be seen as both menacing and play-
ful—much the same way Anonymous itself was being described.
They are believed to have first been used by Anonymous during
their 2008 campaign against the kookiness of Scientology. Not
just a fashion statement, they provided vital anonymity for the
wearers at protests, where cops were constantly trying to identify
Occupiers for future retaliation. The masks became ubiquitous—a
logo of sorts for Anonymous videos, as well as standard apparel at
the wave of protests against banks and corporate greed that began
to characterize the Occupy Movement worldwide.

I've seen many Anonymous videos by now, some with the question mark over the tie, and others with a hovering Guy Fawkes
mask doing all the talking. Although Facebook didn't get blasted
out of existence on November 5, nor did the world order change
in any appreciative way that day, I still counted myself a fan of
Anonymous and came to love their brazen, outlaw panache.

While Occupying America, I came to look forward to proc-
lamations from Anonymous in the same way I used to anticipate
new *Batman* episodes when I was a kid. Only Anonymous was even
better because they were *real* and their shows came on randomly,
with no commercial interruptions. And you never knew when you
were going to log on to your Twitter account and find the link
to another treat from the good folks at Anon Ops. Since my first
exposure to them, I'd been kept in a perpetual OCD cycle of tap-
ping the glass on my phone and gluing my eyes to the screen to
see if there was anything new from them. For better or worse, by
the end of 2011, the social media sites, Twitter, Facebook, You-
Tube, Ustream, were becoming my IV, my lifeline, my unending
connection to Occupy—every second of every day. I who had
often been criticized by family members for being "too into" the
nightly network news, was now almost never bothering to turn

on my television, let alone watch something as behind the curve, shallow, and irrelevant as mainstream media news. In fact, most of the time the "news" famously failed to even cover Occupy events, which often drew thousands of people onto the streets to interrupt the flow of commerce. And on the rare occasions when they did cover an event, they got it wrong, typically ignoring the real story and the important reasons behind it. So that's why I had broken up with NBC and CNN and ABC and CBS and all those other letters. I preferred the unedited truth and immediacy of social media, and all of a sudden, nothing else would do. Social media allowed me to reach out and touch people all over the world with an intimacy and honesty that I could only have dreamed of in the very recent past. For the first time in my life, I was able to witness history in the making, draw my own conclusions and connect the dots in ways that were never before possible.

In early 2012, a series of Anonymous actions came to my attention via my Twitter account. By that time, I'd begun to actively seek out and follow anyone whose Twitter handle included the words, "Anonymous," or "Occupy." Most of the actions were everything from DDOS, (distributed denial of service) to wholesale destruction of the websites of corporate bad guys, as defined by the Anonymous family. I enjoyed reading about the inconvenience and mayhem they caused wealthy criminals. I never disagreed with them about the shadiness of the entities I saw them go after, or thought they unfairly targeted innocent people. I remember breathlessly retrieving tweets with the words TANGO DOWN written in all caps, directing me to open the link to the latest online video, telling me that another evil-doer had been hacked. I thought that employing the phrase *Tango Down* was a wonderful co-optation of the military term used when a terrorist has been eliminated. I read these words when Anonymous brought down Stratfor, a super secret organization of governmental and private sector villains with deep pockets. It was delicious how they disclosed the names and personal information of all its members, as well as published highly classified information about where their money was going and how it was being used to control the American political process and steal from the rest of the world. Not only had they exposed lots of sensitive information about Stratfor, they also broke into member bank accounts and made a series of small donations to good-guy agencies and favorite causes like the Sierra Club and Doctors Without Borders, totalling a million dollars. My heart beat out of my chest for them, as I read about hacks into CIA, NSA, FBI, and Fed websites. I saw them as modern-day Robin Hoods.

Not only had the explosion of technology allowed me to stay current with Occupy—I was suddenly able to communicate directly with people in embattled and impoverished countries all over the globe in real time. One night, I stumbled onto a tweet by an Occupier who was communicating with a Syrian man, named Mulham al Jundi, who was hiding out in the city of Homs. He had recently been shot twice in the leg by a sniper from the Syrian Army. Mulham, along with his friends and neighbors, were rebelling against a bloodthirsty dictator named Bashar al Assad, whose family had ruled the country with an iron fist and a well-equipped, murderous army, for many decades. It was February 2, 2012, that I found myself sitting on a sofa in Pam's hospital room. She had just dozed off when I began monitoring Jundi's live stream.

Mulham had actually been outside the city when Assad began his brutal assault on the Homs rebels and started indiscriminately killing men, women, and children by a number of means, including shelling them with mortars, gassing them with deadly chemicals, and firing upon them with snipers. Hearing of the attack, he had immediately snuck himself back into Homs and joined his countryman in fighting for the right to freedom and self-determination for all Syrians. He and his rebel comrades were mostly unarmed, though some did possess crude, minimal weapons, which they occasionally managed to take out a sniper with. Though it was past midnight in my Wenatchee, Washington hospital room, it was fully daylight in Syria when I began chatting, via Twitter, with Mulham. He looked fatigued and stressed as I began asking him if he was warm and had enough to eat. He replied "no," in English, to both questions. He said it was cold outside and there was very little food to eat inside, but that he was not concerned about that, nor was he worried about his injuries, which he dismissed as "extra motivation to defeat Assad." His calm resolve in the face of extraordinarily precarious circumstance astonished me. He was fully aware of the perils he faced, yet used the deaths and injuries to his friends and family to overcome fear. I asked him about his surroundings and he insisted on walking out into the street with his camera to show me his neighborhood, which had been bombed and shelled beyond recognition. Flattened cars covered in dust and concrete stood parked in the street. Doorways to multi-story brick apartment buildings gaped cavernously open, as exposed rebar and iron framing protruded, twisted and deformed, from upper floors. Occasionally a child or two would emerge from such a building to stand, dazed, in the street, among the shattered remains of their neighbors' homes. Mulham described the constant mortar attacks that had battered his neighborhood to a shambles—where those who had survived, having nowhere else to go, still remained. He said that many of his neighbors on that street had died in recent weeks, and that he too expected to die, but hoped to bring attention to the suffering of the Syrian people before becoming a martyr. The more he shared, the more I came to feel deep empathy and compassion for him and his neighbors, along with a mounting frustration that I could do nothing to help him. He and other Muslims that looked like him were the people my country told me I was supposed to fear and be suspicious of, yet all I could see was a soft-spoken, intelligent, brave, kind man that had placed himself in a horrifying situation, to come to the aid of his countrymen. I stayed with Mulham al Jundi for hours, off and on, as he had to shut down periodically, so that Assad's forces could not locate him by his signal. By the end of our conversation, I felt compelled to tell him that I loved him and his people, and that I would do everything I could to make Americans aware of their struggle against tyranny and oppression. Before I closed down my computer, I "followed" @MulhamJundi on Twitter and resolved to seek out other Syrians to become friends with. I was profoundly moved by our conversation. More than anything I've ever read or seen on television, this intimate, one-on-one interaction with an injured man in a war-torn country showed me that there are few things more precious to human beings than justice and liberty. And the capacity for seemingly ordinary individuals to care for their sisters and brothers, is limitless. People will risk anything to either live in freedom or try to secure it for future generations. He reminded me too, how tenuous the balance between war and peace is on this tiny planet.

At the time of this writing, I am relieved to note that Mulham is still alive, though suffering and subsisting. After he and I talked, I began to search the web for other streamers in Syria. Before long, I was corresponding with a number of them, holed up in the remnants of bombed out buildings, attending to their wounded and dead, or simply sitting in tattered rooms anxiously listening to the explosions coming at regular intervals around them. Some families still had electricity, while others were capturing it from car batteries and inverting it to AC. All were quietly waiting to die. One time I opened a link sent to me by a group of Syrian rebels who'd begun using carrier pigeons to stay in contact with others and relay messages back and forth after an Internet blackout. On another, I logged in with Syrian doctors at makeshift field hospitals who were spattered with blood, frantically trying to save gravely wounded civilians. At one point a doctor began to lament that the hospital itself was under attack by "Assad's Dogs" and, "how were they supposed to treat people under such conditions." Then, a man was brought in who everyone in the room recognized as a beloved rebel live streamer. The doctor cried out in grief, along with many other men who began to embrace him and weep over his blood soaked body. The streamer who was filming this then panned around the small room to show the mutilated bodies of men, women, children, and tiny babies, who were laid out on every square inch of available space. Someone looked into the camera and spoke in Arabic as he began raising the sheets on the infants, and I was overcome with sadness as I observed the beautiful faces of the children, some with parts of their heads missing, others showing gaping wounds and missing limbs. At some point the speaker picked up one of the dead babies and cradled her in front of the camera. She looked as if she were sleeping peacefully in her brown velour jumpsuit, until he raised the jacket and, just above her diaper, I saw holes in her skin, and blood stains all over her tiny body. He gently returned her to her spot, as tears streamed down his face and he continued to speak beseechingly. Time after time, I witnessed similar scenes, as I sought to educate myself about Syria. On February 5 I sat at home in front of the fireplace, watching the Super Bowl with my family, as I scrolled through videos being put up every minute, by Syrian Rebels, of their slaughtered families and friends. It was freakishly surreal being able to ask, those who spoke English, specific questions about their daily reality, even as they turned their cameras on the carnage to reveal their gory surroundings. At the end of every session, I thanked the streamers for sharing their stories with me, I apologized for my government's and the world's inaction, and I told them I loved them. I learned how to say, *Allah Allahu Akbar* which means, "God is Great." Even though I don't believe in God, I wanted to offer something, anything at all, in their language, to acknowledge their grief. Certainly, it was inadequate, but I had heard them say this often as they cried out in agony, lamenting the death of their loved ones. Many, even in their despair, took the time to thank me for my viewership, or my words, which made me feel even closer and more connected to them. The only thing that I was consistently able to do to help was RT, or "retweet", their messages and encourage others to learn about their history and follow them. I was angered by my government's and NATO's failure to do anything substantive to help them. How could one man, Bashar Al Assad, be able to kill and maim so many innocent people, without intervention? Wasn't there something short of entering into World War III, that could be done by the global community to stop the genocide? From my perspective, no one had even begun to exhaust options for humanitarian aid. People were freezing to death, dying of curable diseases, and starving, while we all did nothing. Radical, right-wing, fundamentalist groups, like Al Qaeda and Al Nusra, were finding fertile ground in places like Homs, Damascus, and Aleppo, to recruit rebels who were now willing to go to any lengths to stop Assad's forces. On the nightly news, Hillary Clinton spoke of the brutality of the Assad regime and of the necessity to oppose him in some vague way, while NATO was "unable" to render assistance because of resistance from two members—China and Russia. What the hell good was NATO anyway, if they couldn't get even minimal help to people who were being massacred by the thousands. I sometimes lay awake in bed at night, grinding my teeth as I tried to invent ways to get women and children out safely, until some international coalition could find a way to stop Assad's army from killing. I wondered if something similar to this was how the "American Taliban," John Walker Lindh, came to hold such a fierce love for the Afghani people—so much so that he joined them in taking up arms against their enemies, which included the United States, who'd aligned itself with the Northern Alliance to oppose them and exact revenge on Osama Bin Laden for 9/11. I could never see myself taking up arms against anyone—it's all I can do to put a worm on a hook and kill a fish to eat, but it does seem tragic that such a caring young man could now be serving a twenty-year sentence for having fought with the Afghanistan Taliban army, both before and after American forces were allied with the Northern Alliance to oppose them. Lindh had not known of the September 11 plans when he joined the Taliban, nor had he had any particular affinity for Osama bin Laden, whom he'd heard lecture on one occasion and found to be, "unimpressive." He understood why Americans were upset with his actions, however, rather than some lofty, complicated, political rationale for his membership in the Taliban, he simply professed his love for the Afghani people, who he described as "kind and generous". According to Lindh himself, he had gone for long periods of time speaking only Arabic, rather than his native English, which he admitted having little need for. When asked how he had come to find himself in such a predicament, he was quoted as saying, "My heart became attached to them." Which, the more I think about it, is what I think would happen to most of us if we made the effort to befriend people from other cultures. The "other" gradually becomes "us" as we get to know each other and realize how similar we are. Every day that I spoke with the exhausted, beleaguered Syrians, I felt my heart becoming more and more "attached" to them, regardless of what others said.

After establishing relationships with Syrians, I began to follow and befriend Muslim sisters and brothers from all over the Middle East, as well as in America. I've chatted with Egyptian protesters gathered by the thousands in Tahrir Square, demanding an accelerated end to the military rule which they'd been subjected to ever since the uprising the year before, which resulted in the overthrow of President Hosni Mubarak on February 11, 2011. Mubarak had had a stranglehold on Egypt for thirty years, but was summarily ousted from power in what became known as the Arab Spring, a Middle Eastern populist movement that inspired millions worldwide to rise up and begin a revolution. Less than a year later, many of those who launched the American Occupy Movement, cited the Arab Spring as one of their greatest influences. A short period of transition was expected by the Egyptian people, who understood the necessity of allowing the military to restore order and keep the peace, immediately following the President's ouster, but along the way, many became wary of the military's increasingly menacing presence, and had sought to quicken the pace of the transition to an elected government. It boggled my mind that things I'd only been vaguely aware of the year before were now uppermost on my mind, as I established personal connections with other revolutionaries around the planet. As my Occupy friendships began to take shape, the lines began to blur between news story and personal tragedy. I'd hear a radio story on *Democracy Now*, or read something on the web about a bombing here, or an uprising there, and I'd shush everyone in the room and stay glued to the source, until I could determine if anyone I knew had been affected. Even if the stories' main characters were unknown to me at the time, I knew that many of them were only a click away from being friends. Amazing.

A woman whose Twitter handle is OccPal, sent out daily messages detailing the Israeli army's frequent land and air strikes on Palestinians living in Gaza. Her name came up when I did a Twitter search for accounts beginning with the word, "Occupy." She held the viewpoint that the IDF (Israeli Defense Force) had been radicalized by Israeli Prime Minister, Benjamin (Bibi) Netanyahu, to commit atrocities against her community of Muslims, who were living under Israeli domination. She compared Zionism and the misdeeds of the Israeli army to those committed during the Holocaust against Jews. Facilitated by social media, she made a compelling case that her rights as a human being were being routinely violated by Israel, whose soldiers killed, maimed, and harassed her friends and family perpetually, and whose expanding settlements stole land from her people, forcing them to live in subhuman conditions in an Apartheid-like system of segregation and subjugation. Her volumes of firsthand accounts of deprivation, coupled with links to articles about the indignities she and others were forced to endure, provoked an intense curiosity within me, to know much more about the ongoing crisis in the Middle East. I'd never before had such a burning desire to acquaint myself with the details of conflicts happening a world away, and probably would not have, had I not been reluctantly introduced to the miracle of social media. It was one thing to read a stuffy New York Times editorial about Palestinians being relegated to stark, impoverished ghettos while Israeli settlements grew and prospered, and yet another to actually talk with someone trying to survive in one of those bleak places. I recalled reading dry, distant descriptions of the place 1.7 million Palestinian called home—sometimes referring to their environment as "the world's largest open-air prison," and "a concentration camp." OccPal actually answered my questions, no matter how naive, and gave me insights to the region's complexities from a unique perspective, that no one else could have. Her words prompted me to look more closely at my country's relationship with the country she said oppressed her. I'd known for some time that the United States was one of Israel's staunchest allies, and that America provided Israel with considerable military support, but I'd never questioned that support or wished to probe any further until I began to follow OccPal.

It has long been a slippery slope in America to question Israel's policies toward Gazans because of the fear that opposition to Zionism could be viewed as a form of anti-Semitism. The sensitivity of the issue was clear as I tried to form my own opinions on the issues that confronted Israelis and Palestinians daily. Because Twitter and Facebook had suddenly given me direct access to the players making the news, the personal instantly became the political for me. My exchanges with OccPal and other Muslims living near her inspired me to try to figure out what was really going on over there. So then, I began to ask some of my Jewish friends here in this country what they thought about the whole mess. One of those friends, Penny Rosenwasser, told me of the work she was doing to bring Jewish and Palestinian children and their parents together, to learn to embrace each other's cultures. She was, in fact, writing a book about this work, *Hope Into Practice, Jewish Women Choosing Justice Despite Our Fears*. Another influential voice was that of friend Ed Pearl, who helped make history in the sixties during the Civil Rights Movement, as the owner of the Ash Grove Coffeehouse in Hollywood, California. Ed booked and promoted hundreds of groundbreaking, revolutionary artists during those tumultuous times, including The Freedom Singers, Pete Seeger, Miriam Makeba, Joan Baez, and Taj Mahal, among many others, and was known for his political activism, particularly through music. I met Ed first when he booked me to perform in his club. We became fast friends as I came to understand the depth and breadth of his commitment to social justice. Every day, Ed put out a blog-style newsletter, which was loaded with materials he'd culled, that reflected his own political leanings. After I asked him to add me to his list of readers, I saw how keenly focused he was on the situation in Israel. As a vocal opponent of the settlements and second-class treatment of Palestinians, his writing has been pivotal in helping shape my conclusions. Coincidentally, even as I write these words, I am opening a link sent to me by students at Brandeis University, who are disrupting an on-campus seminar featuring Zionist Israeli speakers. The students at the predominantly Jewish institution are standing up, chanting, "Free Palestine," as audience members look on in amused silence. It astounds me to note that there is almost no area of my life, these days, that has not felt the impact of social media, particularly as a revolutionary tool. It blows me away. For God's sake, my family had a *party line* phone connection when I was a child—look it up. Catholic families that I grew up with scrimped and saved for years in order to purchase the latest editions of Encyclopedia Brittanica, so there kids would have access to an infinitesimal amount of the information that is now easily surpassed with the touch of a button. And these mind-blowing volumes of data come to me, most often, by means of a ridiculously small—hardly larger than a deck of playing cards—hand-held plastic device, that I can operate, even while lying in bed at night.

Sometimes, however, the incessant media input becomes burdensome to me. It's marvelous how contact with people who are outside our ken can change us and inform our positions on ethical dilemmas. Oh, the things we can accomplish when we talk to each other, rather than about each other. However, one unforeseen consequence of this outrageously cool technology is that I often argue with myself, ad nauseum, about whether I am being objective enough. I'm like Tevye from *Fiddler on the Roof*, ("on the other hand . . .") constantly worrying that I have not considered both sides of an issue enough before reaching a conclusion. At these times I find the numerous lengthy tomes detailing every possible angle, troubling, and I want to run from the Internet and its squid-like tentacles, clawing out to me at the strangest times and in the furthest reaches of earth. Is it just me, or is it a universal truth that whichever side one is exposed to, no matter how ostensibly ridiculous or unjustifiable at first glance, if one talks to enough holders of said ridiculous beliefs for long enough, there's usually a kernel of sense somewhere to glom onto. But, surely, there must be such a thing as absolute right or wrong—mustn't there? Before the Internet pervaded every facet of my being, and I had only slanted mainstream media coverage to rely on, some types of issues were easier to resolve in my own head.

I remember during the Rodney King riots of the early nineties, when enraged black people, (who witnessed a film clip of L.A. cops savagely beating Mr. King after a routine traffic stop) were taking to the streets chanting, "Black Justice," in anger and disbelief at the acquittal of the four officers (three white, one Hispanic) who had nearly taken King's life. While I watched the live helicopter news feed coverage, I saw a hapless white construction trucker named Reginald Denny, drive, apparently lost, smack dab into the middle of the scene, where he was converged upon and pulled out of his truck by an angry mob of black folks, who beat him nearly to death because they wanted revenge for the injustice they had just suffered. Denny was battered so severely, he had to spend years in rehabilitation, learning how to walk and talk all over again, which he is now able to do, somewhat. A few of my black friends and acquaintances made light of Denny's ordeal, in much the same way I'd heard whites laughing at Rodney King's thumping. But knowing many good people of all races made it easy to discern that the viciousness shown by those few individuals, (cops and rioters alike), were not representative of entire cultures, but rather a predictable consequence of institutionalized racism in American society. Certain characters had behaved inexcusably, and acts of brutality like these were absolutely wrong, no matter what the rationale. I sometimes long for the good old days.

The more I engaged with other cultures, the more the planet seemed to be shrinking to minute proportions. During the winter, I established Twitter relationships with Occupiers in Athens,

Greece as they fought hard to oppose severe "austerity measures" that continued to be imposed upon them by the European Union, in the aftermath of their government's greed-driven financial crisis. Their economic collapse bore distinct parallels to our own. As a matter of fact, almost every point on the globe was experiencing growing unrest, due in large part to the plundering of wealth by powerful corporations and individuals. February of 2012 was an incredibly productive month for Anonymous Operations and partnerships with the Occupy Movement. On February 12, I sat in my living room, sipping coffee and chatting live with other viewers on a streaming channel called "OccupyTV," while forty-five buildings in Athens billowed smoke and burned with the rage of Athenians, who had just been told that they would be forced to endure another round of belt tightening in order to stave off a bigger economic catastrophe, which the EU warned would ensue if they did not work harder for less money and fewer benefits. I read on the chat line that the insurrection was spreading quickly, and specific businesses were being singled out for destruction. Armies of police vehicles were spraying water cannons and throwing explosives at rioters. A comment scrolled by announcing that fifteen banks were burning, along with Starbucks, and some other multinational corporate franchises. The Twitter feed was atwitter with declarations of solidarity and support for Greece's 99% and I'd just read that one hundred thousand Greeks were in the streets demanding change. "COPS JUST RAN OUT OF TEAR GAS," tweeted an elated onsite protester, who was answered by one of my fellow countrymen, who sarcastically tweeted, "probably manufactured in Jamestown, Pennsylvania—GO USA." I felt awake and alive and ineluctably bonded with my comrades in Greece, as well as in Syria and Palestine.

The next day, while trolling the web, I came across the message, "TANGO DOWN" on the Anonymous feed. On February 14, Anonymous took down the website of Combined System, the tear gas manufacturer in Pennsylvania which was said to have manufactured the chemical dispersants fired on the Athens protesters. Upon further investigation, I learned that a number of Greece's government websites had also been shut down, to protest the ministers' 199 to 101 vote to impose further hardship on their workers. This time, laborers were hit with a 20% reduction in the minimum wage, as well as the elimination of fifteen thousand jobs. Around the same time, I heard an NPR story about a formerly middle-class woman in Athens, who was forced to come out of retirement in her old age, because of prior austerity measures that had already gone into effect. She said that she was struggling to get by on six hundred dollars per month, down from a pension of four thousand dollars, which had allowed her to live comfortably in years past. I learned from the Twitterfeed that, once again, rather than make the wealthy 1% architects of the Greek debt crisis accountable, in the form of direct taxes and fines, the shortfall was being levelled on the backs of the proletariat—the workers, who'd already been pushed to the brink by government takeaways. The constant threat being waved in the faces of Greek citizens was expulsion from the European Union, the EU, which would purportedly spell disaster for the average Greek citizen. More solvent members of the Union, particularly Germany, had pushed hard for the measures, as much, some said, to punish Greece as to bring them back into financial health. German Chancellor Angela Merkel, was accused of sticking it hard to the Greeks, who were stereotyped by some Germans to be an unmotivated, lazy, recalcitrant, funbefore work–loving party culture, whose passion for play had to be reshaped and redirected by feeling the sting of hard consequences for their indolence. I chatted online with a young German medical school graduate who disclosed that she had frequently taken magical family vacations in Greece as a child, which, while relaxing and wonderful, had placed her in close proximity to happy-go-lucky Grecians, who had shocked her for their lack of order, structure, and discipline—qualities that, she admitted, were highly esteemed in her native Germany. She spoke fondly of the Greek people, however, and felt that the culture could benefit greatly from adopting a stricter work ethic. She surmised that this might entail paying a bit more attention to their finances, and a bit less

to Retsina and beach combing. She saw Merkel's actions as painful, yet necessary to instill a little more stick-to-it-iveness in that
otherwise charming corner of the Mediterranean. After the austerity vote, the Greek Prime Minister's website was swiftly hacked by
Anonymous, as was that of the National Police, the Minister of
Finance, and a major TV channel.

The awesomeness of being able to sit there in my Lazyboy
recliner and fire off questions simultaneously to people in Germany and Greece, (while watching buildings blow up and burn
down in Athens) made my head spin. It made me wonder how
history would read if the Romans had possessed Twitter during the
Great Fire in 64 AD:

RomeAnon: NERO had somethin to do w/ the fire up in rome
last nite IMHO—Yo Tacitus U wanna weigh in on this?

TacMan: Imma git the fucktard been spreadin' dat shizzy. My
boy wadnt even there Homey—but when he seen the FB post, he
came runnin home from Antium to set up a OccupyRome relief
effort. Who spreadin' dat shit . . . Cassius?

NeroWorship: Lmfao—that's some effed up bullsh** haters be
blowin up bout Nero playin his lyre and singin up in Antium while
peeps houses burnt up—lotsa smashy smashy tho. moralfags caint
be trusted.

CashIsGud: true dat—your lil emperor fren Nero was jammin
to "Sack of Ilium" last nite all dressed up and actin a fool. totes cray
cray. but he WASNT in Antium, he was in rome.

RomeAnon: Hey Tac, Your boy, Nero is just one G away from
being Negro. Doh! Sriously, I heard it was Christian blac bloc who
set the fire . . . anybody?

NeroWorship: no sense gittin' butthurt . . . haters gonna hate—
gotta bounce. BRB

So . . . I began to get how social media created the platform
that permitted an international groundswell of people to link arms
and connect the dots between the elite forces throughout the
world that collude to determine the living conditions for the vast

majority of us on earth. I'm not particularly bothered that there are rich people in the world who enjoy having more than others . . . that's just a fact of life. I know I am not motivated to spend lots of energy amassing wealth—I'm just not wired that way, and neither, I believe, are most people. Most of us just want to live our lives with a degree of autonomy and some modicum of comfort. But what does gall me, is the realization that the systems the 1% have put into place all over the world, allow a minute portion of society to hoard obscene riches, which relegates a huge percentage of the rest of us to lives filled with disadvantage and suffering. The mental illness of the 1% means a lack of access for many to the most basic needs—food, clothing, shelter, education, health care, and a healthy environment. And that disease must be treated. The world has a finite carrying capacity, and it is imperative that we protect its treasures and distribute limited resources equitably among ourselves, so that we can all survive and have enough. I, and my fellow Occupiers, had come to the conclusion that these sick sons-of-bitches had to start sharing their toys, and we, with the aid of Anonymous, were gonna make them.

Now, through the wonders of technology, people have begun to see a number of encroachments and incursions into the personal freedoms we'd previously enjoyed. It must have scared the living shit out of wealthy captains of industry to see how quickly damning information could be gathered and shared by anyone who had access to a cell phone. Political movements were suddenly born and developed in very short order. Like-minded groups of activists could find each other and coalesce on a moment's notice. As people began to experience and understand the power of social media to alter the course of history, entire nations and private interests scrambled to figure out ways to limit access and regulate content. In essence, the science advanced much more rapidly than most governments' understanding of it. Hence, the cat was well out of the bag and down the road, before sluggish, top-heavy, process-bogged, old white guy—dominated legislative bodies could even grasp what it was, let alone figure out how to control it. While out of touch misogynistic poli-

ticians touted their binders full of supportive women, tech-savvy
social justice warriors and Internet aficionados (some as young as
thirteen) were hacking into top secret websites, amassing databases,
and going for the jugulars of corporate crooks and high-flying criminal offenders in the real Game of Life. As these game-changing
technologies began to figure prominently in political dissent, so did
dampening legislation begin to pop up all over the place. Politicians
argued that United States citizens would accept and even welcome
close monitoring of their Internet activities in order to prevent
another 9/11 from happening on US soil. To that end, Congress
began feverishly pushing to pass all kinds of after-the-fact legislation, like NDAA, PIPA, SOPA, and ACTA. They began flooding
floors with paperwork, which was designed, at least purportedly, to
protect us from terrorists, discourage online piracy of intellectual
property, and stop illegal profiteering from black market/bootleg
trade in such commodities as music, movies, and video games; but
whose additional, (and perhaps even primary), unstated purpose
was to stem the tide of damaging information and put a lid on the
power that came with these revolutionary tools. They knew that
activists everywhere were using the available science to circumvent
them. They saw that, with these technologies, the Occupy Movement had the power to make global alliances that were infinitely
capable of fixing much that was broken with humanity.

As February of 2012 drew to an end, Anonymous declared
open war on the United States government, which it claimed was,
"tyrannical and hurt its people." In a move they called, "OpV,"
they outlined their manifold reasons for wanting to overthrow
the government. Though I agreed wholeheartedly with all the
shortcomings and faults they found with Washington DC, and
their conclusions that wealthy corporate interests were controlling America, I wasn't positive I wanted to hitch my entire wagon
to their star until I knew a little more about them. I might have
even wanted to see something that looked sort of like an election before committing fully to accepting the question mark of
the suit as my new leader. I wasn't ruling it out, I just wanted some

more information. After all, I'd have been horrified if the Tea Bag-
gers had gotten this far with their wacko agenda, even though I
doubted many of them possessed the skills necessary for such an
undertaking. For weeks after the declaration, hacks on the NSA,
FBI, and CIA, as well as other highly protected government sites,
accelerated and became almost commonplace. Shut downs and
Denials of Service were so prevalent among these types of agencies
that even network news programs felt they had to cover the story,
albeit sparingly, and with little detail. Coordinated crackdowns on
politically motivated hackers seemed to begin in earnest shortly
after Anonymous's big announcement. In early March, twenty-five
hacktivists between the ages of seventeen and forty were arrested
in a number of countries around the globe. Later that month, I read
that many of the Anons had been fingered by a man whose online
moniker was "Sabu." Twenty-eight-year-old Sabu—Hector Xavier
Monsegur was the alleged leader of a computer hacking group
called, LulzSecurity or LulzSec. The word *Lulz* is a bastardization
of the abbreviation LOL, which stands for "laugh out loud." It had
become a favorite term among computer geeks to describe the joy
hackers felt engaging in code cracking mischief, especially those
which resulted in DDOS's of high profile targets, like the CIA. A
report that Sabu had been cooperating for months with the FBI
after a low profile arrest in June of 2011 sent shock waves through
the Anonymous community and Occupys everywhere. By early
2012 the United States appeared to have lost all patience with
Lulz of any sort, and began calling groups like LulzSec and Anonymous, "cyber terrorists," as they hysterically decried the threat such
organizations posed to national security. I personally didn't think
LulzSec or Anonymous posed any greater threat to my security
than my own government's annoying habit of attacking countries
that hadn't attacked us first. The US began working in concert
with global police agency Interpol, to compile the evidence which
enabled them to make those twenty-five arrests. Hackers vowed to
remain undeterred by the disheartening development. To illustrate
their unfazed-ness, they broke into the Interpol website and shut

it down briefly the very next day, however, it was irrefutable that the orchestrated sting had dealt a crippling blow to the momentum Anonymous had gained in its notorious spree. A few weeks into OpV, the group decided to indefinitely table the war on the United States government, sighting the unreadiness for the world to fully embrace the changes they had hoped to manifest. They did, however, promise to keep doing many of the same kinds of things that made them famous—that we all knew and loved them for. This promise, while endearing, did not change the reality that many of those twenty-five Anons who were apprehended by Interpol, now faced the same kind of hard time that Sabu had managed to negotiate his way out of by working with the Feds.

It made me sad to hear that Hector/Sabu had turned state's evidence against many of my adored Anonymous justice crusaders. I hated to consider that any one of my crime-fighting superheroes was, in fact, mortal; therefore, capable of cowardice, weakness, indecision, and bad judgment, or perhaps something as mundane as a change of heart—a reordering of priorities. And who could have known the trail would lead so far beyond the initial arrests of the two men in Great Britain, the one in Chicago and the two in Ireland who were known to have been captured based on Sabu's cooperation with the Feds. All of a sudden the Twitterverse was being lit up by people who were threatening and denouncing Sabu as a snitch—a rat and a sellout. In further reading I discovered that Sabu was a family man with two small children. The FBI was said to have applied heavy pressure on him to expose his coconspirators, under the threat of lengthy incarceration, which would have denied him the opportunity to be an active, involved father. It was rumored that they asked him repeatedly how badly he wanted see his children grow up. When I read this I wondered how anyone could be either brave or foolish enough to have risked so much, even for the good of humankind. I contemplated what I might have done in his position. Then I learned he was living in public housing when he was rounded up, had very little money, and was being represented by a public defender. After that, it was impossible for me to hate on him, with any kind of fervor, for doing what he did. As unwise as Sabu's actions may have been, I do understand how he could have gotten so deeply involved with the Movement *and* how he could have crumpled under the pressure. Though most of the Occupiers I ran with were without small children, I often found myself weighing (on a much smaller scale) the potential gain against the cost of my own activism to my family.

Days and weeks of quiet desperation followed the big bust. Tweets filled with threats and recriminations littered the Twitosphere. The hashtag, fuckSabu, came to accompany scores of threads calling for the immediate release of all jailed Anons, except for Hector Monsegur. Ordinary people with little or no computer skills changed their handles to "Anonymous" this, or "Anon" that, in order to show their solidarity with our new cyber martyrs. The hurt and anger that accompanied Sabu's move reverberated throughout the hacker communities, as well as within the Occupy Movement at large. Denouncements and vows to bring down government entities involved with the bust circulated wildly around the Internet. Thinly veiled death threats began surfacing, along with general warnings to any and all other hacktivists who might feel inclined to follow Hector's lead. Palpable fear ricocheted off the walls of social media chat rooms, even as retaliatory statements abounded. I began to notice a general ramping down of the bold rhetoric which I'd come to love and expect from Anonymous. The thrilling days of the ominous videos with the question mark head seemed to be rapidly fading into blackness. The foreboding sounds of dark, tympanic, horn-infused orchestral music which accompanied most of the apocalyptic videos began to disappear from the landscape. I began to long for the return of the Guy Fawkes mask with its stationary lips, hovering atop the crisp suit and tie—the visage which occasionally canted eerily, almost imperceptibly, to one side or the other, as it delivered its sensational message.

Where did Superman go? Did the bandits kill the Lone Ranger? Does Goliath ever really lose . . . anything . . . ever? How's that hope-y, change-y thing workin' for ya? Drill, baby, drill. Bomb, baby, bomb. Surveil, baby, surveil. How in the world could we have deluded ourselves into thinking we could ever do a single thing about the steaming hot bowl of crap we've turned our existence into. We hadn't accomplished anything. Or had we?

Chapter 9

May Day—M1

May 2012

A week in Hawaii had done me good. Sure, I'd felt guilty to be eating coq au vin, drinking aged rum, swilling mai tais, dancing the hula, and boogie boarding with the stars, but I had to admit, living like the 1% in the lap of luxury certainly had its charms. Our ten-year-old daughter, Kristy, was losing her mind every morning as she sprang out of bed and screamed, "Oh my gawd, we're in Hawaii." We were staying in a condo that our celebrity attorney pal, Paula, had rented for us. In fact, the whole pampered vacation was being picked up by Paula, who had magnanimously invited us to come to Kauai for her partner, Woody's, sixtieth birthday bash. Never one to skimp, she had treated us to frequent forays to stunningly spectacular snorkeling beaches during the day, followed by lavish dinners, fireside luaus, pu pu platters, and nonstop island entertainment in the evenings. I did it all. I swam with impossibly gorgeous tropical fish, played in the waves, broke open a ripe coconut with a sharp rock and ate it, saw wild pigs in the brush, and even found myself floating close enough to caress a friendly sea turtle as she cavorted balletically in the warm Pacific ocean

surf. Our time there was filled with laughter and the excitement
of communing with the other friends our host couple had invited.
There wasn't a jerk in the bunch and we all got along beautifully—
though we were all from wildly disparate backgrounds. One of us
was a renowned breast cancer surgeon, another, an upper echelon
career military specialist who was also an advisor to the Pentagon
on matters of national security and cyber intelligence, another a
sought after wedding photographer, yet another a San Francisco
city planner, and so on. Ostensibly, the only thing we had in common was our friendship with Paula and Woody, yet I'd been pleas-
antly surprised and relieved to discover our shared love of nature,
and humanity in general. We all agreed that our planet was in dire
straits and that corporations, corruption, banks, and bought politicians were primarily responsible for the awful state of affairs. All
were open and tolerant, some even enthusiastic, about my passion
for the Occupy Movement. I had a deep discussion with one of
the few men among us, the military adviser, about the power of
nonviolence and the importance of listening to the perspective
of those we most disagree with. His name was Dan and he spoke
candidly, respectfully, even tenderly about his interactions with
Muslims in the Middle East. He outlined his commitment to influencing the American military to rethink its mission and adjust its
attitudes toward other cultures, who many Americans now see as
"enemies." He openly referred to himself as a dedicated pacifist,
which fascinated me given his extensive military background. All
in all the week in Kauai was lovely. Were it not for a late-night visi-
tation by a walnut-sized cockroach in close proximity to my bed,
I'd have to say that it was a perfect vacation. Even the giant bug
had done little to dampen my spirits, as I envisioned the darling
geckos (which were running around on the ceiling, making kissy
sounds to one another) plotting an ambush on the insect and all its
creepy crawly buddies, wherever they may have been.

Before we left for Hawaii, I feared I'd be champing at the bit to
hit the streets and get back to the revolution—sitting on my hands
the whole vacation, trying not to rock and pace back and forth

like a caged animal, but thankfully, that had not been the case. However, as soon as Mary, Pam, Kristy, and I landed in Seattle, I felt a surge of restlessness overtake me—I wanted to be underway fighting the powers that be in Oakland and San Francisco. The three of them were going to drive home as I flew out the next morning to board a plane for the Bay Area. In the three months since I'd left Oakland, after the debacle of Move In Day, I spent much time following the Occupy Movement by smartphone, with much interest and concern. I'd seen police in cities like New York and Chicago ignoring and making up laws as they went, in order to brutalize and arrest protesters who were beginning to show up everywhere to oppose bank foreclosures, wage/benefit cuts, unemployment, environmental crimes, and the like all over America. Cops were arresting Occupiers for filming them, for sitting or lying down in public places, for attending corporate shareholder meetings, asking for their badge numbers, and all manner of other legal activities. They'd even resorted to planting marijuana and cocaine on arrestees to pile on more charges. I'd read accounts of big city mayors up-armoring police forces and buying millions of dollars of military grade weaponry to thwart Occupiers. In Chicago, Rahm Emanuel was reported to have been quietly negotiating with the state of Wisconsin to evacuate the entire city in the event of a full scale riot on May Day 2012, or the ensuing NATO summit later that month. In addition to Oakfosho, I received much of my Bay Area activism updates from a fellow whose Twitter handle was, "PunkBoyinSF." PunkBoy, who was also known as J'Tao, struck me, just as Oakfosho had, with his brazen, in your face, unrepentant coverage of tense confrontations with police during Occupy events. PunkBoy in San Francisco had somehow remained unfazed and above the fray during an expanding backlash against streamers, many of whom had fallen out of favor among Occupiers, who contended that their feeds had incriminated them in charges filed against them by the police. They complained loudly that the ubiquitous coverage was being combed through by Bay Area cops looking for suspects. Petty jealousies began to sprout up everywhere as some indie journos were accused of losing political focus as their popularity soared. Some activists cried foul as people like Spencer Mills (Oakfosho) and Tim Pool (Timcast) in New York City were achieving rock star status and getting job offers, while putting them in jeopardy by exposing details of their activities and whereabouts. PunkBoy, in addition to being highly intelligent, had many endearing qualities, as well as a general ability to break bad in a heartbeat and boldly go forward where others feared to tread. From my point of view, it appeared that Bay Area police were intimidated by him, as they failed to arrest him when he called them out or pushed back against their aggressive tactics. On numerous occasions, I'd seen him holding his camera phone high, while leaning into throngs of police officers actively engaged in cudgeling groups of demonstrators at direct actions in front of banks, CEO's houses, or corporate offices. Not once did I see the cops turn their focus onto him. It was as if they had a hands-off policy with regard to harming J'Tao, even though his live-streams were punctuated with his own brand of color commentary and dotted with expletives like, "Whatssamatter, Pig . . . why'd you cover up your badge? Scared of getting doxed? . . . cuz that's what's gonna happen if you keep fuckin' with Occupy . . . You ever heard of the Internet, motherfucker? . . . Do you know how the Internet works? . . . you know who Anonymous is moron? . . . you know how to work a computer asshole?" His bravado and unrelenting style was impressive for sure, so I established a friendship with him by joining his chat line whenever I saw that he was on air.

After several months of tweeting back and forth, I direct messaged PunkBoy to tell him I was coming back to the Bay Area for May Day and asked him where he would be that day. He'd tweeted back that he would be dashing all over the place, covering the event, and asked if I'd like to join him for a drink when I got to town. After I checked with my friend Laura, we agreed to meet with PB after visiting "Occupy the Farm" in Albany, just outside of Oakland, that afternoon. Laura met me at Southwest Airlines baggage claim around 1:00 p.m., and off we drove to the

"Farm," which I'd been keeping tabs on by way of a tweeter named Courtney, who enthusiastically took it upon herself to keep folks up to date on a brassy move by activists, who had taken over an unused ten-acre parcel of land, owned by UC Berkeley, to create an organic garden commune to raise food and provide housing for their members.

As we pulled into Albany we were greeted by typical city noise; cars whizzing by every which way and horns blaring to make sure you stepped on it as soon as the light changed. Then, I looked forward, and saw a huge expanse of rare, green, open space, populated by three or four dozen dusty, parched people pushing wheelbarrows, kneeling before neat, newly tilled rows of soil, spreading straw, and carefully planting each seedling from the many flats spread out on the ground around them. The sun beat down on their reddening skin as they hand watered each transplant from two plastic, 275 gallon containers parked on the center path. Opposite the main entrance was a large banner that said, WHOLE FOOD, NOT WHOLE FOODS, which pointedly referred to UC Berkeley's intentions to sell the "Gill Tract" to the controversy-plagued, mega-grocer (Whole Foods), which was headquartered in Austin, Texas. The chain's purported plan was to pave over the parcel and build another "healthy" food outlet on this land. Whole Foods CEO John Mackey had recently found himself in a shit storm of his own making by voicing such beliefs as, "Climate change is perfectly natural and not necessarily a bad thing," and also contending that health care is "not an intrinsic right," in interviews he granted to magazines such as *Mother Jones*. To make matters worse, he was considered on some fronts to be ethically challenged, as he was known to promote and sell sugar- and preservative-laced GMO-laden foods as healthy choices to his largely liberal, educated, diet-conscious, clients across the nation. Then, there was that brief, but noteworthy phase in 2009, when Tea Party members found so much to like about Mackey's public political pronouncements, that they vociferously encouraged their members in places like Dallas, Texas and Phoenix, Arizona to purchase a week's worth

of groceries from Whole Foods, in what they called a "Buycott" of
support for their newly anointed kindred spirit.

However precarious its future, the Gill Tract was, at that
moment, ten acres of organic beans, peppers, carrots, onions, let-
tuce, greens, peas, potatoes, herbs, and all manner of edible offer-
ings. One of the first things I did was ask a farmer in overalls and
a straw hat where they'd procured their water. "Well, till Friday we
had running water from the University, but they cut it off a couple of hours before we were supposed to meet with them to ask if
we could stay till the crop was in. Then, when we all went to our
scheduled meeting to discuss things, they never showed up. Now,
we just been filling these containers up from friends' garden hoses."
That sounded like a lot of work to me. I couldn't even imagine
keeping up with a ten-by-ten-foot plot that way, without putting
myself in the hospital, let alone ten acres. As I walked through
the grounds, I was delighted to see kids running around naked, or
nearly so, as they fed, watered, and played with dwarf goats and
chickens in moveable "tractors," which furnished fertilizer to the
rows. There was also a plethora of dogs and puppies who were
allowed to roam in certain nonplanted areas of the joyful environment. A child artist had crayoned a sign asking us not to disturb
the nesting turkeys, who were making themselves scarce to get a
little peace and quiet while they sat and waited for their brood to
hatch. Overhead were gaily decorated archways announcing areas
such as "Ladybug Patch" and the "Library." An enthralling marriage
of industry and fellowship rewarded me wherever I cast my eyes.
There was a small, canvas-covered stage that protected musicians
from the hot sun as they played to entertain workers and planners.
A young woman was giving a free "herbal health for female-bodied
people" clinic from a circle of straw bales, which provided seating
for me, my friend Laura, and the other people attending, one of
whom was an inquisitive man who listened intently as homemade
tinctures and remedies were passed around for all to sample, along
with free instructional printouts. I learned lots of fascinating stuff
about the abundance of easily grown, readily available herbs that

can alleviate a whole host of issues we women have around our unique physiology. Just as we were leaving, four ominous looking uniformed police officers strode in officiously and singled out a man to corner for questioning. I stood within four feet of them as I filmed them talking gruffly to the man with their clipboards out. One stern-faced officer lowered his clipboard in exasperation as he turned sharply to face me and spoke sternly, "Look, could you just step back and give us some privacy here. We're trying to investigate a crime scene and we need you to get back, okay. We need you to cut the camera off too." "Oh, okay," I said, wondering what sort of crime this tousle-haired, Norman Rockwell–looking farmer had been involved in, besides transporting lady bugs without a permit and watering vegetables.

After being told to back off and stop filming, Laura and I reluctantly departed the "crime scene" in order to convene with PunkBoy at his apartment in the Haight so we could share a drink or two before our big day in the Bay. Just before we got to his place, I called to say we were nearby and asked if could we bring anything to his flat. "Nope, I'm good," he said. "I got a houseful of people and just bought beer and food for them, so just come on by." So that's what we did. We practically had to turn sideways to get into his small apartment, since nearly every flat surface was overtaken by visiting guerilla journalists from all across the nation. Some had even taken the time to construct laminated press badges with their Twitter handles on them. "Oh, you're Korgasm," or, "Hey, that's Hicksphilosopher," I exclaimed, starstruck. There were bodies sprawled out everywhere, heads bent over computer screens—fingers flying, as occasional bouts of conversation broke out between tweeters, who were sitting so close together their skin touched. J'Tao had laid out a large large, foamy mattress on the floor of the unit's only bedroom, which was almost entirely obscured by visitors from places as far flung as New York City and Chicago. A chubby, pimply, black-garbed teenager who was sitting against the bedroom wall began rocking back and forth as he excitedly repeated, "I can't believe I'm in

Oakland!" until someone close by glanced up from his computer and said, "Well, no, actually dude, you're in San Francisco."

"Well yeah, but that's *almost* Oakland," retorted the manic kid, who appeared to be slightly off-plumb in some way. "I *knew* it was gonna be awesome in Oakland on May Day," he continued, "so I took a bus and hitchhiked all the way out here from Kansas to get here. Do ya think the cops're gonna shoot *tear gas* at us like I saw on Oakfosho's channel? I bought a gas mask, just in case. Is Oakfosho gonna be there? How close is the Golden Gate Bridge to Oakland? Where do you think the most action's gonna be tomorrow?"

His rapidfire ejaculations did nothing to dispel my feeling that he needed guidance, or supervision of some sort, so I faced him, with some misgivings, and asked him if he was here by himself.

"Let's just say . . . when Georgie wants to go somewhere, Georgie takes off and goes somewhere . . . no matter what his *retarded* parents say," he answered, obliquely.

Oh Lord have mercy, that's not what I wanted to hear.

"So, Georgie," I began.

"*No!* It's *George*," he violently corrected, clutching his head in his hands and clawing at his temples as if to stop it from exploding off his shoulders.

"My *parents* call me Georgie, but my name is *George!* I'm eighteen and I can do whatever the fuck I want now."

I felt a hand pressing lightly against my back, so I turned slowly to face PunkBoy, who began gently tugging me to the overcrowded living room.

"So, I see you've met George," he said, painstakingly pronouncing every letter of the name, almost converting it into a four syllable word.

"Yes, it seems so," I replied, cautiously.

"He just showed up on my doorstep this morning, saying he was an Occupier that needed a place to stay for the 'May Day riot', so what could I do. He's just a kid, so I couldn't tell him no, but I think we need to keep an eye on him to make sure he doesn't get into too much trouble. He's totally broke. He says he spent his last dime on food and a gas mask, so I'm hoping he doesn't think he lives here now. I wonder if his parents even know where he is."

"Well, he's got a cell phone," I offered. "He could probably call them if he gets totally stuck." Then, I recognized Courtney from her Gill Tract, OccupyTheFarm coverage, so I excused myself and squeezed over to her to say how appreciative I was for all the up-to-the-minute news from Albany.

This was an electric, alive, hope-filled, convergence—infused with passion and purpose—ground zero for the revolution that we would kick into high gear the next day. We were going to hit the streets, shut down the Golden Gate Bridge, and "raise a ruckus," just as Robert Reich had urged us to do when he delivered that dynamic speech on the Berkeley campus back in November. From there we were going to keep on rolling forward, gathering momentum wherever we went—to the ports and legislative houses, to Oakland, Seattle, Los Angeles, Omaha, Chicago, Saint Louis, New Orleans, Memphis, Tampa, DC, New York . . . every square inch of the planet earth was going to hear us roar and jump aboard our freedom train. We were going to end corporate rule—to right the ship to create the world that we all knew was ultimately achievable. They may have been able to raid our encampments and shut down our demonstrations, but we were convinced that they couldn't evict an idea whose time had come. And that time was now. Looking into that packed room, filled with smart, motivated, visionary young people who were reaching out and touching each other, gave me a sense that anything was possible. We had attained critical mass and were, at that point, unstoppable. To spur us further, PunkBoy began to play a new PBS Frontline episode documenting the Occupy Movement's meteoric rise to the forefront of the conversation in America about social justice and income inequality. I watched the video from a cot that had been placed in the living room for PunkBoy and his husband, Tim, to sleep on while their bedroom was occupied by Occupiers. My face was inches away from the television screen as I heard excited voices proclaiming from behind me that they had been here, or there, as scenes of unrest from coast to coast played out. "I know that person," or, "That's me," or, "I was right there," were phrases that kept bouncing off my ears every so often as the documentary unfolded.

Just as the show was ending, someone shouted out, "Hey, you guys, listen—I just picked up a tweet from OSF [Occupy San Francisco] that said they're calling off the bridge shutdown tomorrow." *What!* I thought. *What is he talking about. That can't be right. There's a whole apartment full of people here, (and presumably throughout the Bay Area) that came out specifically to do just that.* The next day's plans were so openly discussed that even the mainstream local news stations, like KRON and KTVU, had warned commuters to avoid the anticipated mess if they could. How now, could a message of such magnitude, ordering us to call off a major uprising, be reaching us by way of a flippant, eleventh-hour, 140-character tweet. Why not just tweet everything. Hey how about tweeting your best friend that his parents just died in a car crash. Why even bother with the formality of an email when you've got important news . . . that's two steps more than you need. And direct messaging is time consuming. Just put it all out there on your feed. Let's litter the airwaves with tweets like, "Dr. Mason frm Oncology @Mayo—Yup u got cancer. smh. Btw its pretty fast moving so u shld get up to date on wills, DNRs, powr of attorney etc"

I mean, what in Sam Hill was going on here? The room quickly erupted into a state of confusion as bewildered people, like me, hastily logged onto their accounts to make some sense out of the announcement. Speculation about the trustworthiness of the source began to abound as folks tried to glean who the person(s) behind OSF tweet was, and we wondered aloud amongst ourselves if we could reach him or her. It was baffling to me that no one in that room full of insiders seemed to be able to identify the real-life human being that had pushed the buttons to send that tweet.

Someone else clicked onto a link sent in the body of a tweet that led us to a statement that had come, supposedly, from OSF, outlining the reasons why they (whoever they were) had decided to call off the bridge closure. The main reason cited was that the Port of San Francisco had just put out a press release announcing their own plan to preemptively close the Port of San Francisco the next day in order to encourage Occupiers to call off their action. Since the Golden Gate Bridge is one of the main routes in and out of the Port, OSF was now claiming victory, in the form of a one-day disruption of service in the commercial operations at the Port of San Francisco. It occurred to me momentarily that I may have been letting my frustration get the better of me when I vented, "I just flew here from fucking Hawaii to shut down the Golden Gate Bridge and now some voice from the clouds is saying we've won and it's off? I mean . . . how can anyone call a one-day port closure "victory?" We gotta get out there tomorrow to show the world that *We* are the ones who decide when, how, and *if* business gets done in this country!" Some nearby heads nodded in approval, while others seemed anxious to distance themselves from my rant. Perhaps revealing that I'd just been vacationing in Hawaii hadn't been the best strategy to win the hearts and minds of my mostly impoverished companions, some of whom were eating Top Ramen in styrofoam bowls as they sat on the floor. As I searched the room for consensus, I heard PunkBoy's calm, rational voice in my ear, "Well, Sweetie, it is a victory of sorts that they're freaked out enough to go as far as to shut themselves down for a day *and* I just don't think we'd have the numbers to pull it off anyway. SFPD's been saying they've got an army waiting to shut *us* down if we try to shut the bridge down, and we all know what that means. They'll probably bring out the paddy wagons and the heavy artillery and if we don't have thousands and thousands of protesters out, we'll get creamed. We'd probably get creamed either way." The only one in the room who seemed as crushed as I was Georgie, who seemed on the verge of tears. As the news sank in, he dejectedly offered, "Well, maybe Oakland's got something

big up it's sleeve, or Blac Bloc, or something." Laura Koch and I
ended the night by making a plan to meet up with PunkBoy early
in the morning to decide what to do.

We arrived back at his apartment at 6:00 a.m. May Day morning. We walked the many stairs to his door and knocked. No
response. After a few more knocks, J'Tao's face emerged, bed-
headed bleary-eyed, from the cracked door. "Oh hey guys. Yeah,
c'mon in . . . no one's quite up yet." We hung out as some began to
stir within their sleeping bags or under bedding on the floor. An
hour later, he and two other streamers crammed into Laura's car to
make an exploratory run across the Golden Gate Bridge. A block
before we reached it, we saw a group of police standing around in
their uniforms with their helmets on and their batons showing. At
the entrance to the bridge stood dozens of riot cops, standing at
the ready—waiting for our arrival. Very few cars crossed with us as
we stared out at the hundreds of officers stationed along the entire
span of the bridge. "Yup, they're here . . ." observed PunkBoy,"
there's no sense in trying something cute."

I agreed that it would be unwise to try to resurrect the plan,
particularly since there was hardly any traffic on the route anyway,
so we returned to PB's place and gave the news to the others. Most
everyone seemed to take it in stride, as they hopped onto their
social media and began checking in with others to formulate a
Plan B. After breakfast, Laura dropped me off in downtown San
Francisco at Market Street before heading home to put in some
billable hours, as a lawyer, for her employer. A large, friendly
gathering of performance artists, dancers, musicians, and peaceful protesters was amassed there. Thousands of people mingled
about on the blocked intersection, some with small children, others
with signs, chalk, and washable paint, to decorate the entire area
with temporary installments of colorful scenes bearing inspira-
tional, revolutionary slogans. The sun shone brightly on us all as
we cavorted under the watchful eye of the police, who were maintaining a fairly low profile while patrolling the perimeter. As disappointed as I was that we weren't forcing the issue on the bridge, it

was gratifying to see everyone enjoying themselves, unmolested, on that beautiful day. An hour or so in, I picked up a tweet from Occupy Oakland 3 saying that there was a skirmish at City Hall, and some had broken out windows and were engaged in a struggle with the OPD. I squinted to locate the nearest BART train to head over there quickly. Georgie, who was hovering near me, had just picked up the same tweet, and instantly recruited me to help him navigate the complexities of taking the BART to Oakland . . . and to pay his way there. "Is Oakfosho gonna be there? Are they going to arrest us? I left my gas mask at PunkBoy's house . . . I'm hungry," came the ceaseless prattle of poor, confused, curious, George, who never seemed bothered that I only occasionally answered his infinite array of questions. We got off the train at Twelfth and Broadway, just outside City Hall, and hit the ground running. Indeed, there was a smattering of broken glass evident on the front of the building, as well as a dozen or so police pacing the grounds, but other than that, nothing particularly urgent was afoot. If there had been a confrontation, it had all been resolved by the looks of it, and either the participants had fled or been arrested and were clean out of sight by then. George wailed piteously at my side as he took it all in. Not wanting to witness his disappointment bloom into a tantrum, I put on a brave face, hoping to mask my own feelings of doubt and despair. It looked as if the revolution I'd invested so much hope into might be dying. "Let's get you something to eat. I bet that'll cheer you up," I proposed gaily to my forlorn little buddy with the hangdog face. His mood brightened considerably as he jumped up and down and pointed excitedly to a big fat corporate Burger King he'd been eyeing for awhile, right across the street. Minutes later we were sitting opposite each other, inhaling our Whoppers and fries, as I wondered where the revolution had gone.

Chapter 10

Occupy NATO—M20

May 18-21, 2012

Two weeks after an underwhelming May Day in the Bay Area, I boarded a Greyhound bus in Omak, Washington, to stay the night with friends in Seattle. The next morning, Friday, May 18, I hopped the new Sound Transit light rail link to the airport, and then settled in for the three-and-a-half-hour flight to Chicago. I'd spent those intervening weeks at home, regrouping for the next action, while I planted my organic, open-pollinated, vegetable garden in the warming spring sunshine. I hoped I wouldn't be as plagued by pocket gophers as the year before, when I'd lost nearly all of my green beans and carrots, which were literally being yanked underground, (just like I'd seen in Bugs Bunny cartoons) the moment they were ripe and ready to eat. En route, I thought about all the daunting tweets and Facebook posts I'd been picking up, describing the formidable police response Chicago Mayor Rahm Emanuel was planning to unleash on any misguided fool who dared think s/he could breeze in to Chicago and Occupy his NATO conference without an unpleasant consequence. Rahm, whose previous job title had been White House chief of staff for President Barack Obama, put the entire NATO Summit area in downtown Chicago, on highest threat alert status, and expressed his determination to thwart us in every way possible. He promised to hit us hard with everything at his disposal. It was widely publicized that he had spared no expense in outfitting his law enforcement professionals with lots of new gadgets, some of which were military grade weapons systems that were identical to those currently in use by US armed services in the Middle East. Rahm said he would stop at nothing to make sure the NATO Summit went off without a hitch. He had hurriedly enacted a law making it illegal to assemble within a certain distance from NATO events. Then came the assertions that he would scramble the Internet, deploy a massive, cooperative, interagency police force of thousands, close Chicago Transit Authority stops into the antiprotest zone, and use tear gas and other "nonlethal" weapons to disperse us if he deemed it appropriate. He also purchased an LRAD system(long-range acoustic device) for use by the CPD, which emitted an eardrum-splitting sound that could cause permanent hearing loss, and even possible organ damage, along with helicopters and tanks if necessary. He assured NATO participants, as well as the citizens of Chicago, that he was ready for us. It was dawning on me that the mayor, and the country at large, considered Occupy to be public enemy number one, and wanted to eradicate it at all costs. WBBM Newsradio Chicago was reporting that an email had been obtained from Milwaukee Red Cross volunteers, saying that the NATO summit "may create unrest of another national security incident. The American Red Cross in southeastern Wisconsin has been asked to place a number of shelters on standby in the event of evacuation of Chicago." Although officials at Chicago's Office of Emergency Management and Communication said the directive did not come from them, a chapter spokesperson disagreed by stating, "Our direction has come from the City of Chicago and the Secret Service." It felt for all the world like I was preparing to go into combat—the only difference being, our side was unarmed. I thought there was supposed to be a thing called the Posse Comitatus Act that limited the government's ability to use the military as a police force against its citizens. I was so concerned about the blurred lines between the military and the police, that I did some research, and indeed, the law does exist, and it's been in place since 1878. I googled the statute, which also yielded me discouraging revelations that certain politicians around the country were pushing hard to alter it, or do away with it altogether. John Warner, R-VA, chairman of the Armed Services Committee under George W. Bush, had signaled his desire to change the law as an impediment to effective policing. Former Pentagon spokesman, Lawrence Di Rita called Posse Comitatus "a very archaic statute that hampers the president's ability to respond to a crisis." I guess, technically speaking, the mayor wasn't planning to turn the army on us, he was turning the police into a domestic army . . . to turn on us.

Though I was apprehensive about going, I needed to feel like I was doing something to counter the doubling down on dissenters that I was seeing everywhere I traveled. The language coming from politicians and corporate mouthpieces was alarming to me. New York City billionaire mayor Michael Bloomberg had recently been quoted as saying, "I have my own army in the NYPD, which is the seventh biggest army in the world." I'd also read a request from Oakland police officers, who told local newspapers that they needed additional funds to purchase a bigger arsenal to respond to counter threats like the, "IEDs [improvised explosive devices] and pipe bombs that were coming out of the Occupy Movement." I'd never seen so much as a firecracker being thrown at any of the demonstrations I attended—broken windows, yes, graffiti, yes . . . an overturned garbage can set alight . . . yes . . . even plastic water bottles being thrown on one occasion—but IEDs? Pipe bombs? No. Another recent development I noted, was the growing emergence of partnerships and alliances between municipal police departments and military contractors, (like Halliburton and Bechtel), resulting in disappearing distinctions between cops and soldiers. Fox News, (which we all called Faux News), Rush Limbaugh, and others of that ilk, were representing people like me to be the pitiful remnants of a dying fad—a bunch of lunatic, fringe, lazy, homeless, stinky hippies that belonged in mental institutions, rather than sullying city streets. Conservative on-air personalities such as Sean Hannity and Ann Coulter were doing their utmost to convince their viewers that America was fed up with our inane rot, and had had it up to here with our rants about police states and corporate greed. According to them, we were little more than outliers on a perfect bell shaped curve. The Heartland Corporation had bought and placed a number of billboards around Chicago, before NATO, showing images of infamous villains Charles Manson and Ted Kaczynski. The captions read: STILL BELIEVE IN GLOBAL WARMING? SO DO THEY. The comparison of environmental activism to mental illness, and the association with convicted murderers had infuriated so many, that the outcry prompted Heartland to remove them shortly after installation.

My friends Ellen and Barbara, whom I'd met ten years earlier at one of my Chicago concerts, had offered to pick me up at O'Hare airport, as well as to put me up at their house in Algonquin, (a suburb about forty-five minutes from the city) while I was Occupying NATO. That seemed like a great option to me, so I said yes, and prepared to stay with them. But just before I left Seattle, I picked up a handful of messages from event organizers, saying that Mayor Emanuel's promises to severely restrict access to areas near the conference should be taken seriously; therefore, it would be wise to seek lodging within the city limits, for fear that some of us would find it difficult to re-enter if we left. Could they just do that? Could mayors and other politicians invent laws on the spot that closed off large areas of a city (or country) to people who planned to assemble to protest their government's nefarious activities? What if you happened to live in one of those cordoned off areas, and all of a sudden, you had no public transportation to and from your home, nor could you log onto the Internet, or make calls from your cell phone, even in the case of emergencies? What if, in order to be allowed into your neighborhood, you'd be asked to produce copious documentation proving that you did indeed reside there, which may or may not suffice to convince the police to let you in . . . especially if you looked "suspicious" to them in any way. What if you'd forgotten your ID, or had none with the current address on it? Would you not, then, be able to reach your children to escort them off the school bus, or get into an apartment where you were pet sitting? Was this an acceptable trade-off for whatever security and safety assurances you'd been given?

Fortunately, Ellen and Barbara took my change of plans in stride, and in their kindness, even purchased a tent, along with a sleeping bag, which they placed in my hands as soon as they greeted me at O'Hare airport's, Vestibule 3H. I'd learned online at Occupy Chicago.org, that a downtown church, St. James Cathedral, had generously offered to let us stay on their property as a place of refuge and shelter from police brutality. We arrived at 65 E. Huron, where the church was located, and Ellen escorted me, sleeping bag, tent, and all, through the open door. It was a grand old house of worship, possessing rich stained glass windows and antique oak pews. Ellen and I saw that the church was about a third full, perhaps a hundred fifty people, and everyone was listening to a speaker at a podium on the altar. Relief washed over me as I took in the scene of my temporary home. We were walking toward the aisle to sit and listen to the speaker when two women intercepted us. One said, "Excuse me, who are you?" as she eyed my sleeping bag suspiciously. Though I was taken aback by her clipped tone, I could understand why Occupy Chicago would exercise caution to ensure that I wasn't a cop, or an agent provocateur, or something equally offensive. After all, having just landed, I was still clean, coiffed, crisp, and dressed fairly conservatively. And, at fifty-two, I was well past the age of many of my fellow revolutionaries. "We're here with the Occupy Movement, and I saw your offer to house us, so I was planning on staying here for the next three days." The woman's eyebrows shot up as she tried to contain her hostility. She then turned to her frosty colleague who said, "This is a *private* meeting ma'am, you aren't allowed to join this group." Startled, I looked at the other woman and said, cleverly, "Ummmmmmmm, really? Uh, are you sure? I mean, 'cause like, we were told by Occupy Chicago, on their website . . . that we could stay here during NATO . . . so, like, what exactly *is* this meeting." The first woman snapped, "It's a *private* meeting and that's all I can say." I didn't know what to say next, so my friend, Ellen, queried, "What exactly is this meeting, and who are these people?" The woman began to reiterate, "It's *private* . . ." when her colleague interrupted, "It's Alcoholics Anonymous, and if you aren't here for that meeting, you should go, or maybe, I could take you downstairs to the office and you can ask them all your questions." That didn't sound very encouraging to me, however, I still believed we were in the right place. I could imagine that, in a large city like Chicago, there could possibly be 150 alcoholic Occupiers who'd called a special AA meeting for themselves, as well as for the benefit of visiting alcoholic Occupiers.

Downstairs in a small basement office, a husky man in casual clothing eyed us warily as the AA woman left. I explained to him that we had been directed by Occupy NATO to the church, and that we understood that the head priest had offered us shelter and sanctuary there. The man could not have been less welcoming as he said, "Oh no, no, no . . . uh uh. I do not know where you got that information, but it is most *definitely* not true. I'm not sure how you all got in here . . . but you gotta go right now. You're not the first one that's barged in here today, and you need to just turn around and go back to wherever you came from." By then Ellen's wick had shortened considerably, prompting her chilly rejoinder, "We got in here because the front door was *wide* open, which *usually* means you're welcome, *and* we were told that Occupiers could stay here. The only reason we know your address is because it was *posted* on the Occupy NATO website. We were invited." The man seemed to know more than he was admitting to, as he spat, "You need to leave this place right now—*period.*" Neither Ellen nor I could understand why he was so angry with us, since our demeanor had been friendly and pleasant until that last exchange, however, we simply did as we were ordered, turned away from him, and began to mount the stairs we'd been led in on. "Not that way," the man barked venomously. "You need to go out the *back* door." And with that he stomped us out a small basement exit, which he closed loudly behind us and locked audibly.

"That went well," I said to Ellen, whose hackles were still up. "I'm so glad we didn't just drop you off, Laura. What the fuck was wrong with that asshole," she fumed. "I dunno," I answered, "but I remember getting another text about the 'Wellington Ave. Church,' that said they would put us up too." We got back into the car to investigate that lead. After we told her what was up, Barbara began driving a long way across town, to 615 W. Wellington, where we came upon a much more inviting scene—a group of scraggly, travel-weary road warriors, brimming with as they immersed themselves in the political discourse I'd become so accustomed to in my adventures.

There were blacks, whites, Latinos, queer people, transgender—you name it, all clustered around the closed side door of the church, some spilling out onto the sidewalks and parking strips of the surrounding dwellings in the city neighborhood. One of the first I recognized was a young man named Maupin, whom I'd met in Washington DC while Occupying Congress and the Supreme Court in January. I recalled his engaging personality, rail-thin body, and the mop of unruly, dark hair atop his head. When he'd introduced himself in DC, I immediately changed it to "Moppin" in my mind, because of that outstanding volume of hair. I also remembered the deep husky voice, ever present cigarette dangling from his lips, and the dirty, bagging-at-the-butt blue jeans. He had a craggy, earnest, working-class face, with a depression-era vibe, like Tom Joad (Henry Fonda) in the *Grapes of Wrath*. I could easily envisage him as a black and white Dorothea Lange photo, gracing the pages of her books, chronicling hungry, poverty-stricken Americans fleeing dust bowl states. I pictured him traveling westward among whole families of Okies and Arkies in rickety jalopies during the thirties, as they sought employment picking fruit for opulent landowners in California, Oregon, or Washington state. The sight of him warmed the cockles of my heart, and we embraced like kin as I told him how nice it was to see him. His infectious grin enveloped me as he held out a handmade 99% patch for me to wear. Ellen and Barbara felt it safe to leave me there, as I was certainly in the right spot. Then I saw "OccupyFreedomLa" and Sky "CrossXbones," streamers from Los Angeles, which also eased my anxiety. They'd both ridden one of three buses from L.A., (paid for by some generous Occupy supporter) which ferried Occupiers to this church, which we were now calling, "The Convergence Center." Just then, the side door to the church swung open, and it was announced that the dinner was ready and we were free to come in and eat.

I knew most of them were flat broke, so the words were met with great enthusiasm as famished, tired folks filed into the brightly lit room, which was adjoined by an industrial kitchen, staffed by volunteers who had prepared our supper. The meal was offered to us by an organization called Occupy the Seeds, who had cooked up huge pots of brown rice, organic, home grown greens, and produce. They also provided sesame tahini dressing, fresh condiments, and a whole host of other real foods that were nourishing, visually appealing, and tasty. Watching the ragtag crowd descend ravenously onto the feast strengthened my associations with impoverished, opportunity-robbed soup kitchen patrons of decades past. Jacob Riis studies popped into my head, as I merged this scene with his sepia-toned photographs of shockingly poor tenement slum residents in New York City, after the turn of the twentieth century.

After the repast, I looked around the space and wondered aloud to FreedomLA if I could set my tent up anywhere in the room after we folded up the tables. "Oh, the church is only offering us meals and a meeting place. I'm afraid there's no overnight camping here," was her response. What was with this vexing habit of Chicago churches to giveth and taketh away in the same breath, I wondered, as I mulled over my options. A few moments later, as I was talking with someone else, FreedomLA interrupted and said, "Hey, they're talking about lodging over there, so you should listen in." A young woman had mic checked the crowd to say that we were being offered lodging on the South Side of Chicago by the head priest at St. Sabina's Church at 7800 Racine Street. She said it was only one short bus ride off the Red line, which we could catch about a mile away. Knowing nothing of Chicago Transit stations, I scrambled to write down every bit of information in sharpie, on my right arm, as she read off the instructions to St. Sabina's. It was approaching 11:00 p.m., Seattle time, and I was fried from my long day of travel, so I stood there trying to order my thoughts and gather the energy to walk to the bus stop carrying my backpack, sleeping bag, and tent. Barbara and Ellen were probably just arriving home in Algonquin by then, and I wasn't even considering asking them to turn around and retrieve me. They both worked hard at their day jobs—Barbara, as a production manager for scholastic book publishers, and Ellen, as a talented, yet meagerly compensated photography teacher at a local community college. In addition, Ellen also attended classes in political studies. Knowing their crazy schedules, I'd rather have slept over a heating grate than call them back at this late hour. If all else failed, I probably could have gotten myself a hotel somewhere, though I was loathe to do so. It was probably safe to assume that few, if any of the others in my group, could afford to plunk down a credit card (as if they even had credit cards) for a night of comfort in a big, expensive city, so I was damned if I would either. Just having the option put me at a distinct advantage to many of my comrades and I felt the weight of my privilege in every step I took. A young woman among us climbed the base of a street lamp to be seen as she shouted out that two bicycle rickshaw cabbies were willing to cart up to three people each to the Red line station. I looked where she was pointing, and saw two skinny, sweaty guys, both professional peddlers, sitting on the seats of their oversized three-wheeled tricycles. Both had spent the entire day carting around sight-seeing tourists to pay their bills, and earn the privilege of living in the Chicago metropolitan area. How exhausted they must be, yet here they were offering me and my fat ass, a mile ride to the CTA station—for *free*. I was grateful in the extreme, as my younger, fitter counterparts beckoned me forward to mount the narrow seat with a slender girl named Audra, who'd arrived that morning on one of the L.A. buses, along with a slight, elderly black man named Lendon, who lived in the deep South Side of Chicago—a long bus ride from the last stop on the line. All together, with our bodies and our bags, we must have weighed over 500 pounds, yet our driver cheerfully bade us aboard his buggy, and told us that he too was a dedicated Occupier, and wanted to support us in any way possible, in addition to attending NATO actions in the coming days. Ten minutes later, we exited his chariot, and I begged him to take a five dollar tip, which he steadfastly refused. Sneakily, I shoved it into his jeans pocket as he turned to leave. He smiled back at me, as I thanked him profusely for his personal contribution to the quality of my life that night.

Lendon was a distinguished man who possessed a straight back and three-foot-long salt and pepper dreadlocks, which nearly touched the floor as he sat regally in the train seat. He was colorfully dressed in an assortment of vintage clothing from head to toe. He was a feast for the senses—his rich mahogany skin providing the perfect backdrop to his unique attire, as his mellifluous voice articulated his affinity for Occupy, and his hopes for the future of the 99%. He advised us to exit the train at the Seventy-Ninth Street stop, and then to catch the bus toward Ford City, which would take us to Racine Avenue. He leaned in and lowered his voice, "Just so you know, it is a black neighborhood, but the main priest at Saint Sabina's, is a white guy by the name of Michael Pfleger. He's been there a long time and he's a good man. He's notorious for rabble rousing and supporting liberal causes and social justice movements. He's well known in this neighborhood, so if you get lost, just ask someone where Saint Sabina's is and you should be fine." Until I met Lendon, my only working knowledge of Chicago's South Side, was that it was the "baddest part of town,"

which I had gleaned from Jim Croce's monster seventies hit, "Bad
Leroy Brown." So now, I was adding a Catholic Church named
Saint Sabina's to my base of wisdom, though it rankled me that
I was having such a hard time remembering how the locals pronounced the word "Sabina." I wanted the "I" to sound like the one
in Tina, but no—it was not to be. Every time I went to say it, I had
to back up and start again until I got it right. That is until I came
up with a handy mnemonic that involved me imagining the priests
referring to their Sunday sermons as the Sabina Monologues.

I hadn't seen a section of town like this in years, but as Audra
(who admitted to being uneasy about our surroundings) and I rode
the bus past the numerous boardedup buildings interspersed with
thriving ghetto industries; liquor stores, pawn shops, beauty par-
lors, bars, churches, usurious check cashing marts, Newport cigarette billboards-, and the like, I was instantly reminded of my
childhood days spent in the depressing Omaha, Nebraska ghetto
of the 1960s. North Twenty-Fourth Street, in Omaha, shortly after
the riots in L.A., was not a pretty place. The bloody Watts Riots,
in South Central Los Angeles, had started in August of 1965, when
a young black man named Marquette Frye was pulled over by a
white state patrolman, who suspected him of driving under the
influence of alcohol or drugs. The relationship between the police
and the underserved community was already strained, at best,
but as a gathering crowd of residents watched the officer, Lee W.
Minikus, arrest Frye, they became agitated and angry, eventually
resulting in an insurrection that played out for six chaotic days and
left millions of dollars in property damage, as well as thirty-four
deaths and scores of reported injuries. Fourteen thousand National
Guard troops were called upon to restore order to the area and
a curfew was imposed over forty-five square miles. When it was
all said and done, very few changes were implemented to ease
the suffering of the neighborhood residents, despite the fact that
then Governor Pat Brown and a gubernatorial commission found
the schools there to be inadequate, the housing substandard, and
unemployment rates to be unacceptably high.

That uprising had triggered nationwide civil rights unrest and upheaval, which spread from city to city, until it finally reached the Nebraska town where I lived. In a matter of days, my poverty-plagued, mostly African American, Midwest neighborhood had turned into a shot-up, burned-out, still-smoldering, brick and plywood jungle, newly remodeled by the seething rage that had propelled black folks to rise up and demand change. Some had asked peacefully, while many others were out of patience with due process and preferred to achieve it "by any means necessary," from a color-consumed nation run mostly by wealthy white men, who were no more willing to do right and soften the stranglehold they enjoyed on the means of production than they are now. At that time, as in these times, they wielded ultimate power and control over the quality of black people's lives and were mainly responsible for the deplorable conditions that most lived under. I remember in 1969, seeing a large gathering of very angry people assembled near our dilapidated shack off North. Twenty-Fourth Street. They were on the verge of setting the whole block on fire—again, after a white Omaha policeman shot a fourteen-year-old black girl, who was coming home from the store, walking through an abandoned lot with some groceries when she was spied by the officer, who said he mistook her for a tall, heavyset male suspect, who had allegedly robbed a liquor store nearby and was still at large. The officer said that he thought she was the perpetrator, as he pulled out his gun and shot her dead. His attitude was far short of contrite, and his words had been delivered with indignation and disdain. They were seen by many of us to be more of an explanation than an apology. That incident sparked days of demonstrations and uprisings in the Omaha ghetto where residents had gathered spontaneously outside the police station and chanted things like, "Burn, baby, burn" and "Hell no, we won't go." Those public displays of outrage instantly struck me as the way to go to get people's attention and leave a lasting impression when things were intolerable. I remember my mother listening intently to the local radio station to hear what was happening in our little corner of the world. She'd just come home from her mind-numbing, short-lived factory job (at a place called Components Concepts Corporation—what the hell does that mean?) and was telling me and my sister what her coworkers were saying. The job, which was to assemble plastic gizmos of some kind, required little or no thought, so she and her fellow employees helped to alleviate the crushing boredom by talking to each other throughout the day. My mother was almost giddy when the riots broke out near us, because the conversation at work suddenly veered away from mundane small talk and insipid gossip, which my mother abhorred, to topics that mattered to her. If she couldn't interest any of them in discussions about art, literature, opera, and classical music, then this was the next best thing. Before the unrest, she would come home from work, throw her purse down on the floor and scream things like, "If I ever have to hear another woman describe how happy she gets when her baby pees on her, I'll hang myself." We knew she was not to be toyed with when making such statements. In fact, scarcely three years earlier, Mom had done just that, during a particularly stressful time in our lives where we were living in a neighborhood surrounded by racists, had very little money, and she was trying to complete her college education, so we knew she was capable of following through on such things. Trying to free her from the yellow braided laundry rope she swung from after she'd stepped casually off a chair, noose encircling her neck, had not been pleasant, and I never wanted to go through that again. She was never given to selfcensorship when it came to talking to her children, so, my sister Lisa and I were thrilled to hear her rattle off terms like, "racist honkeys," "pig motherfuckers," and "blue-eyed devils," to describe the fury she and her colleagues were feeling. We were tickled by her gift for constructing ghetto sentences that somehow managed to smoothly integrate bits of classical literature. We found the juxtaposition delightful, when she'd string together phrases like, "Those rabid jackals think we're all just a bunch of animals. Goddamn peckerwoods just shot that little girl down like she was a common cur. Hath not a nigger eyes! Hath not a nigger hands, organs, dimensions, senses, affections, passions! A pox on all those crackers' houses!" At nine years old I didn't know exactly what it all meant, but I do remember being enthralled by watching people who'd had enough, reached their boiling point, and just gone off.

The South Side of Chicago exuded the same bleak, forgotten, broken, hopeless feel that Omaha had back then, and the familiarity of the scene made me all the more anxious to revive some of that "Burn, baby, burn," "Hell no, we won't go," spirit that had so affected me back in 1969. Audra and I got off at the intersection of Seventy-Ninth and Racine, on the advice of the heavy black woman who drove the bus. Her voice was loud and authoritative, making her sound mad, even when she wasn't, and her breasts were so large they almost obscured the steering wheel beneath them, which made it hard for me to focus on anything else, but she was every bit as knowledgeable and helpful as Lendon said she'd be. We stood there momentarily, and saw a large stone building that looked like it might be St. Sabina's, but upon closer inspection, was not. We ventured into an alley where we encountered half a dozen or so young black men, who were hanging around outside a rundown neighborhood bar.

"Come on over here ladies—it's my birthday," hollered one.

"Uh oh." Audra said, quietly.

I walked toward them, smiling, as Audra shadowed me.

"Happy birthday, sweetheart," I said to the hollerer. "Do you know where Saint Sabina's church is?"

"Awww yeah, it's right over there," answered the birthday boy, pointing, helpfully.

"Thank you so much. You have a great birthday."

"Thank you," the young man replied, respectfully, bowing slightly and tipping his dark green Kangol cap to us.

A hundred yards later we stood directly in front of one of the large wooden entrance doors to Saint Sabina's Church. A man that Audra knew from her long bus ride from L.A. was already there, enjoying a cigarette at the curb. Audra threw her arms around his neck and scolded him for allowing them to be separated. Her relief, however, at reuniting with her friend in this strange and foreboding place was almost palpable. I tried the door and found it unlocked. Inside the cavernous, dimly lit church gym were a dozen or so bedraggled, scruffy human beings, lying on the ancient varnished wood floor, all along the walls of the hot room. One or two industrial fans blew at full blast, providing some modicum of relief from the hot, stale air.

Home. A kid who introduced himself as Franklin approached me with a clipboard, and asked for my name and contact information. He said that he was in charge of keeping track of everyone, and making sure we got onto his list, so I happily complied with his request. No sooner had I finished, when he began regaling me with stories of the physical ailments he was afflicted with, which included, but were not limited to; vomiting, nausea, and excessive mucous discharge. He surmised that all of these problems had been caused, and/or exacerbated, by the medication he was taking to prevent him from contracting HIV-from a total stranger he'd slept with the week prior. A sizeable cold sore was blooming underneath the peach fuzz of his upper lip, as he explained how the man had only revealed his HIV-positive status to Franklin, *after* they'd had sex. "I mean—I didn't ask—we were both kinda in a hurry, and neither one of us talked much—but still . . ." he trailed off. Franklin informed me that there was now a course of medication, similar to the "morning after pill," that had a 50% efficacy rate for preventing HIV transmission after unprotected sex. Apparently, though, for the highest chance of success, the medication was to be taken no longer than seventy-two hours after the encounter, which troubled him, as it had been at least a week after the tryst before he'd been able to afford the drugs. He was twenty years old, short haired, zaftig, and clearly concerned, as he worried aloud about his chances of remaining healthy. "I don't know if I should even bother taking the meds. I mean—I gotta take them for a whole month and every time I do, I end up puking in a trash can somewhere and I don't even see it coming. It's like—what would you do if you were me?" I was unnerved, and even recoiling a little bit, at his willingness to divulge the most intimate, even somewhat disgusting, details of his life, however, I did notice how his graphic banter had taken the edge off the hunger that had crept up on me earlier. "What are the odds you'll stay HIV negative if you keep the meds up?" I asked. "The doctor said it's like . . . 10% or something, since I didn't start taking them right away," Franklin answered. "Well, it's certainly a personal decision," I stalled, not really having a definitive answer. "But people *are* living nearly normal life spans, in good health, many years after diagnosis," I offered. "I do think I'd *consider* abandoning the procedure if it was me, since you feel so awful and the drugs have so many horrible side effects." Franklin's face immediately registered relief that someone had given him, what he interpreted as, some sort of permission, to abandon the drug regimen that was making him so miserable. His brow unfurrowed all the way, and he declared us to be a team, which I had no particular objection to, other than being tired and hoping my hunger would remain at bay. I helped him to greet and check people in that night before going to bed, and the next morning I assisted him in waking people up. We'd been kindly informed by Father Pfleger himself, the night before, that we were welcome to sleep at his church, but we were to be out by 8:00 a.m., and could not return until 8:00 p.m.—a small price to pay for all the comforts Saint Sabina's represented, compared to sleeping outside, under a bridge somewhere, in downtown Chicago. I thanked him, and said how much I appreciated the accommodations. With my own private tent and a gym mat Franklin scored me from the basement, I was the envy of all the squatters at the church—the 1% of the 99% as it were. No one seemed to hold my relative riches against me however, since I was older than everyone there, and the kids understood how a fossil like me might need a little extra comfort. In fact, some of them began asking me questions, as if I were the den mother, and I quickly came to enjoy that role. "Is there gonna be a bus to pick us up tomorrow?" "Is there anyplace to store our gear?" "Can you get Wi-Fi?" "Is somebody gonna feed us?" The next morning as Franklin and I gently woke people up with phrases like, "Good morning, sweetie . . . it's 7:25

and you've got about half an hour before we have to leave," or, "Rise and shine, Valentine." Sleepy, blinky, Occupiers mumbled, "Okay," and "Thanks," back at me. There were times when I half expected them to call me "Mom," which would have made me smile. One couple was nestled together, deep in slumber inside a double sleeping bag. When I touched the young woman's shoulder, she began to stir, and a tiny puppy wriggled out of the bag. It had slept pressed against her stomach all night, and nearly fell over backwards while yawning expansively at me, and wagging its curly little tail. The two humans told me it was female, and that they'd found her on the roadside as they hitchhiked to Chicago to Occupy NATO. They tumbled out of their bedding, and reached down into a backpack for some puppy chow they'd bought somewhere along the way. By eight o'clock, we all stood outside the church in the morning sun, hoping that the ride another camper had spoken of would be coming soon. "I dunno," one kid said, "yesterday at the Convergence we waited hella long, and the bus never came." That was all I needed to hear to convince me that I should hoof the half block to bus seventy-nine, and transfer to the Red line to reach the Convergence Center on Wellington Avenue. "Hey guys, I think that the Walgreens by the bus stop sells CTA transit passes for like, three bucks, that covers the whole day on buses and trains. I'm not going to take the chance of missing any marches waiting here for a free bus that might not ever come. If anyone wants to follow me to the Walgreens, that's cool." Suddenly, I found myself standing in the middle of a dozen panic-stricken youths, who wanted to kill the messenger who'd just delivered this abysmal news. "How'm I 'sposed to come up with *three fuckin' dollars*," one barefoot brown girl, with an adorable short afro, no shoes, and a leather halter top wailed. Another, with freckles and long red hair, let out a woe-filled gasp, and buried her face in the crook of her arm so that none of us would see her beginning to weep. Then Franklin and a cute gay boy who'd showed up late the night before, named Von, looked pleadingly at each other, desperately hoping that the other could produce the unimaginable sum I'd quoted, to ride public transportation into town. "I guess I'll just have to walk to the Convergence," Von whispered to Franklin, who said, "Yeah, me too." I didn't know Chicago at all, but judging by the time it took us to get to Saint Sabina's on the train and bus, it had to be at least fifteen miles away, if not more. Though I had previously considered myself to be of limited funds, I could see that I, who possessed not only a credit card, a checking account, and about a hundred twenty dollars cash, may as well have been Bill Gates to them. I couldn't stand it any longer, and began doing the math to figure how much it would take to buy the most desperate among us, two-, or three-day CTA passes. I came up with around thirty bucks, and tried not to start a riot as I quietly offered to purchase them for the neediest kids. By then it was approaching nine o'clock, so we walked to Walgreen's and got in line at the counter to buy the passes. As I waited there with everyone, I speculated that, since it was getting late, we might be better off to head directly downtown and meet up with marchers, rather than go all the way to the Convergence and then ride back into town for the planned Mental Health Clinic Solidarity march, to support patients who were protesting the recent shutdown of the clinic due to a "lack of city funds." I didn't want to miss anything, but quickly realized the blunder, when my suggestion was met with sideways glances and anguished faces. The mysterious reaction resolved itself when someone sheepishly said, "Well, yeah but we're starving and none of us has any money to eat. They're feeding us on Wellington, so we gotta go there first." My general lack of awareness made me feel like an idiot, as I compared mine to Mitt Romney's latest remarks. "Oh yes, I just love Nascar . . . I don't attend much, but I've got several friends who own teams." It had amazed me that those words could come out of his mouth, right on the heels of his declaration weeks before, when he'd said, "I just love American cars. My wife has a couple of Cadillacs that she just loves, too." This was apparently the best he could do to right the ship after it surfaced that the Romneys had a vehicle elevator installed in their garage for easier management of their personal fleet. My suggestion to forego the visit to the Convergence because of time constraints was almost as out of touch as Mitt's latest remarks. It disturbed me to note how quickly a few years of comfort and good fortune had made me forget how hard it was to live in this country without money. At the time of Mitt's Nascar statement, I had shaken my head in disbelief that anyone could be so clueless about the hard realities facing millions of Americans every day. Those comments, along with daily revelations of Mitt's unscrupulous leadership at Bain Capital, incensed me to the point that I'd begun sending out a rash of snarky tweets, with rants like, "Romney" unscrambled is "R Money." Even though I held little sympathy for Mitt, it wasn't particularly difficult for me to understand how he'd come to be so ignorant about a huge segment of the population, but my own lack of sensitivity frustrated me. I, like many of them, grew up poor, and knew on a visceral level what is was like to yearn for things I needed or wanted, yet had no means of acquiring—save stealing, or some other illegal pursuit. Those were the realities that had inspired me to get out into the streets and "Raise a Ruckus" in the first place, yet, here I was, oblivious to their circumstances. I might as well just pack my dog into a crate, put him on the roof of my Cadillac, and go on home.

And so it was, that it began to sink in that many of the activists I hung with were without even the slightest margin of protection against calamity in their own lives. Despite that, they'd somehow gotten themselves to this place, by hook or crook, to oppose the excesses that threatened to steal their futures. They wanted to gain some control over their destinies, and they'd heard that one of the most important actions in a participatory democracy is just showing up, so that's what they did. They'd taken it to heart and showed up, even though they didn't have any idea how they were going to feed or shelter themselves once they got there. They'd jumped off the cliff and begun building their wings on the way down. For them, social justice wasn't a lofty ideal to aspire to— their lives depended on it.

"Why don't you guys go grab some snacks to tide us over till we get to the Convergence, and I'll wait in line for the passes," I said, pushing a twenty at them. Relief dominated their faces as they thanked me, before darting off into Walgreen's aisles in search of something edible to mollify their discomfort. Soon they were inhaling fistfuls of chips, popcorn, and candy aboard the seventy-nine bus that carried us to our Red line station. The sight of them devouring their food like vagabonds in a Dickens novel compelled a middle aged black woman sitting nearby to take pity on them and ask if anyone wanted to finish the barbecue potato chips she had in her purse. They pounced on the offer, swiftly accepting the half-full bag from her hands. It was painful to watch them forcing themselves to slow down long enough to divide portions equally on the way to the church on Wellington Avenue. The woman asked if we were locals, or if we were just in town for the NATO protests (how did she know?). I remained silent, as I listened to them launch into colorful stories about their former lives in the cities and towns they came from. One thing they had in common though, was that all of them had left their homes and/or low-paying service jobs to roam the country and join up with other revolutionaries to act on their conclusions that things had gotten so bad, they had no recourse but to abandon their worlds, and get out in the streets to try to change things. As we arrived at our Red line station stop, the kind woman told us that she agreed things had gotten really bad, "especially on the South Side." Then she told us that she supported us and hoped we wouldn't get arrested. As we poured off the bus and onto the sidewalk, she hollered that God would be with us.

First we rode the Red line, then transferred to the Brown line, eventually arriving at our final destination, 615 W. Wellington, where the Convergence was located. People milled about inside and out, as we entered the building and took in the rows of boxed cereal, bags of bagels, cream cheese, butter, coffee, tea, jams, and other breakfast foods displayed on the tables before us. I worried that my crew may have filled up on junk, but saw otherwise as they loaded their plates with nutritious fare. A wide opening into the kitchen allowed me to see the hive of volunteers who were rush-

ing about, scrambling eggs, slicing fruit, frying bacon, flipping hot-
cakes, and washing mountains of dishes. Nearly everyone I struck
up conversations with had ridden into the city on any one of a number of free buses that were still arriving from around the country.
A few people were still curled up in the corner of the dining room,
after arriving late the night before with no lodging lined up. The
church leaders had relaxed their rule at the last possible moment,
and graciously allowed them to to bed down there, when it became
apparent they had no other safe choices. Spirits were lifted to diz-
zying heights, as the hungry began to feel full, the tired began to
feel rested, and the smokers among us began to share tobacco and
weed. The sun was shining, the weather was warm, but not too
hot yet, and life was good. I mingled contentedly with folks, forg-
ing new friendships, for about an hour before starting to walk with
them to a Brown line stop that would connect us with Occupy
Chicago members who were protesting the closure of vital mental
health clinics that were said to be indispensable to those who used
them throughout the city. I was excited at the prospect of getting
to meet some of the people that I hadn't been able to take my eyes
off as I'd watched, on an OccupyChi livestream months earlier.
Somehow, patients had managed to organize and bring attention to
the issue, in spite of their challenges, and even chained themselves
inside one particular clinic for several days before being forcibly
evicted. I found it difficult to leave my home during that time, as I
nervously observed vulnerable clients, whose heartbreaking stand
was being documented by a handful of individuals who were on
their side. Many of the unlikely activists who had come into my
living room, via Ustream, were also elderly and physically disabled,
in addition to having manageable mental health concerns.

I followed the procession of demonstrators, since I didn't
know which Brown line stop to get off on, but to my pleasure,
we ended up directly in front of the same clinic the patients had
locked themselves inside of a few months ago. We teamed up with
those already in position, and found spots to listen to a few short
speeches before we embarked. I found it fairly easy to distinguish

the client activists from others on hand, because of their endearing, idiocentric mannerisms. The most visually arresting was a tall, dark black man, who was dressed only in white hospital sheets, pinned and draped upon him to look like a robe and veil, along with leather thong sandals. His hands trembled as he clutched a brass topped staff in one hand, and a weighty Bible in the other. A nearby friend called the man "Cowboy," despite his distinctly non-Western garb. He seemed at ease, though shaky and physically fragile, as he stood on unsteady legs and gazed serenely through slightly haywire glasses. He asked if any of us were wondering why he was dressed that way. I was eager to validate his wardrobe choices, but not sure whether it was a rhetorical question. And if it hadn't been, I certainly didn't want to give an answer that would push him over the edge, since I knew from his own admission, that the clinic's closing had deprived him of the care he relied heavily upon to function. As I deliberated my response, he moved on to explain that he had purposely outfitted himself to look like Moses as he parted the Red Sea and led his people to the promised land. He said that he, like Moses, would lead us on the march to show people how desperately they needed these facilities to stay open. He spoke eloquently about the false economy of closing places like this in Chicago, which had the potential to throw patients dangerously off-kilter, and could unintentionally cost the system much more than it saved, in the form of increased emergency room visits and elevated crime rates from those, who, with clinics like these, found their lives manageable and even enjoyable. Cowboy Moses argued that he had been able to live independently for years, with minimal assistance from this newly closed clinic, which Mayor Emanuel contended was too costly to continue operating. His sweetness and vulnerability drew me in, and made me want to make everything better for him. I wanted to defend him against the Mayor and the other city officials that had taken away his lifeline. I also wanted to get my hands on the nearest sledgehammer and bash the doors to the shuttered clinic wide open for all to enjoy and get their equilibrium back. It was approaching ninety degrees

outside as I strained to hear Moses' waning voice above the din
of traffic and passers by. Something on the periphery caught my
eye, and I looked across the street to see a large number of police
officers gathering, with helmets, shields, zip-tie cuffs, and batons,
which seemed uncalled for, given that we were perhaps only two
hundred peaceful protesters. Sure, some of us had signs saying
things like MAYOR EMANUEL KEEP OUR CLINICS OPEN, but the amount
of cops seemed a bit heavy-handed. Similarly incongruous, was
the helicopter that had begun to hover overhead and monitor
our movements. Moses was completely hoarse by this time, so he
wrapped up his speech and began leading us up the street, toward
a large city park, that was to be our lunch stop before marching on
to Rahm's house.

Sadly, our leader was physically unable to march more than a
few feet at a time, very slowly, before stopping to rest, so there
were several awkward moments when all of us realized we'd be on
the two-mile journey to the park for hours if we allowed Moses to
stay at the helm. Respectfully, many among us began to ease up
on him, some patting him on the back, even bowing their heads
or thanking him as they excused themselves to scuttle past him. I
stayed with him until the crowd was blocks ahead of us, before asking if he would be okay if I followed suit. "Oh yes, Ma'am, I don't
need no help, " he assured me. Reluctantly, I began trotting to catch
up with the group. so that I wouldn't lose my way to the park.

I arrived, tired and thirsty, to a lush green opening, which was
halfway between our starting point and the Mayor's house. Like
magic, a rusty old pickup truck pulled up to the park entrance
and began unloading huge coolers, which they placed onto metal
folding tables they'd also brought for the occasion. Like a well-
rehearsed squadron, they quickly set up two feeding stations,
which they furnished with paper plates, plastic utensils, condiments, beverages, and garden fresh organic greens and grains.
Tabouleh, quinoa, homemade dressings, and an abundance of produce, fed those who came from the mental health clinic, as well as
the several hundred more that were already on site for the Mayor's

March. As I glanced toward the edges of the park, I could see almost as many police, standing with their hands on their batons, as there were marchers. I looked skyward and saw that the law enforcement helicopter was still with us as well. Then, I looked out into the throng of people gathered at the park, and noted that Moses, inexplicably, was already there, sitting comfortably in the shade on a lawn chair, as he held court for his many friends and admirers. How in the world had he gotten to the park before me, and how come there wasn't a drop of sweat on his brow, I wondered. And where did the chair come from? Nice touch. Get down witchyo' bad self, Sir Moses. Contemporary music began to play from a sound system that had also magically appeared, followed by political speakers, who outlined abuses foisted on us by city leaders and the megarich in recent years.

Shortly after the lunch break, we were underway to Rahm's house, rested, refueled and ready to rock. We trekked for half an hour, until we stood directly in front of a light-colored, two-story Victorian, with a nice front porch and a decidedly Midwestern feel. Many of the people marching looked like locals and young professionals. They wore clean clothes, were freshly showered, and had combed, blow-dried hair. The signs they were carrying were mostly asking the the mayor to do such things as, open the mental health clinics back up, funnel more money into education, employment, and social programs, and decrease spending on jails and policing. There was one in particular, however, that caught my eye. It was easily eight feet long, and required two people to hold it upright. The bearers took special care to position themselves right on the Mayor's lawn, with the message, RAHM IS A [BLEEP] [BLEEP] UNION BUSTING PRICK.

Oh, I'm sure he'll get a kick out of that, was my first thought. My second was surprise that a man as wealthy, controversial, and high profile as Mayor Emanuel, lived in such an accessible place. I'd expected him to inhabit a giant castle that was completely surrounded by iron gates and guards and the like. The neighborhood certainly was well-to-do and close to downtown.

And its lovely, old, well-kept homes did have lots of appeal—
but for God's sake, his nearest neighbors were only a few feet
away. If his windows were open, they could hear the toilet flush.
Some of them were sitting on porch swings, gawking at us like
we were from Mars. Sheesh, this must be some prized block.
The battalion of cops who'd followed us all the way from the
park did exercise some restraint by staying on the fringes of our
protest, which I took as a good sign. Maybe it was to spare rich
people the ugliness of a violent outbreak next to their homes.
Most of us stayed on the street and curb, however there were
those brazen few (like the sign bearers) who'd pushed the issue
by encroaching onto his lawn.

From Rahm's house, we walked and walked and walked and
walked until my feet were blistered and bleeding. We ended up
somewhere downtown, but by then, I could walk no further. I would
limp a few steps and have to stop and lean against some structure to
get relief. I fell far behind the rest of the group, and wondered how
I'd make it back to a train stop, until a kind man on a bicycle noticed
me struggling and approached me. The short but muscular man was
returning from fishing on Lake Michigan somewhere, as evidenced
by the silver pole protruding from a panier attached to the front
fork. "How was the fishing?" I asked, trying to affect a smile.

"Better than the walking, I'd say," he answered, affably. Then
I looked down the street he came from, and saw a tall, slender
woman, with similarly coffee-colored skin, a pleasant, engaging,
countenance, and a silver fishing pole, identical to his, tucked in
to her bike bag. "Ooooh, shoot, you look like you in a world a
hurt, chile . . . ," she opined, sympathetically. "How far you trying
to go?"

"I'm not sure," I replied. I just need to get on the nearest bus or
train that can take me to Saint Sabina's."

"Oh, honey, that's a least half a mile away. You ain't never gonna
get that far on them feet. Why don't you let my husband ride you
there on the back of his bike. It ain't no limo, but it'll get you there
better than trying to walk."

"I don't know . . ." I replied, I'm sure I weigh a lot more than he does."

"Yeah, but my man is *strong* girl. He ain't gonna let you fall. We been married twelve years and he ain' never let me down yet," she said, winking at him, coyly.

I was touched by the kindness of the two strangers, but hesitant to hoist myself up onto his saddle. Before I knew it, they were both gently supporting me and lifting me onto the seat. In no time, we were underway, him pedaling, me leaning heavily on him as we glided smoothly to our destination. A few minutes later, they helped me down at the train stop and watched as I took off my shoes, which were too painful to wear. The husband then reached into his handlebar basket, dug around, and produced a pair of black rubber flip-flops, which he extended to me. "You need these more than I do, so take them, Ma'am . . ." he sweetly ordered, as I shook my head in disbelief at their unflagging generosity.

"I don't know how I can ever thank you two enough for saving me, today," I choked out. "I didn't know how I was ever going to make it back."

"You just heal them feet up and stay out there and keep marching to get a little justice for us, honey. We lost our house too, and we see what Occupy's been trying to do, and we appreciate it." My train arrived, and I hobbled onto it, wearing his flip-flops, holding my old shoes, and waving back at them as we pulled away. Sitting on the hard plastic seat, I pulled my throbbing feet up to my chest so I could examine the wounds. All of my toes sported blisters of varying sizes, but the most ghastly sight was the oozing discoloration and bruising under both of my big toes. I nearly gagged when the nail covering the mess pulled off easily, with a light tug from my sweaty fingers. Later that night, as I lay in my tent, talking with Franklin and Von who were stretched out beside me, I wondered if my infirmities would repair themselves enough for me to participate fully in the next day's NATO protest.

Tens of thousands of raucous, fired up, Occupy NATO protesters greeted us the next morning in Chicago's Millenium Park.

The infusion of energy coursed through me like current through a copper wire, as I jumped, enthusiastically, into the gathering with both feet. An enormous concrete amphitheater stage provided the platform for a dozen speakers, who educated us about the kinds of activities we should be monitoring closely around the NATO conference. They warned of the dangers we all faced, as international leaders assembled together behind closed doors to make deals and forge unholy alliances with each other, that would ultimately lead to future wars, increasing economic inequality, and the continuing degradation of the environment. Many contended that these types of collaborations would create unbreachable cabals that threatened to make our planet a generally unlivable place, designed to further accommodate corporate interests, and serve only the super wealthy few at the very top. Their conclusions were that we had to watch such organizations as NATO, the G8, the WTO, the Federal Reserve, Wall Street, the IMF, the NSA, and myriad others, with utmost diligence as they continued to exceed themselves in running over us and stealing the world's resources, which, by the way, included our labor.

I mostly stood in place to see the stage, but found that my feet still hurt badly when I tried to take more than a few steps. My anxiety began to mount, as speakers wrapped up, and we were given the overview of the day's events. Our next move was to be a medium distance hike to the closest point we were permitted to get to the actual NATO Summit, over a mile away. I was certain that I couldn't make it, so I sent out an APB on Twitter and Facebook, asking if anyone could help me figure out a plan. Once again, my friend Ellen came to the rescue, and quickly texted me the location of a nearby bike rental shop that could help me out. I hailed a cab that was traveling a few feet from where I stood, and struck up a conversation with my driver, who, as it turns out, was from the West Bank of the Gaza Strip. As we chatted, he told me he was surprised I knew so much about a region that he said most Americans ignored. He gave me his full support of the Occupy Movement, which he credited for bringing attention to the conflicts he said were raging in his homeland. His accent was thick and hard for me to understand, but much better than my Arabic, as he said, "Every person I pick up from Occupy . . . knows something about my country. I am very . . . impressed by this. So, I tell you a story now—if you let me."

"Please do . . ." I encouraged.

He went on to describe the horrors of daily existence for most Palestinians in his Israeli-occupied and controlled homeland. He called the Israelis "barbarians," who stole Palestinian land, and murdered their children with impunity. "They act like the Nazis treated them—however," he blurted, stabbing the air with his finger, interrupting his own train of thought, "each person have the ability to think for *himself*. I tell you, I can say 100% that I know, *myself*, that there are good people there too. I have friend . . . who is Palestinian, like me, who go to door of Russian family, who are Jewish, and who have come to my country to live and settle on my friend's land. My friend—he knocked on the door and told the Russian man that this house was the house *he grew up in!* It was his family's home! The Jewish man and his wife, who have lived there for many years by that time—they say, 'No, this cannot be your house. We were told that we can move here to this place with our family, from Russia. We have been told that the houses here have been built here just for us . . . and that *No* people will be displaced. We made sure to ask them and they *guarantee* us.'"

"My friend, he say, 'Yes, this was my house and it was taken from my family by the Jews. I can tell you that upstairs in the closet, there is a cat drawn onto the wall, which my daughter has done, when she was very young . . . and in the bathroom is a crack on the floor which looks like a fish . . . and in the back yard are two olive trees, which have carved stones at their base.'"

The cabbie became more and more animated as his story unfolded, "Finally, the Russian man—the *Jew*—he says to my friend, 'Okay, okay, I believe you. Everything you have said about this property is true, so you must be telling the truth. And so, we have no choice but to tell you how sorry we are about what you have suffered and what has happened to you. My wife and I feel responsible for your loss. Our children are now grown, as are yours, and you say you are now alone, because your wife has died. Please accept our offer for you to live here with us. We will share this house. We insist.'"

My mouth was agape with incredulity when he finished talking, such that I scarcely noticed we'd been sitting in front of the bike rental place for a few minutes with the meter ticking. "So . . . my friend—he thinks about it, and he agrees to stay with the couple and they have lived together as very good friends ever since then. I get letters from him . . . still. This is a very good story."

"That is the best story I've heard in . . . *forever!*" I exclaimed. The tale was so uplifting my heart was pounding in my chest, as I clasped his hand to hold and shake it before I left. I stood outside the passenger side, digging in my pocket for cab fare, as he leaned over and touched the window. "'This ride is very short . . . you don't have to pay me. Please tell your friends about my friend though. He has taught me that not all Jews are bad. They are brainwashed too—and *everyone* can decide for *himself*, what they are going to do in this world."

My head was still abuzz with his happy ending as I pedaled away from the rental shop, back to Millenium Park, for the march to NATO. The bike was a little too tall, but it had been the closest they had to my size, so I settled for it. My crotch, having been inactive for much longer, was far less tender than my feet, so the occasional landing on the bar wasn't nearly as painful as walking. Thousands of us proceeded to within a mile of the international summit, where a stage had been set up to contain the long line of military veterans who had traveled here from across America, to deliver short speeches, before returning their medals of honor at the NATO Summit. To a person, they expressed disillusionment, sorrow, anger, and betrayal for the lies they said their government had told them, in order to coerce them into fighting an unjust war under a false pretext. Every branch of the armed services was represented by the young men and women in uniform, who stood waiting patiently for their turn at the podium. One spoke of being "robbed of his humanity," after being forced, once in Iraq, to wage a brutal war against civilians. He recalled being told he'd be fighting a "vicious enemy," and that he would be "welcomed" by Iraqis as a protector and liberator. Instead, he had found himself thrusting his gun into the faces of terrified old men, women, and children, who had had nothing to do with 9/11, or Al Qaeda. The awards, which he referred to as, "meaningless trinkets," had left him "broken and hollow," as he struggled to make sense of the whole affair and regain his balance. Another spoke of being told by his government that he was in Afghanistan to "save their women from the horrors of the Muslim religion," but once there, saw how woefully underconcerned our government was about the welfare and safety of our own service women, who he professed to have repeatedly witnessed being sexually assaulted by enlisted men—some even from his own unit. He said he grieved every day for all these women, as well as for countless Iraqis and Afghan citizens who lost their lives in the "pointless" wars. A Syrian-American woman who was Muslim, and also a US Army soldier, described her feeling of shame after having signed up to "serve her country," post 911, only to discover that the reasons she was given were, "all a bunch of made up lies." She contended that she had "only wanted to do (her) patriotic duty," and was even willing to die for our freedom. "And now I feel deceived and tricked—I can hardly bear to face my own family after what I've done," she lamented. One of the last to speak was Scott Olsen, the veteran Marine from Oakland, California, who'd been lucky enough to survive two tours of duty in Iraq, only to be critically injured by aggressive OPD cops, who'd split his head wide open when they intentionally lobbed a tear gas canister at him and his colleagues, while he was protesting with Veterans Against the War at an Occupy Oakland rally. The device had exploded against his skull, resulting in a near-fatal fracture, which had caused him serious brain damage that required months of intensive rehabilitation as he relearned to walk and talk again. I noticed a handful of police officers in riot gear, (some who were likely former soldiers) surreptitiously wiping away tears with black-gloved hands, under their light blue riot helmet shields. They were visibly moved by Olsen's frailty and halting speech, as he recalled aloud his orders to "eliminate the enemy, wherever he found him." "Once I got there, I couldn't find any 'enemies' to eliminate," he reflected. "All I found were frightened people—who just wanted to live their lives and be left in peace, like you or me, or anyone else." Then he, like all those before him, turned his back to face the mile of road which separated us like a moat from the conference itself, and hurled the hardware with all his might toward it, leaving it lying impotently on the ground with the others—despised by their owners—in the middle of the heavily guarded, closed avenue.

No sooner had the last bauble hit the pavement, when the glut of omnipresent, heavily armored police, began feverishly erecting barricades and shoving people away from the collapsible stage, while simultaneously broadcasting harsh orders to disperse. A couple dozen protesters, dressed in black, began pressing forward, storming the stage area, ignoring the dispersal order, and trying to get into the newly decreed "No Protest Zone." Fearing for my safety, I stopped filming and jammed my cell phone into a zipped pocket, just before being smashed between my bicycle and the row of metal stanchions police were erecting. Cops began yelling obscenities at startled Occupiers, who began screaming to be released from the enclosure. Many other protesters, who had managed to wind up outside the crush, began fleeing hysterically from the scene, which cleared a passageway for me to see city buses, loaded with law enforcement personnel, rolling onto a side street. As soon as officers exited the coaches, the drivers remained with the vehicles, which had been appropriated by the city of Chicago to serve as overflow paddy wagons and processing stations for arrestees. I overheard one of the cops relaying that he was, "securing the area to move some heavy artillery into the theater of operations," over his police radio. Once again, I was struck by the use of military terminology, which seemed to be becoming more commonplace, as

I eavesdropped on radio communications between cops across the nation. I was getting used to hearing words like, "deploy," and "neutralize," when I joined a political action and tried to exercise my right to peacefully assemble in protest of my government's activities. I hoped the "artillery" he was referring to might simply mean one of the two LRAD (long range acoustic device) units that the Chicago Police Chief had shown off to a news crew the week prior, and not a Howitzer or live cannon of some kind. I could live without my hearing, but a direct missile hit would be hard to recover from. At the LRAD demonstration, given to the local ABC affiliate on the South Shore Beach of Lake Michigan, the CPD announced they'd purchased the pair of twenty-thousand-dollar apparatus, as a "communication tool," to help project the directives they anticipated needing to give to the crowds who were planning to Occupy NATO. The anchorman referred to it as merely "a modern day bullhorn," which would be used solely to give "fair warning" and "clear messages" to help avoid "breakdowns in communication" that past protesters had experienced in being able to hear orders to disperse during political protests held years earlier. He said that many participants had claimed they "just wanted to go home," but had been caught off guard when they discovered they could not do so, after failing to catch the underamplified police command. Though he did mention that the machines were capable of emitting "high-pitched alarm tones which are not fun for the ear," he assured the viewing public that there was no intent to use them in that way on antiNATO activists.

"We're (now) able to broadcast over a great distance. It's clearly understood, so there's no miscommunication. It's more effective than using a bullhorn," a uniformed Police Sergeant, Chris Bielfeldt, said innocuously in the interview. He went on to add, "We're using this as a messaging device. We're not using an alarm tone. We're using this to communicate messages."

"So alarm tones to those people who might think this is going to be used to bring people down by using alarm tones . . ." interrupted the newsman.

"No. We're here to broadcast messages with the device," came the swift response from the Sergeant.

What the story did not elaborate on were the numerous controversies and issues swirling around the use of the LRAD "Sound cannon." A recent article, posted by Roberto Baldwin at Gizmodo. com website reported that:

"The Occupy Movement has become one of the longest large-scale protests in US history, and all that protesting had pitted the activists against police departments and their crowd-control weapons. One of the more controversial of those is the LRAD Sound Cannon."

So what's the harm in a little noise? Well, a lot, actually.

The LRAD Sound Cannon is an acoustic weapon and communication device . . .

Developed by the LRAD corporation to broadcast messages and pain-inducing "deterrent" tones over long distances, LRAD devices come in various iterations that produce varying degrees of sound. They can be mounted to a vehicle or handheld. The device produces a sound that can be directed in a beam up to thirty-degree wide, and the military-grade LRAD 2000X can transmit voice commands at up to 162 dB up to 5.5 miles away.

. . . that blasts "non-lethal" sound waves . . .

The LRAD corporation says that anyone within a one hundred meters of the device's sound path will experience extreme pain. The version generally utilized by police departments, (the LRAD 500X) is designed to communicate at up to two thousand meters during ideal conditions. In a typical outdoor environment, the device can be heard for 650 meters. The 500x is also capable of short bursts of directed sound that cause severe headaches in anyone within a three-hundred-meter range. Anyone within fifteen meters of the device's audio path can experience permanent hearing loss. LRAD claims the device is not a weapon, but a "directed-sound communication device."

. . . and keep birds from hitting planes . . .

LRAD systems are deployed at airports to sonically deter birds from residing in the paths of aircrafts. The bio-acoustic deterrent helps minimize bird strikes like the one that caused the ditching of Flight 1549 in the Hudson river. In this context, the LRAD broadcasts tones and predator calls that frighten birds away.

. . . but has also been used against activists . . .

The LRAD device has been used on several occasions against activists in the US. The first documented use was in Pittsburgh during the G20 summit in 2009. The Pittsburgh police used it again following the Super Bowl in 2011. The LRAD has reportedly been used against Occupy protesters in Oakland and recently against Occupy Wall Street protestors in Zuccotti Park.

. . . and has potentially long-term side effects.

Use of the device has come under fire because of the potential for permanent hearing loss. Human discomfort starts when a sound hits 120 dB, well below the LRAD's threshold. Permanent hearing loss begins at 130 dB, and if the device is turned up to 140 dB, anyone within its path would not only suffer hearing loss, they could potentially lose their balance and be unable to move out of the path of the audio. The device is also entirely operator-dependent, which could lead to serious ramifications if the officer in charge doesn't have sufficient training.

As a professional touring musician, who's sung through hundreds of state-of-the-art outdoor sound systems across the globe, I must say, I do love a good sound system. I've even purchased a few over the course of my career. However, the idea that any police department in the United States would find it necessary to buy an LRAD Sound Cannon, whose main purpose is—let's face it—sending dissenters (and all other living creatures) running for their lives to escape the ear-breaking blasts, rather than a conventional sound system, is ludicrous. We are continually being told that municipal budgets are stretched to the limits and need to be slashed to the bone, so the reasoning leaves me cold. Any police department in the country could easily outfit itself with enough volume and clar-

ity to knock off a mastodon from half a mile away for far less than
the twenty-thousand-dollar price tag that came with the LRAD
"attention getter." I wondered if investments like these were part
of the reason the Mayor felt he needed to close mental health clinics. If the intended purpose was, as they insisted, to "communicate
messages," there are scads of systems that would do just that, for a
fraction of the cost, although they would not be able to drop you
to your knees with organ-damaging frequencies at the drop of a
hat, like LRAD can.

I knew from having seen the ABC broadcast that the LRAD system would be, "on standby" at the NATO rally, but I didn't expect
to see what looked like beefed-up Humvees advancing toward
us, down the same street that I saw the city bus/paddy wagons
stationed. I also saw what looked like a tank, amidst the other
armored vehicles on that side street. The pain of being mashed
on all sides by police barricades, my rented bike and panicked
Occupiers, coupled with the frightening approach of paramilitary
troops, proved to me more than I could easily handle, so I began
pleading with some of the yelling officers in front of me to let me
out of the kettle. At first they refused, but one finally took pity on
me and relented, after I fell against the bike and tumbled to the
ground, inadvertently pushing a small opening in the metal barricades. The cop didn't stop me when I used the fall to my advantage and pushed as hard as I could to widen the wedge enough
to let me squeeze through. It was almost as scary to be standing
among the officers without a barrier between us, as it had been
to be on the inside of the scrum. Still, I did feel fortunate to be
able to get out of there, as it seemed I'd come close to being flattened. Part of me wanted to ride as fast as I could to the nearest
airport and highjack the next flight out to anywhere—while the
other wanted to witness what lengths Rahm's army might go to.
Once out of immediate danger, I walked with others toward the
street with all the armor, and climbed to the edge of an elevated
apartment parking lot, hoping to videotape the carnage. Shortly
after that, my cell phone battery, inopportunely, ran out, leav-

ing me to oversee, without documenting, what happened next. Our original numbers had declined dramatically after the riot squad rushed in, leaving what looked like about five hundred of us in attendance. At first glance, I judged there to be more police officers than Occupiers, which gave me little solace, as I watched them start swinging their bludgeons at the small group of Black Bloc anarchists, who continued trying to breach the barricades and get onto the forbidden avenue. I looked behind me and saw the familiar round speaker of the LRAD unit, which had been moved into position for possible use. Cries of pain from downed demonstrators registered upon my ears, as a riot cop strode up to me, clenching his baton like a baseball bat. "Get the fuck off the concrete and get out of here, right now," came the crude order, from the husky officer in the kevlar vest. I wasted no time leaping down from my perch and jumping onto my bike, before he took a notion to take a swing at me with his club. I moved so fast that I made bone bruising contact with the bicycle's center bar, before getting up to speed. But once I did get going, I zoomed past the parked buses and armored vehicles until I got a few blocks away and darted up another street, wanting to gain a vantage point that wasn't so tightly patrolled. Every street I went down had cars and cops stationed at every intersection, making it well nigh impossible to penetrate the compound they'd set up. If I wanted to see what was happening, the only method was to head back the way I came, past all those buses and tank-looking things—which is what I tried to do. This time, I only got within two blocks of my original perch before I was stopped by a group of law enforcement personnel, who advised me to go no further, "If I didn't want to get hurt." I took them at their word and dismounted my bike to stand on an upraised apartment lawn, craning my neck along with some mostly black building residents, who had also come out to see what they could. "Oooooooweee, they just tore that little motherfucker's ass up!" exclaimed a dark-skinned man with binoculars, (a resident, I presumed), who was glued to his post. He handed them over to another young brother, who began cringing and grimacing as he gave us a running commentary on what was taking place up the street. "Bammmmmm, Dawg! Oooooh shit! Ahhhh, hell no . . . *No, boy* . . . don't get up—just stay down, Nigga. Ohhhhhhh, snap, they got 'im again. They done beat that other white boy's face bloody. He a damn mess . . . Oh, lookout Homie . . . now there go another one . . ." I wanted badly to ask for a turn on the glasses, but could see the police eyeing us contemptuously from the car, so I resisted the temptation.

"How many are there?" I burst, no longer able to contain myself.

"You mean cops or them other people?" the commentator replied, never taking his eyes off the action.

"Both," I answered.

"Shoot, it looks like there's maybe twenty or thirty of them protesters . . . and like . . . eighteen . . . *million* cops!" he finished, cracking himself up as his neighbors erupted in hysterics.

Soon thereafter, one of the officers who had been leaning into a car talking to his coworkers, straightened to turn and address us. "Okay, look folks, we're going to have to ask you to leave now and head back up to your homes if you live here, and . . . if you don't live here, you'll have to head back that way . . ." he said, motioning behind him.

I appreciated that this one's tone wasn't as bossy as I'd heard near the kettle, but I knew he meant business, so I turned to leave, just as one of the residents beside me said, "Why've we got to leave? We live here. This is *our* building and this is *our* yard."

"I understand that sir, but I'm asking you and the others to go back inside to your apartment now—for your own safety," was the officer's response.

The man turned, grumbling, and slowly walked toward the apartment entrance, as did the others. Another man mumbled under his breath, as he walked past them, "The only danger I see here is *you*." He was closely followed by a woman, balancing a toddler on her hip, who defiantly tossed a denuded pork rib bone out onto the street near the police car before flouncing toward the entrance door that another man was holding open. "I 'spose you gon' charge me for littering now," she hissed, belligerently.

Oh please don't make him mad, I mentally pleaded with her.

"'Asking'—you say it like we got a choice. Hmmmph, I really don't see why the hell we cain't just stand here in our own damn *yard!*" She concluded, all lathered up, as she tried to slam the shock-absorbed door behind her.

Chapter 11

Vaginista

July 18, 2012

Sitting in the balcony of the Michigan State Legislature had an allure all its own. Especially when compared to the hard work of trying to outrun CPD riot cops on bloody stumps and racking my junk on oversized bike bars. I'd returned to Pagan Place two months earlier, reeling from Occupy NATO and the combat zone-iness of it all. On my flight home, I once again vowed to find safer, easier ways to protest, that didn't involve travel, tear gas, or tanks. Perhaps it might behoove me to become proficient at writing compelling letters to my elected representatives, from the warmth and comfort of my living room. For a full two weeks I happily immersed myself in domestic projects that may have bored me in the recent past. By the third week, I was gnashing my teeth and sitting on my hands trying to endure the silences that gave me so much time to ponder the great distance we had yet to cover before even coming close to achieving our goals. Unscrupulous lenders had blinked for a brief moment in time, but houses were still being plucked daily out from under desperate families. Big Oil, gas, and coal were still providing us with reams of nightly news footage featuring oil-soaked marine life, flaming faucets, and destroyed riparian ecosystems. Wall Street bankers and corporate CEOs were still reaping outrageous profits while labor unions got crushed under the pressure to accept takeaways in order to placate the "job givers." And the country's highest legislative body was still earning its nickname, the "Supreme Koch."

I lay in bed at night, restless and heartbroken, dreaming of new ways to foment the revolution and restart the momentum we had in September, 2011. Right about that time, an interesting/infuriating story was making the rounds on the mainstream media. In a June session of the legislative House, Michigan Representative, democrat Lisa Brown had taken the floor to voice her opposition to HB5711, a republican-authored bill that would essentially make the cost of abortion prohibitive by imposing so many new regulations on providers, they could no longer practice the procedure. In her concluding remarks she said, "I'm flattered you're all so interested in my vagina, but no means no." White, male, republican speaker of the house, Jase Bolger had been so inflamed by her indecorous utterance of the "V" word, that he had exploded into a fit of gavel pounding, declaring Ms. Brown to be "out of order," whereupon he informed her that she was no longer allowed to speak. The wave of indignation that ensued washed like a tsunami over the bodies and minds of women nationwide, resulting in five thousand angry Lisa Brown supporters descending, like hornets, on the state capitol steps to rebuke the offending men. Though Americans are notorious for their short attention spans, I vowed to attempt to revive the conversation about the "War on Women," by theatrically disrupting the next legislative session on July 18. To that end, I began working my social network to see if there was any interest in helping me put together a demonstration in Lansing, Michigan for the reconvening of the state Legislature on July 18. A Washington State woman named Diane Jhueck answered the call, which got the ball rolling for a direct action I dubbed, "Twattergate." To prepare for any eventuality, I procured a used, king-sized bedsheet, which I converted into a giant banner, emblazoned with the enigmatic blood red message, VAGINAS ARE REVOLTING. Diane, who predicted the need, created a website for the occasion, whose address she suggested I paint on the bottom of the sign. Before long we had carved out a plan to assemble a small choir in the balcony of the legislative chamber, which would leap to its feet when the signal was given and erupt into a loud song and dance routine. Our aim was to infuriate and embarrass Speaker of the House Jase Bolger, along with the bill's author, Bruce Rendon and their other republican colleagues, whom we saw as arrogant, controlling, and out of line, in the censure of Representatives Brown and Byrum. Our choir consisted of ten women from the Lansing area, as well as one man, (our lone Vagangsta), who were all set to launch into the song, "Vagina Yeah Yeah Yeah," which I had written to the tune of the Beatles song, "She Loves You." The lyrics were:

> Vagina yeah yeah yeah, vagina yeah, yeah yeah,
>   vagina yeah yeah yeah yeah
> We think you lost your mind, when you told her
>   what she couldn't say
> It's her we're thinking of—it's why we came to sing
>   today
> She said vagina—and you know that can't be bad
> She said vagina—and you know you should be
>   glad—oooh
> Vagina yeah yeah yeah, vagina yeah yeah yeah
> With a rep like that you know you should be glad
> You good ole' boys are through and you can't push
>   us around
> 'Cause you may have the floor but we've got Lisa
>   Brown
> She said vagina—and you know that can't be bad
> She said vagina—and you know you should be
>   glad—wooo

CHORUS

We think that you're absurd, and we think you ought
    to know
If you can't say the word, then we think you ought
    to go
She said vagina—and you know that can't be bad
She said vagina—and you know you should be
    glad—wooo

I recruited my friend, PunkBoy, to accompany me to Michigan and livestream the day's festivities, so that others around the nation could watch our antics. The rehearsal we scheduled the night before went well so we met up the next day on the steps of the Capitol Building for the real thing. Several speeches were already scheduled to take place prior to the beginning of the session, which we hoped would inspire us to deliver a flawless performance. Coincidentally, an antifracking rally was also taking place there at the same time, which I threw myself wholeheartedly into before our special serenade. The leader of the group of sign waving "fracktivists," gave a sobering description of the frightening consequences that came with hydraulic fracturing of shale gases buried deep beneath the earth's surface. A cluster of moms, calling themselves "lactivists" held their babies to their bosoms to nurse, while standing next to signs bringing attention to the hostility they felt when trying to breastfeed in public. Planned Parenthood had a booth surrounded by employees and patrons who passed out flyers and engaged in conversation with others. Next up was Representative Barb Byrum, who spoke compellingly about the raw deal women get when men take control of their health care and reproductive rights. I conspicuously displayed my, "Vaginas Are Revolting," bedsheet, twenty feet in front of her while she spoke, which guaranteed its inclusion on the local nightly newscast. As her speech wound to a close she bade us accompany her to Bolger's office to deliver the 115,000 signatures she'd gathered from her constituency, demanding an apology from the Michigan Speaker of the House. PunkBoy and I positioned ourselves toward the front of the pack so we could witness, firsthand, his reaction upon receiving the package. Ms. Byrum swung the door open wide to admit us, as a startled aide named Ari, swallowed a gasp and backed into a corner of the office. His mouth remained open as Representative Byrum asked the receptionist if the Speaker was available. "No, I'm sorry, he was called away," she replied, patronizingly, through the plastic smile glued on her face.

"Is there any chance you could get ahold of him to talk with us?" asked Byrum.

"I'm afraid not," she dripped, apologetically.

Barb then turned to face us, shrugged her shoulders, and said, "Well, I guess Mr. Bolger is too busy for us today."

"Awww," we chimed, in unison.

"There you have it," concluded the Rep. So . . . thank you all so much for coming, and there's probably room in the chamber for some of you to sit in on the session if you like."

PunkBoy and I turned to exit the office, elbowing each other gleefully about the good fortune to have an invitation to the session. We turned to our choir, who comprised a large portion of the audience, and beckoned them to accompany us up to the balcony. We sat in nervous silence as roll was called, followed by a prayer, which raised eyebrows within our ranks. The prayer leader asked us all to bow our heads in silence, as he prayed to the Lord God for wisdom and guidance in performing his legislative duties. "So much for the separation of church and state," I whispered to PB. "Right," he agreed, fixing his camera on the scene. The wooden oak bench seats were far from crowded as I scanned our environs for signs of future trouble. A pasty-faced, plump white guy stood in his security guard uniform, with his head bowed next to the entrance behind me on the right. On my left was a handful of cherubic teens, who were sitting together in their Sunday best, in close proximity to some of our members. After the prayer ended, the man at the podium gestured upward to direct the room's attention to the young people beside us, who, he reported, had been selected to attend the session as a reward for having distinguished themselves in an interstate choral competition.

"Maybe they wanna sing with us," joked PunkBoy under his breath, as we sat poised for our big debut. An appreciative silence fell over the room as the legislators took time for us to reflect on the kids' achievements. I spotted Lisa Brown looking radiant in a pink blouse and paisley skirt that gave me the courage to proceed. Nervous grins were still frozen on the youngsters' faces when we seized the moment. "One, two, three . . .Vagina yeah yeah yeah." Our voices carried well, enhanced by the natural reverb the aged wood afforded us. All heads in the room whipped around to stare in astonishment at the spectacle. My breathing became labored with the exertion of projecting my vocals, coupled with the extreme energy expenditure of executing the wild gesticulations that accompanied my singing. They were all contributing factors that served to take their toll on my flagging stamina. After the second chorus I glared imploringly at the security guard, who, by that time was doubled over in hysterics, wiping tears from the corner of his eye. I criticized myself, roundly, for not being in better physical shape, as I tried to will the amused employee to draw his gun and shoot me dead, rather than force me to continue the exhausting performance to its conclusion. The guard's giggling turned to snorting guffaws as he pounded the balcony railing, struggling to straighten himself up and catch his breath. His unexpected reaction, combined with our animated delivery, created a party atmosphere, which prompted some representatives to go as far as to clap when we finished, while many of the older white men greeted our outburst with shaking heads and scowls of disapproval. Spent, I collapsed onto the bench, waiting in vain for the expulsion that never came.

After resting for a while, we silently communicated with hand signals, and rose as a team to meet outside. Once on the Capitol lawn, we hugged one another and doled out congratulations to each other for our bravery. None of us had expected to get through the whole song, uninterrupted, which contributed to the general merriment we felt. One excited Vaginista pulled me to her and gushed, "Gosh Laura, that was a blast. I had so much fun with you today, and I meant to bring this up to you earlier, but did you ever notice how the phrase, 'Vaginas are Revolting,' could maybe be misconstrued by some people." Her quizzical expression contained not even the slightest hint of playfulness, as it dawned on me that the intentional irony of the double entendre had completely evaded her, so I hid my incredulity and tried to say nothing that would make her feel foolish. Hugs were exchanged before going our separate ways to tell the story to our friends and families. PunkBoy and I drove our rental car back to the nearby home of Yvonne LeFave, who'd graciously volunteered to host us during our stay in Lansing. We tossed back a few beers as she listened, with laughter in her eyes, to our sordid tale. "I just can't believe Jase didn't whip out his gavel and pound us out of there," marveled PunkBoy.

"Me neither," I concurred. "But he still doesn't get it. Maybe we should find out where he lives and take our banner to his house tomorrow."

PunkBoy nodded his approval for the deliciously juvenile prank, and the next day we embarked on our journey to the Speaker's home on 216 Mansion Street, in the neighboring town of Marshall, Michigan. At first I tried to drape the unwieldy cloth over a bush, but a stiff breeze kept dislodging it from its moorings. There were cars in the driveway, which made us both nervous, and the large picture windows in the living room were adorned with lacy curtains, that appeared to part occasionally as we mulled over our options.

"How about you hang it between the columns on the front porch," PunkBoy suggested, impishly.

"I don't know . . . his neighbors are probably all watching us, and tons of cars are going by. I bet you anything we're about to get busted," I worried.

"Yeah . . . well, it's up to you, my friend."

Steeling myself to the risks, I hopped up onto the deck and secured the sheet onto the perfectly spaced supports on the porch. I paused briefly to capture the image on my iphone along with the declaration, "My name is Laura Love, and I just tied that banner [pointing] to Speaker of the House, Jase Bolger,'s actual *house!* I did that! Vaginas are Revolting! Expect us." Pleased with myself, I darted back into the driver's seat of the car, where PunkBoy sat filming the hijinks. "Jeez, whaddya have to do to get arrested in this town!" I squealed mirthfully as we peeled out of the space.

Chapter 12

Expect Us

July 2012—Intentional

I was still chuckling to myself at home the next week, when I picked up an email from a Michigan newspaper reporter, who had taken the time to jot down the website address I painted on the sheet. I called him back to learn that our mischief had caused quite a stir among republican men in Michigan, who were now calling on their democratic counterparts to draft a formal letter of apology, distancing themselves from the banner prank, which they speculated, might have been instigated by one of them. The democratic reps had bristled at the idea, claiming the allegations to be preposterous and unfounded. One democrat rolled his eyes when talking to a local reporter as he scoffed, "For goodness sake, she gave her name when she posted her video all over the Internet, why don't they just go after *her*?" Speaker Jase Bolger was said, by the reporter, to be livid that a woman would have the temerity to violate a man's private space, impose her beliefs on him, and infringe on his rights. "Well now he knows how it feels!" I shouted, triumphantly, into the phone.

While the blowback from our Twattergate caper thrilled me no end, it did nothing to ameliorate my fears that the Occupy Movement had seen its greatest days, and the revolution that I'd poured my heart and soul into, was dying. Few of our encampments still remained, having been crushed with overwhelming force that included chemical dispersants, concussion grenades, rubber bullets, armored tanks, helicopters, M-4 assault rifles, inflatable cages, and even an LRAD device. Municipal police departments across the country had thrown everything they had at us. I'd been shocked by the look and feel of modern police forces. We'd been chased, gassed, shot at, kettled, clubbed, cuffed, and caged and we were tired. Some of us were bone weary from the effort.

The most common police response to Black Bloc anarchist vandalism had been to stand aside and allow the perpetrators to escape, preferring to terrorize and arrest thousands of peaceful protesters instead, often beating them senseless in the process. Infighting had invariably broken out between divergent factions of Occupy—some insisting on a peaceful movement, while others wanted to employ a diversity of tactics, including destruction of property and other retaliatory measures against police armies and the power elite. Tensions between anarchists and pacifists had reached a fever pitch after the scenario of small groups of Black Bloc rabble rousers drawing firepower to the majority of us began to play itself out over and again across the nation.

Some live streamers had imploded under the pressure of instant stardom, accompanied by the brutal onslaught of vicious trolls and jealous rivals. Oakfosho vanished entirely from the picture, after having been pilloried by Occupy Oakland members for threatening to turn the camera on them for throwing plastic water bottles at police who were poised to harm us. His trolls had come out of the woodwork with messages like, "Get a job and take a bath," as well as brutal personal insults, such as, "Hey triple chin, why don't you put that camera down and go Occupy a salad," and, "Hey moralfag, you turn us in, and it'll be the last thing you ever do." OccupyFreedomLa had her iphone ripped from her hands by an unknown assailant, who ran through a rally and was never caught. Oakland Elle had been arrested for standing outside a jail and livestreaming while trying to reason with police to release unlawfully detained protesters. Outspoken, informed, intelligent Bella Eiko of Occupy Oakland had made a tearful retreat from political activism, after tweeting messages from a City Council meeting lamenting that Oakland's plans to institute NYPD-style, "Stop and Frisk" policies would poison the future for her unborn son, who would mature to "match the profile" of the young black men being thrown into prison for life every day in America. Police forces nationwide adopted a "hands off" policy toward the most famous streamers, fearing that all hell would break loose if their army of adoring fans and fellow occupiers saw them roughed up and hauled in. Oakfosho, Punkboy, and Tim Pool(@Timcast) from New York City, were among the superstars of independent journalism who were allowed to operate, largely unscathed, throughout Occupy's heyday. Their raw footage and unedited comments were a breath of fresh air to activists who were fed up with corporate news coverage, or the lack thereof. Television news networks, such as, FOX, CNN, and MSNBC, had begun complaining they were losing market share to the amateur feeds. They began looking for creative ways to stop the hemorrhaging. Some desperate networks had even resorted to plucking indie footage from the Internet and airing it as their own, since streamers gave unlimited access to viewers and had no copyright protections on their work. But by this time, the cat was out of the bag and we, as consumers, had already tasted the sweet fruit of truth, and many of us were acquiring nearly all of our information from sources unbeholden to corporate bosses. Rumors that lucrative employment offers had been extended to a few wildly popular guerilla journalists were confirmed by those very journalists, who tweeted that they had declined to accept them. Television news programs struggled to remain relevant in light of the reality that some postings by Anonymous were garnering hundreds of thousands and even millions of views as they made their way around a shrinking planet in a matter of seconds.

Many Anons and other cyber activists that had been apprehended and locked up were now facing years of costly court appearances, as well as lengthy prison time. Government agencies had rounded them up like cattle, in ostentatious displays of force, coming down so hard on them that a few, like Aaron Swartz, would be unable to handle the stress and would take their own lives. The United States Department of Homeland Security proclaimed them a threat to our national interests, and formed special committees to deal with what they were calling "cyber terrorism." America lost some of her best and brightest minds—talented people, whose extraordinary powers could have just as easily been harnessed to further our own standing in the realm of computer science and Internet technology, had they not been locked up. It is tragic to consider that many of these brilliant young citizens concluded that their government had so betrayed them, they were better served by risking everything and working against it rather than for it.

College students had been assaulted, handcuffed, and pepper sprayed at close range by campus police, for daring to sit their ground and plead with wealthy chancellors to consider their plight. They asked these officials, who all too often did double duty on the boards of major financial institutions, to recognize that they held their futures in their hands. They took their case directly to the wealthy decision makers, who controlled their fate, asking them to understand how the skyrocketing tuitions that lined their pockets, acted also to saddle the young students with unpayable debt and severely limit their choices.

At several points during and after my tenure with the Occupy Movement, I'd been gripped by several crises of confidence. As I lay in a Seattle emergency room, unable to talk or sing, inhaling steroids and laboring to breathe, after OPD tear gas triggered an unshakeable asthma attack, I wondered if it was worth it. As I tuned in to one of my favorites, #OO's Bella Eiko, crying pitifully after revealing that what little money she earned working three jobs, had gone toward her cell phone bill and its costly data plan, which allowed her to livestream color commentary of the revolution, and I wondered if it was worth it. She implored anyone who watched her fiery, gritty street coverage, to send any sum of money to help cover some of her other financial obligations that month. By her own admission, her phone had become one of her most precious possessions, so she had prioritized that bill over others, because livestreaming had been the only thing that enabled her to keep her sanity in a world of eroding rights, extreme wealth inequality, legalized racism, wholesale planetary destruction, and vanishing freedoms. It was almost more than I could bear, listening to her explain how, although she put in over forty work hours each week, she still did not have the funds to continue her education, pay her student loans, put gas in her dying automobile, pay rent, or buy health care.

A number of my favorite activists had dropped everything to jump into the Occupy Movement. Some had immersed themselves so deeply in the culture that they'd foregone all other pursuits. One such person was a woman named Amber Lyon, who was reputed to have quit her high-paying day job as a CNN correspondent to hit the streets with little more than her iphone and a Ustream account. But these defections from civilized society—these elopements from obedience, did not come without heavy psychological consequences. During one particular Ustream broadcast, Oakfosho looked as if he was on the verge of tears as he read the same chat line comments we too could plainly see, questioning his motives and making fun of his weight. Though he showed a fierce indifference to peril when confronting out-of-control cops delivering savage blows to dissenters, I knew from closely monitoring him, that he was also emotionally fragile, and ill-equipped to bounce back easily from the hate-filled remarks. His backstory included graduating with honors from a California University after obtaining a master's degree in Business Administration, only to find himself drowning in debt, stuck in a low-paying service job, unsure of himself, and depressingly overweight. He'd pulled himself, up by his bootstraps and started exercising in earnest at a local gym, spending nearly every non-work moment running laps and pumping iron. His affability, unfailing kindness, and dogged determination to get physically fit had gotten the attention of the facility's manager, who encouraged Spencer to apply for a job opening that they'd recently posted. His effort and dedication paid off, and he was able to shed nearly a hundred pounds before paying a visit to the Occupy Oakland encampment. He arrived at Oscar Grant Plaza shortly after Marine Scott Olsen made headlines by narrowly surviving the impact of the exploding tear gas canister, maliciously thrown by the OPD.

Prior to that, his main online presence had been as a rabid sports fan. Most of his Internet communications had been focused on lively discourse around his beloved Oakland Raiders and athletics. Spencer Mills instantly demonstrated himself to be a knowledge-able, caring, intuitive journalist, and became famous overnight after his first Occupy Oakland broadcast on November 2, 2011, the day of the General Strike/Port shutdown. He'd been bowled over by the unanticipated reception, and recoiled from the harsh glare of the spotlight that seemed to give others license to take cruel potshots and throw flaming daggers at him. The blows had taken a huge toll on his public and private life, prompting him to abandon his routine, and eventually causing him to regain the weight he'd so painstakingly lost. Ultimately, the online battering wounded him, despite repeated warnings by friends and admirers alike, for everyone to simply focus on the revolution and ignore the critics. "Don't Feed the Trolls" became the mantra of many #OO followers, urging everyone on board not to encourage the haters by responding to their taunts, even in defense of our dear comrade, whose name had become synonymous with Occupy Oakland. The pressure levelled him and sent him staggering for the shelter of his former life. I had to force myself to accept his decision to leave and not beg him to return. As I watched him dive back into the world of debating the merits of professional sports teams, I felt hollow and jealous, as if those players had somehow stolen my hero from me. I fought the selfish compulsion to call him up and tell him how much more we needed him than they did—to remind him how few sports teams there would even be to watch if we allowed the 1% to continue robbing us blind and fracking the planet to smithereens. It was almost as if he'd died. I cursed myself for once thinking that it would almost be better if he had died. At least we wouldn't be left with all these unanswered questions about why he dropped out of our revolution. But hard as his departure had been to accept, it was much easier than reading the sad, defeated tweets coming from his Twitter account in response to other fans who had not resisted the temptation to throw themselves at his feet and wrap their arms around his ankles pleading with him to come back. His life was in shambles and his heart was broken. In the end, his legions of friends and fans had not been able to lift him out of the abyss. He was done.

When I got home from my last planned action, (Twattergate— July 2012) I had what can best be described as a combination of PTSD, withdrawal, and a general feeling of letdown and sadness. I felt rudderless and adrift—almost as if I'd just broken up with a long time lover or prematurely lost a treasured friend. I didn't know what to do with myself. I was financially broke, having spent many thousands of dollars racing across the nation from one hotspot to another, foregoing my musical career by not writing songs, rehearsing, or touring with the band. I felt as if the critics, in some respects, may have been right in telling us to go home, take a bath, and get a job. We were said by them to be lazy, bratty, and spoiled—unlikable and ungrateful for the opportunities this country had given us. We had goaded law enforcement into action and gotten what we asked for when we were beaten, sprayed, locked up, and fined. It took me awhile to shake myself out of those doldrums. Punkboy and I spoke on the phone every so often and I never lost my constant Twitter and Facebook contact with almost all of my coconspirators, from livestreamers to street activists and Anons worldwide. I owed them an unpayable debt for not only keeping me safe when the tear gas and rubber bullets started flying, but also teaching me how to use my smartphone by scrupulously honoring my repeated requests to "tell me, as if I were a two-year-old," how to perform such mundane tasks as sending out a tweet, or posting a video to YouTube or Facebook.

But little by little, I started to pick up the pieces and reconstruct my life. I spent a lot of the following winter thinking about what I'd learned and what to do with that information. It was hard for me to focus on any one thing and compartmentalize all the knowledge I'd gotten about how our country and the world works in the realms of banking, farming, the stock market, big business, branches of government, etc. I was frustrated that we hadn't come away with a tidy, quantifiable victory that could be summed up in a few pages of a history book—that encapsulated our entire struggle for social, economic, and environmental justice. I yearned for a clean sentence that sounded similar to: "The Civil war ended slavery with the Emancipation Proclamation, or World War II defeated Hitler and freed the Jews." Perhaps, "The Occupy Movement ended corporate corruption and saved the world." I moped about that for awhile, until I was sick of myself, and then began taking inventory to see what others were doing to move on and make sense of what had happened to us. In essence, it looked as if many viewed their days in Occupy foxholes as a smorgasbord to sample areas of activism they wanted to acquaint themselves with or already felt passionate about. They floated around, as I did, from issue to issue, march to march, throwing themselves into whatever worthwhile cause was being protested right then, but filing the most compelling things we learned and people we met to revisit and get to know better when things calmed down. We were all fed up and angry about a host of worrisome conditions that exist today, and none of us seemed inclined to limit ourselves to any one concern. They treated the experience as a primer in civil disobedience and personal empowerment.

One such individual was Kshama Sawant. After Seattleites set up their own OWS encampment at the downtown campus of Seattle Central Community College, Sawant, who'd already been a long time social/economic justice advocate, showed up to join in the struggle. She did the same things most of us did—marched against capitalist excesses and the corporatocracy, risked injury and arrest, and spoke with all walks of life from the downtrodden to the wellheeled. Wherever she spoke, she put her own socialist beliefs front and center, in an attempt to enlighten and enroll others to the manifold benefits of governments based on equitable distribution of wealth, rather than personal acquisition and overblown displays of military might. Kshama grew up, middle-class, in India, observing the painful injustices of the caste system there, which she found abominable and unacceptable. After graduating from the University of Mumbai, she moved to the United States and was shocked to encounter the depths of poverty and inequality here as well, which had many parallels to that of her home country. These images affected her deeply and she decided to abandon her training in computer science and pursue answers to her newfound interest in systemic denial of access to social justice, both in America and points beyond. To that end, she earned a PhD in Economics from the University of North Carolina, followed by a move to Seattle in 2006, where she began teaching at Seattle Central College shortly thereafter. It was there that she surrounded herself with others who wholeheartedly rejected our country's pathological obsession with wealth and status and replaced them with her own brand of compassionate advocacy for all citizens, not just the top 1%.

My path to revolution may have been markedly different from hers, but I'd reached the same conclusions that she had: *tax the rich!* Eliminate special privileges for corporations and billionaires, and demand sweeping reform to how business is done in the United States. Her incredible journey toward becoming what some have described, "the most powerful socialist in America," was predicated, in part, on her remarkable conduct in the days leading up to her victory. She cut her teeth in the trenches of Occupy Seattle and then went on to launch an outrageously successful campaign to become a member of the Seattle City Council, whose most compelling hue and cry was to increase the minimum wage in that city to fifteen dollars per hour, which she deemed to be the lowest reasonable amount to compensate a full time worker, in order to elevate them above poverty level. And then, against all odds, she won! Not only that, she unseated a longtime encumbent, Richard Conlin, who was viewed by many to be untouchable in the race. By doing so, she became one of only a handful of socialist candidates to ever win council posts in the entire history of the United States. Then, she took her heartfelt commitments directly to Seattle voters, who agreed with her position and, in May 2014, became the first to adopt the fifteen dollar minimum wage ever seen on our shores. We who Occupied for this too, lit the Twittersphere up like a Roman candle when the votes were finally tallied and we realized one of our own had accomplished the impossible, so quickly. And it was not just OWS supporters who took to the streets and danced with joy, it was labor rights advocates across the country, many of whom I witnessed, clapping each other on the back and tearfully embracing, even as they wielded their FIGHT FOR FIFTEEN signs in front of WalMarts and McDonald'ses nationwide.

We saw Kshama's spectacular gains to be Occupy's as well, but there were scores of others who did not attain quite that level of fame, who also discovered superpowers and found their capes along the Occupy Trail. Consider Dorli Rainey, the tiny, 84-year-old, Austrian-born grandmother who was pepper sprayed by Seattle police as she joined in a protest there on November 16, 2011, along with hundreds of others. I ran into her at Occupy the Rose Parade weeks later, where we spoke before her scheduled appearance there. She told me that many of her friends who were in nursing homes and assisted living centers thought that she was both crazy and heroic. "They ask me—they say, 'Dorli, aren't you afraid that you're going to be hurt or arrested with these people' and I say *no!* This is what I must do—This is what all of us must do. Why would I want to be sitting around, playing cards or watching TV and waiting to die. This keeps me alive!" A photographer named Joshua Trujillo captured the agonized look on her face—dripping with chemical spray, as two younger protesters came to her assistance and held her steady. Shortly afterward, she told MSNBC interviewer Keith Olbermann, that the pain and stinging were gone from her eyes, but she still felt a heaviness in her chest and was battling a persistent cough, which I was all too familiar with. After that incident, which was blasted all over the Internet, she became the face of Occupy Seattle, and as such, found a much wider audience for her message than ever before. Around that time I also heard her talking with Amy Goodman on *Democracy Now* about her Occupy experiences. Go Granny, go!

And as for me, here in Okanogan County, Washington, halfway into my fifty-fifth trip around the sun? I am a little more arthritic than even three or four years earlier, and perhaps a little less inclined to walk headlong into a hopped-up army of militarized police than I was then. It's been ages since I've seen so many colorful and intriguing humans gathered together, as I did on that adventure. When I first came home from my time with Occupy, I'd been confused by the volume of conflicting feelings I was having. There were days when I found it difficult to fold back into my normal, ordinary life, filled with normal, ordinary people. Certainly few people in my present could lay claim to explosively inspiring the kinds of questions and deep internal dialogues that many larger-than-life OWS cohorts sparked within me, then, though at the time, during the height of my fear and discomfort, it had been hard to come up with something even moderately attractive about some of the characters surrounding me, and I desperately craved normalcy and civility.

But, that was then and this is now—and these days, it's no trick at all to come up with dozens of things I can not only tolerate, but even love about virtually all of them, even the red-eyed, foul-mouthed litterbugs; pitbull possessors; mentally ill; tone deaf midnight serenaders; the chemically dependent; and chicken wing combatants. And after all, wasn't that one of the main points of Occupy—to push the boundaries of understanding, compassion, and tolerance way out, in order to create new visions of what was possible? No small part of the original appeal of joining OWS had been the certainty that I would be exposed to people and situations that would expand my worldview, shake up my reality, and force me to encounter opinions and personalities that challenged my narrowing notions in my staid existence at Pagan Place. Living in the country and learning how to get along with people of differing political stripes had been mostly marvelous, but I'm not proud to own up to the ignoble encroachment of some degree of provincialism and small-minded judgments, which had somehow managed to creep into my psyche during my time away from the liberal bastion of Seattle, no matter how hard I'd tried to resist them.

One of Occupy's greatest gifts to me was the way it made me embrace some of the glorious contradictions I encounter all the time as I move through time and space. It meant relying on tweakers and crack addicts to warn me when trouble was nigh, tweeting out dog food requests for snarling canines who wanted to tear me to pieces, and sharing a laugh with a policewoman who'd just had a breakthrough about our shared goals, shortly after calling my friend and cellmate a cunt. I'd even shaken my head in wonderment when pondering how one of my fellow incarcerees, a six-foot-something white male with a low voice, high heels, miniskirt, and sharp adam's apple, had not been beaten to a pulp by the OPD, who seemed eager to do that, for any reason, at all times. He had shaved his face and legs, applied makeup, and insisted to arresting officers that he was a woman. I didn't have much of a problem with that, or sharing a cell and exposed toilet with her, but it knocked me off my feet to see Oakland Police be so evolved on this particular issue, while so backward on the rest. It gave me hope that even they could be trained into behaving with a modicum of civility and sensitivity if the majority demanded it. The Occupy Movement also facilitated my reaching the uncomfortable conclusion that I, even as a gay, black woman, am sexist too. Not only that—I'm racist, homophobic, looksist, ageist, and all that. We all are. It is impossible to grow up in America, be hammered with all the spurious, reprehensible messages we are inundated with, and be anything else. Yet and still, most of us doggedly refuse to acknowledge this disquieting fact. Instead, we have whittled the only responses to this inconvenient truth down to A) admitting we are these things, and being stoned to death; or, B) denying we are these things, when accused, and then being stoned to death. It is only because we stopped defining them as just plain bad people, that it is now perfectly fine to confess that some of us are alcoholics. Indeed, it's common knowledge that the first step to recovery is admitting we have a problem, followed shortly thereafter by getting treatment, learning more about the disease, and finding ways to manage the unfortunate condition and stop offending. But we've never come up with realistic, kind, gentle ways to cope with our ongoing battles, as flawed human beings, with the "isms." I was mortified when watching NPR's Juan Williams being summarily dismissed, thrown under the bus, if you will, when he admitted to feeling nervous when seeing people in "Muslim garb" boarding the same flight he was booked on. Ashamedly, I thought, "there but for fortune go I." If every one of us told the truth and were dealt the same consequences, there would be millions more people out of work than there already are. I, too, was something other than perfectly okay with the fact that Williams had been doing double duty as a commentator for both NPR and Fox News, and was not entirely happy with some of the comments he'd made prior to the career-derailing gaff that got him canned, but I was utterly baffled by how so many NPR listeners instantaneously stuck him right up there with Clarence Thomas, Herman Cain, Ben Carson, and Condoleezza Rice, as one of the most detestable Negroes in America. Millions of them could not fathom how he, a person of color, could harbor such unevolved notions. And he stayed canned, even after he went on to try and make it "clear that all Americans have to be careful not to let fears lead to the violation of anyone's constitutional rights, be it to build a mosque, carry the Koran, or drive a New York cab without the fear of having your throat slashed." I could be dead wrong here—I don't know all that went on behind the scenes—he may have been a real backward, hate-spewing pain in the ass to his co-workers, but I'm trying to give him the benefit of the doubt by surmising that much of his ignorance could easily be interpreted as a predictable response to the barrage of hate propaganda that followers of Islam received after 9/11. Can't we just admit that we are all, to some degree, influenced by the crap that hits us 24/7/365 in the Land of the Free/Home of the Brave Melting Pot we reside in? And then, after we do that, can we reasonably conclude that it's not up to Muslims to disavow their religious beliefs, or look and act in ways that put our istic, phobic selves more at ease. It's up to us to grow the fuck up, learn some shit, and go out and make some Muslim, black, gay, transgender, crazy, homeless friends. What is evolution anyway, but a naturally occurring anomaly/abnormality, or mutation, that winds up redefining a species in ways that increase its future odds of survival? The first guy who rejected the plumbing he was born with, placed an "s" in front of "he", and insisted that psychology trumped physiology, changed us as a species forever. As did the first cop that broke with tradition and understood the rightness of allowing a person to be accepted as the gender s/he-they identified with; or the drug-addicted homeless vet who recognized he had a right to protest the pretense that thrust him into an unjust war, crippling him physically and emotionally for the rest of his life. These rogue individuals set in motion the future-altering butterfly effects that are necessary for us to progress, and thrive. The eighty-four-year-old woman who chafed at the idea of resting in a home until she died—who chose instead to risk her safety by rallying against injustice, was also one of those rare mutations that may be our only chance (as life-forms capable of rendering the planet to rubble at the touch of a button) to survive our own propensities. These exotic examples have the anomaly/abnormality thing in spades, and as such, should have spawned crazy adulation in me straight away for offering the only shred of hope I see for ferrying homonids safely through climate change/religious wars/ nuclear proliferation/genocide, etc. In order to get to the point of gratitude and fondness, I had to take a few years to mull them over and deconstruct the quandaries they unleashed in my mind. Wouldn't it have been so much better if I had gotten there right away? The beautiful thing though, is that I *did* get there. I did finally discover that one of my superpowers was adapting to those whose methods, madness, and message did not precisely mirror my own. They had undoubtedly stretched me, and helped me to rejoice in diversity, while strengthening my conviction to only use my newly discovered powers for good. And, as has been said, "with great power comes great responsibility," and knowing what I now knew, made me feel more motivated than ever to dedicate myself to changing, at least some of the things I could no longer accept.

In order to do that, I knew I'd have to make some hard choices and decide on the one or two things I most wanted to do, and could pull off in the near term, that wouldn't cost a lot of money, or involve risking life and limb. It was my friends at Occupy the Farm that hammered home the criticality of taking back control of our food supply by avoiding genetically altered produce like the plague, and never using chemical fertilizers or pesticides. In years past, I simply visited the nearest chain store that had garden seeds or plant starts on sale, be they hybrid, GMO, or whatever—paid my money, and put them in the ground. #OTF drilled into me, the radically revolutionary aspects of planting *only* open-pollinated crops, which would allow me to select the best and brightest producers in my garden to go to seeds, which could then be harvested, dried, and planted the following year. "Save Your Seeds," was their mantra, and it has now become mine. They said that huge agribusiness and chemical companies, like Monsanto, had so compromised the food supply that ancient varieties of common grains and vegetables were going extinct and being replaced by toxic, "Roundup Ready" strains that did not produce viable seeds, but rather had to be purchased each year from these companies, who controlled the prices, quality, and supplies. Food crops in America, like corn and wheat and soybeans, were being genetically engineered to withstand the chemical onslaught of Roundup weedkillers and insecticides, that corporate farms drench our food in, and contained (among other really bad stuff) neonicotinoids, which kill pest insects and bees (and other pollinators) alike by making their stomachs explode when they are ingested. They are making people (particularly Americans, who've not banned them as many other countries have) very sick too, and account for untold illnesses that are associated with their consumption—everything from cancers, to Crohn's disease, gluten intolerance, obesity, allergies, birth defects, autism, heart disease, diabetes, infertility, and the like. The list is long and being added to regularly. These and other depressing realities about how the planet has devolved and the 1% come to control everything we hold dear, continue to make me angrier than ever, even after my adventures with Occupy. However, at a certain point, I had to take inventory of my talents, tolerances, and weaknesses to decide what I could do to give meaning and purpose to those hair-raising experiences and put that sacred knowledge to the test. If I couldn't compel Monsanto to label their deadly produce, I could refuse to buy it. Even though the conscienceless corporation had spent millions to defeat initiatives requiring them do so, I still had options to avoid and thwart the poison peddlers.

I started out by making a concerted effort to find open-pollinated, non-GMO, organic seeds to plant in my garden. I combed the Internet to find seed companies that specialized in exactly that. As it turned out, there was a local business in my area, the Glover Street Market, which sold products by Uprising Seeds and Seeds of Change, two of the companies I was attracted to in my online search. I've heard it said that we humans vote three times a day when buying and consuming food, which seemed to me to be a golden opportunity to get cracking right away to put some fresh faces in office. While I was off Occupying, I'd neglected my 880 square foot greenhouse, and the roof collapsed due to an unusually heavy snow load. Normally, I'd have been right there after every storm to rake and pull the snow from the plastic roof, but, in my absence, it did not get done. My first order of business was to extricate and reconstruct the splintered rafters, gas up the backhoe, lift them into place to secure to the frame, and repair the structure for use. Next, I brought over load after bucket load of manure that our horses had been busy manufacturing in their corral all winter long. Later that day I put up a YouTube video of me dumping it onto my garden, offering each "steaming pile of manure to my friends at Monsanto." Shortly afterward YouTube removed it as "inappropriate content."

I am proud to say that in the last two months I have not prepared a single bite of produce I did not either grow or buy from a local organic farmer, who employs the same methods that I practice. Last night's supper featured an arugula salad, with sesame oil, garlic, rice vinegar, baby spinach, tamari, and toasted pine nuts. Every time I walk into my garden and select succulent greens, strawberries, beans, or vine ripe tomatoes to grace my table, I feel like I am doing something tantamount to printing my own money. The thrill of it consumes me. Throughout the last few winters, my family and I have enjoyed canned and frozen vegetables that I grew myself, as well as bushels of potatoes, beets, and carrots which were stored safely in the root cellar we recently built. Almost everything I planted this spring was from seeds I saved from last year's bumper crop. I even fenced in an additional four thousand square feet and planted an heirloom wheat, which I will harvest and grind by hand soon. With any luck, I should be able to harvest at least one hundred pounds of whole wheat grain, which I will thresh by hand against a wooden box and throw into the breezy air to winnow in a basket, just as was done in this country for hundreds of years before modern machinery came along. When I checked today, thirty or so of the hundreds of wild asparagus seeds I harvested last year from a hillside, had germinated and were reaching their whispy fronds heavenward. What it ultimately came down to was this: I may not be able to abolish corporate wrongdoing, but I can grow a tomato so delicious and nutritious, it'll throw you into a tantrum that'll make your head spin off its axis and steam come out of your ears every time you have to choke down anything less.

And, there were lots of small things I found that I could do every day to make my immediate environment a better place to

live. I'm not able to completely eliminate homophobia in my
obscure micropolis or the surrounding farming communities,
but I discovered I could help our first ever Methow Valley Gay
Pride Festival become a ringing success by holding my rainbow
flag up high and dancing my booty off on a June Sunday in 2014.
I, along with my gay, bi, straight, trans, and non-binary friends,
could shake my moneymaker to Madonna and The Village People,
right there in broad daylight in our main street city park. I can
keep smiling and ignore the occasional redneck gunning past us
in disgust as we link arms and step out, to show everybody how
groovy and fantastic it is to be loving, tolerant, and inclusive. And,
I can forever cherish the memory of a shy teenager named Tiffany,
with black hair, clothes, makeup, and fingernail polish, jumping
up and down—crying and shrieking like a contestant on *The Price
is Right* when she won the grand prize of a day spa makeover and
pampering session, in our cross-dressing, "drag race" relay. After
winning, she grabbed the microphone from the MC and breathlessly announced, she "finally felt like she belonged somewhere,"
and that she was so proud and grateful that our valley had come
together and done this so boldly, which, she said, had given her
the courage to help start a GSA (Gay/Straight Alliance) chapter at
our only, small, high school. Priceless.

A few months ago, I spoke up at a packed Town Hall meeting
where a bunch of suits were toeing the water to take the tempera-
ture of our community regarding their hopes to construct an open
pit copper mine on a pristine mountain nearby, which is home to a
number of threatened and endangered species. Many of my friends
and neighbors were there, politely questioning the Forest Service
and mining experts about the possible harmful consequences of
the mine, as well as expressing their doubts and concerns about
the whole idea. Before my tenure with Occupy, I may have been
hesitant to throw my two cents in, fearing I'd embarrass myself
somehow by being too emotional, tripping over my tongue, or
not having enough facts in order. I'd have kept quiet, for fear of
reprisal, or thinking I hadn't lived here long enough to have earned

the right to speak up in a room full of locals, some who'd been in the Methow Valley for generations. Not so anymore. I thrust my hand into the air and bounced on the edge of my chair like a grade-schooler waiting to be called upon. When my turn finally did come, I said that I did not believe the company's assurances that they'd run a squeaky clean mine that wouldn't harm the ecosystem in any way, because I knew for a fact that no mine has ever in the history of humankind been able to do so. I said that there was intrinsic value in having a mountain left intact that didn't have a "goddamn copper mine on it," and that Flagg Mountain shouldn't have to justify its existence by making money or creating jobs. And further, that we, the citizens of Okanogan County didn't have to get caught up in that ridiculous argument. I said that the mountain's only job was to stand there and be beautiful. I concluded by shouting that I "would throw myself on the gears of the machines before I let another jerk trying to make a buck destroy something I love." Not once did I replay the scenario in my head that night, riddled with self-doubt and recriminations. I just closed my eyes, smiled, and slept great.

It seems that many of my comrades from the movement reached the same conclusions I did, as I observe them choosing sensible portions and taking manageable bites from their plates as they operate, post-OWS. I'm regularly seeing many of their current projects blossoming and coming to fruition. I just saw a post from an activist friend I met in Oakland at OGP, who was outlining her intentions to "Carpe the shit out of this diem" and get bodies in the streets to raise a ruckus over the recent construction of a building known as the DAC, or Domain Awareness Center, which is a surveillance hub that happens to be located very near where our commune existed. Several days ago, I saw that my Washington DC, Occupy the Supreme Court/Congress friends, Tighe Barry and Medea Benjamin, along with other members of their organization, Code Pink, were on the NBC Nightly news . . . again—this time for disrupting the Senate Armed Services Committee hearing in the Nation's Capital, where members of Congress were trying to sell the idea of redeploying American troops and weapons to defeat the latest swarm of Muslim extremists called "ISIS" or ISIL, depending on whom you talk to (which stands for Islamic State in Iraq and Syria/Levant). This latest incarnation of the furious faithful in the Middle East arose in wrath-filled retaliation for US military war atrocities committed against them over the past decade. Medea, Tighe, and their co-conspirators stood before the panel holding signs, loudly calling out, and shaming individual hawks, like Republican Senator John McCain and Secretary of Defense Chuck Hagel for relentless fearmongering and war baiting. Code Pink accused the committee of trying to foist another chapter of America's endless wars onto our broke, obese, unemployed, debt-straddled, under-educated, over-medicated populace. She and others accomplished a brief halting of the proceedings by loudly shouting, "Don't drag us into another war," while holding a sign aloft that said, MORE WAR = MORE EXTREMISM. Their strident voices created such havoc in the room they prompted Democratic Chairman Carl Levin to pronounce, "You're acting very war-like yourself," idiotically, to the assembly of elected officials. Secretary of State John Kerry was so undone by their affrontery, as they chanted, "Your invasion will not protect the homeland," that he began to engage in a rare counterargument of unscripted debate, saying that he understood dissent . . ." but that the protestors "should care about fighting ISIL" because of their record of committing rape, mutilation, and other barbarities against women that, "frankly comes out of the stone age, making a mockery of a peaceful religion." Wow, I thought as I watched the video, if an aerial bombing campaign is going to be our new standard response to violent, women-hating religious extremism, maybe we could go after the NFL next . . . or even the Church of Latter Day Saints.

Practically everywhere I look there are signs that our populist revolution is not only far from over, but growing exponentially worldwide and poised to burst even more forcefully into the forefront of global awareness. Last Sunday, September 22, 2014, a crowd estimated as high as four hundred thousand people, comprising everything from the great unwashed, to captains of industry and presidential hopefuls, descended upon New York City and marched for hours to protest stultifying inaction on the urgent life-threatening crisis of global warming on our home planet. Marchers drew compelling, science-based connections between such occurrences as the out-of-control wildfires in the American West to the rapid spread of the Ebola virus in Africa to the onslaught of record-breaking temperatures caused by carbon emissions and unsustainable addictions to fossil fuels. Experts said that the heat was throwing everything out of whack, producing super-fires, super-floods, and super-germs that threatened mass extinctions to all life forms . . . including us. I was particularly receptive to their message after having had to evacuate my own family, along with our horses, bunnies, cats and goldfish, down the highway this past July, as out-of-control, record-breaking wildfires bore down upon us with unprecedented speed and fury as we raced to outrun the flames. Scores of my dear friends and neighbors lost their homes and their beloved animals as the fire consumed 360 homes around mine and devastated our tiny community—leaving it almost unrecognizable as I drive to our daughter's school. Inexplicably, the network news, on the night of the largest climate march in history, was jam-packed with everything but that, as anchors devoted all but a few paltry seconds to detailing the intricacies of a man hunt for a "crazed cop-killer on the loose," and a missing college co-ed, who just happened to be blonde, white, and pretty, from a Virginia campus. After those compelling stories of grave national security and importance, came the coverage of the latest barbaric ISIS beheadings against Westerners. The broadcast that evening seemed wholly devoted to hysteri-cizing the urgency to devote more massive-scale counter campaigns in the Middle East, as well as to chasten those who dare challenge our moral authority and military might.

The day after that historic rally, there were over three thousand, mostly young people, who showed up in Battery Park and surrounded the bronze bull, declaring their willingness to be arrested if need be, in order to attain their goals, which were declared,

"To shut down Wall Street and end capitalism in America." *Go big or go home*, I thought, as I read their optimistic mission statement and watched them through the lens of familiar Occupy livestreamers who noted that the NYPD had "wisely chosen" to eschew riot gear and other paramilitary shows of force that day. The streamers attributed the modified police attire to the unanticipated groundswell of activism by people of color in the wake of recent Ferguson, Missouri protests that had erupted after jacked-up law enforcement personnel gunned down a black teenager accused of shoplifting in that town. As I watched the wide-eyed kids in New York City, linking arms and looking up fearfully at cops for hours, my heart filled once again with compassion and a fervor to support their efforts to undo some of the damage my generation has done to them and their future prospects. As I monitored their uneasy, hours long-standoff with the cops, I checked the Internet for airline deals as I considered joining them if they were still there in a few days, which was the time it would take me to reach them from my remote perch. As I observed police slowly drawing a noose around them, and preventing them from re-entering after brief, "comfort breaks", I even debated the relative merits of going astronaut style and sitting in an adult diaper with them, should I choose to fly out there and try to get inside the circle. Even if this particular stand was dismantled, I knew that others would soon arise in replacement, as it dawned on more and more of us that breaking the law was our only hope for survival. Even normally reserved college students in Hong Kong are amassing in droves to give birth to a new movement called, "Occupy Central with Love and Peace," which urges its participants to demand fully democratic elections from Chinese leaders and "Disobey and grasp your destiny."

My dear friend Laura Koch is now volunteering to defend activists like us with the Bay Area chapter of the National Lawyer's Guild. We texted each other excitedly as we watched indie journalists cover the Climate Change Rally in NYC. "I'm afraid I'm not going to get much work done today," she texted me as we glued

ourselves to our social media with glee. Punkboy continues to
advocate and agitate for the rights of the 99% both in the streets
and from an online newspaper he calls, *The Punkboy Times*. One of
his latest endeavors has been to call out a recent push by corporations and their political backers to create a fast lane for Internet
users, who are able to pay higher premiums to providers to access
them. He has even launched an online talk show called *Wake Da
FuQ Up Radio*, where I have called in to chat with other guests and
voice my opinions. A short time ago thousands of his followers
were alarmed to see that he'd been arrested, along with several
others, while protesting at Google's San Francisco headquarters.
They were trying to encourage the huge, multinational Internet
service provider to be more vocal, proactive proponents of net
neutrality, which is crucial to our ability, as citizen activists, to use
social media as a means to quickly inform, organize, and coalesce
people around an issue. Luckily, he was only detained briefly and
then released, much to the relief of many of us, who were already
discussing strategies to mobilize and help get him out of there.
As soon as he got out he began an additional campaign to begin
registering black voters to elect representatives who shared their
concerns and would advocate for their best interests.

To be sure, the 1% is noticing. So much so, that they're starting to complain—a lot. The ripple effect of Occupy is still evident
and expanding. It never ceases to amaze me when I read about yet
another bloated bigot complaining about the audacity of activists
for daring to expose and confront them. The January 25, 2014 edi-
tion of the *Wall Street Journal* included a letter to the editor by billionaire venture capitalist Tom Perkins, who cried foul for what he
perceives to be an alarming trend of unjustly demonizing the rich.
He said that it was "absurd to attack the rich for doing what the
rich do." In that same letter he compared the persecution he suf-
fers as a person of wealth in America, to that inflicted on the Jews
of Nazi Germany. And then he likened the Occupy Movement's
injuries to him, to those suffered by *Kristallnacht* victims—the infamous night in November, 1938, which saw over ninety Jews killed

in a series of coordinated attacks on Jewish-owned businesses and synagogues. Wow.

Panicky pronouncements like this reveal how opposing forces are getting to them—the engorged entozoa that have made things such an untenable mess lately and threaten to kill the host. Movements such as Occupy and the groundswell of focus groups that continue to spin off as a result are punching through the facade and hitting the hoarders where they live. Inch by inch, hour by hour, they are seeing the handwriting on the wall, in the form of more frequent and effective campaigns to end the wholesale theft of our futures. Today I read that Monsanto, feeling the heat, just announced what is called, an "accelerated share repurchase," because of a 5% drop in earnings in the third quarter of their latest fiscal year. Much of that drop was due to plunging sales of their genetically modified seeds (especially corn) which numerous groups, such as GMO Free USA, have been tireless in educating the public about—never missing an opportunity to out them and the role they've played, among many horrors, in the rapid evolution of superbugs and superweeds all over the world. In an effort to stop the bleeding, the company is buying back ten billion dollars worth of their own stock, hoping to restore consumer confidence in their products.

We're reaching and influencing them, the pompous plutocrats and overstuffed oligarchs, in countless ways, and they are responding in every imaginable fashion, from furiously striking out at troublemakers to keep a dying model in place, to occasionally making positive changes and forward thinking adjustments to how they operate. Many of us will be amazed to see how our past, present, and future actions have, do, and will continue to alter the course of history, just as a group of startled protesters discovered, once upon a time, way back in 1970, just days after National Guard troops killed four students on the Ohio Kent State campus during an anti–Vietnam War rally. Sometime around four thirty in the morning of May 9, President Richard Nixon approached a clutch of young people bedded down at the Lincoln Memorial, accompanied by his personal valet, Cuban immigrant Manolo Sanchez. In a bizarre chapter in history, the leader of the free world spontaneously decided to pay the campers an unannounced visit. From subsequent interviews with his former secretary of state, Henry Kissinger, we know that Nixon felt the country was falling apart, which had thrown him into a tailspin, and put him in a delicate emotional state. He'd taken to obsessively calling Kissinger at all hours of the day and night, for guidance, comfort, and reassurance. Nixon later recalled this as "the darkest period of [his] presidency." His version of the interaction with the kids was captured on tape as he dictated his recollection to his chief of staff, H.R. Haldeman, shortly afterward, ". . . And I said I was sorry they had missed it because I had tried to explain in the press conference that my goals in Vietnam were the same as theirs—to stop the killing, to end the war, to bring peace. Our goal was not to get into Cambodia by what we were doing, but to get out of Vietnam. There seemed to be no—they did not respond. I hoped that their hatred of the war, which I could well understand, would not turn into a bitter hatred of our whole system, our country and everything that it stood for. I said, I know you, that probably most of you think I'm an SOB. But I want you to know that I understand just how you feel." Until I read that quote from our former leader, I had no idea, and could barely imagine Richard Nixon giving a fig about what the country's young people thought of him. Now, looking back, I can clearly see that the times they were a' changin'.

After my wheat crop is processed, I'm thinking about joining up with a growing legion of antifracking organizations who are assembling worldwide to put an end to the wasteful, planet-frying practice of extracting deeply embedded energy reserves through hydraulic fracturing of fossil fuel seams. If some other gigantic wave of activism doesn't grab me first, I've got my eye on a group of anti-Keystone XL Pipeline fracktivists called The Cowboy/Indian Alliance, who are helping to unite and bolster resistance networks in both Canada and the US. Their motto is, "Reject and Protect," and they've already pulled off several well-attended, high profile events. I admire what they're doing and wonder if I could lend a hand with upcoming campaigns. They were all over the S22 Climate March on Sunday and it thrilled me to see their faces and hear their voices.

Who knows where the journey that Occupy Wall Street started, will eventually lead me? I don't, but I do know that the masses will eventually prevail, because we will not stop until we do. The one thing I am absolutely certain of is, I will never sit in my living room, do nothing, and be complacent again. Not only will we ultimately succeed in righting the ship, but in a sense, we already have. This revolution, as in all others, is won the moment We The Many recognize that the insults we've come to endure every day are far worse than anything the few can do to us. When that recognition reaches critical mass, as it invariably does, all the other pieces will fall into place. Hurled insults, or even tear gas canisters may discourage or slow us down, but we will keep coming. Neighbors looking askance at front yard vegetable gardens that have replaced sterile, weed-free lawns won't kill anyone, but toxic turnips will, so plant and save heirloom seeds until Monsanto goes out of business. Register the poor and people of color in your area to vote. A revolutionary action as simple as moving money out of, "too big to fail" banks, with shameful foreclosure records, into smaller, community-oriented institutions, like credit unions, can be every bit as radical and effective as strapping on a gas mask and facing down a tank.

And I say unto you this day, it is my firm belief that the Occupy Movement will be judged as a phenomenon of great moment in American history—a watershed occurrence that changed the course of events in ways we have yet to clearly understand. It changed the national conversation from far-flung esoteric exercises in irrelevance, to monumentally important discourse about the urgent crises we must solve as a nation and a planet, right now. It's greatest achievement may someday be determined to have been to redirect the country's focus onto real problems, hurting real people, real bad. However desperately we may want to define its significance and portent, we cannot even hope to do so for perhaps generations to come. I don't know about that—but I do know that I believe what Mahatma Ghandi once said, and that is, *"First they* ignore you, then they *laugh at you,* then they fight you, then you win."